Think About It

Critical Skills for Academic Writing

JOHN MAUK • JAYME STAYER • KAREN MAUK

Illustrations by Benjamin Busch

WADSWORTH
CENGAGE Learning

Australia • Brazil • Japan • Korea • Mexico • Singapore • Spain • United Kingdom • United States

WADSWORTH
CENGAGE Learning

Think About It: Critical Skills for Academic Writing
John Mauk, Jayme Stayer, Karen Mauk

Publisher: Monica Eckman
Acquisitions Editor: Margaret Leslie
Senior Development Editor: Leslie Taggart
Development Editor: Stephanie Pelkowski Carpenter
Assistant Editor: Sarah Turner
Editorial Assistant: Cailin Barrett-Bressack
Media Editor: Cara Douglass-Graff
Brand Manager: Lydia Lestar
Senior Content Project Manager: Corinna Dibble
Art Director: Hannah Wellman
Manufacturing Planner: Betsy Donaghey
Rights Acquisition Specialist: Ann Hoffman
Production Service and Compositor: Lachina Publishing Services
Cover and Text Designer: Dare Porter
Cover Image: istockphoto.com/ iLexx

For product information and technology assistance, contact us at
Cengage Learning Customer & Sales Support, 1-800-354-9706
For permission to use material from this text or product, submit all requests online at **www.cengage.com/permissions.**
Further permissions questions can be emailed to **permissionrequest@cengage.com.**

Library of Congress Control Number: 2012955973
ISBN-13: 978-1-285-07252-4
ISBN-10: 1-285-07252-9

Wadsworth
20 Channel Center Street
Boston, MA 02210
USA

Cengage Learning is a leading provider of customized learning solutions with office locations around the globe, including Singapore, the United Kingdom, Australia, Mexico, Brazil, and Japan. Locate your local office at **international.cengage.com/region**.

Cengage Learning products are represented in Canada by Nelson Education, Ltd.

For your course and learning solutions, visit **www.cengage.com.**
Purchase any of our products at your local college store or at our preferred online store **www.cengagebrain.com.**

Instructors: Please visit **login.cengage.com** and log in to access instructor-specific resources.

Printed in the United States of America
2 3 4 5 6 7 16 15 14 13

Brief Contents

Think About It

Preface

For years, we've watched college students struggle in first- and second-year courses. We've watched the most earnest, the most disaffected, and those in between try to understand what instructors want, what intellectual behaviors warrant success, what qualities beyond format and content get most rewarded. In short, we've watched students struggle with the shapeless and evasive nature of academic thinking. With this book, we've tried to call out and give shape to the curricular dark matter, the epistemic stuff that gets most valued in college life.

Think About It explains how to recognize, understand, and perform common intellectual maneuvers in academic writing. In these chapters, we have charted out the critical moves—the particular things that scholars, good thinkers, and professional writers do to develop insights. Throughout the book, we show that good thinking is not magic, that it is not exclusive to those who are "naturally smart," and that powerful ideas come in tandem with learnable moves.

Part I, "Learn the Moves," includes nine chapters that describe and model common and critical moves for academic writers. Each chapter presents a series of excerpts and detailed explanations so that students can perform those moves on their own. *Talk About It* activities appear throughout the chapters and serve as in-class discussion starters. *Write It* prompts appear at the end of chapters and offer students suggestions for their own projects, which in turn are supported by corresponding generative outlines in Part III.

⬧ **Part II, "Read the Moves,"** begins with brief advice on reading in academic life—for instance, how to grapple with complex terms and how to interact with different genres. It then offers a range of essays, articles, book excerpts, and blogs written by popular authors, scholars, and college instructors. The essays directly illustrate the moves taught throughout Part I. *Study the Moves* boxes accompany the essays and chart out the specific intellectual moves operating in the paragraphs.

✓ **Part III, "Apply the Moves,"** offers a series of *generative outlines* for common assignment types: explanatory/descriptive, analytical, argumentative, and reflective projects. The outlines help students to develop and map out their own thinking—not to think first and *then* write, but to think in terms of common patterns that yield insights. While the outlines are narrow enough to keep students focused, they are adaptable enough to transport into a range of writing situations.

SUPPLEMENTS

Online Instructor's Manual for *Think About It*
ISBN: 978-1-285-16992-7
Available for download on the book companion website, this manual contains valuable resources to help you maximize your class preparation efforts. It includes sample syllabi and teaching tips for each chapter in the text.

Companion Website for *Think About It*

At the *Think About It* companion website, students will find downloadable, printable outlines corresponding to those in Part III of the text. The website provides an ideal online environment for mapping out and developing their ideas.

Interactive eBook for *Think About It*

Think About It is available as an interactive eBook! Now students can do all of their reading online or use the true-to-page eBook as a handy reference while they are completing other coursework. The eBook includes the full text of the print version with navigation, search, and highlighting tools. Find this and additional resources at www.CengageBrain.com.

Enhanced InSite™ for *Think About It*

Printed Access Card ISBN: 978-1-285-19507-0
Instant Access Code ISBN: 978-1-285-19508-7
Easily create, assign, and grade writing assignments with Enhanced InSite™ for *Think About It*. From a single, easy-to-navigate site, you and your students can manage the flow of papers online, check for originality, and conduct peer reviews. Students can access a multimedia eBook, private tutoring options, and resources for writers that include anti-plagiarism tutorials and downloadable grammar podcasts. Enhanced InSite™ provides the tools and resources you and your students need plus the training and support you want. Learn more at http://www.cengage.com/insite.

Editor's Choice CourseReader for *Think About It*

Editor's Choice CourseReader is an online reader with essays selected for their illustration of the intellectual moves featured in *Think About It*. These readings represent a range of disciplines, including business and economics, computer science, humanities, science, and social science. The CourseReader is loaded with convenient features such as downloadable MP3 audio files and allows for easy highlighting, printing, note-taking, and more.

ACKNOWLEDGMENTS

We thank our students and colleagues who helped us boil down these critical skills for academic writers. We're especially grateful for the essays in Part II that were contributed by our colleagues—writers and instructors throughout the country: Michael Anderson, Shawn Burks, William J. Carpenter, Steven D. Krause, John McCormick, Stephanie Mills, Ann-Marie Paulin, Astrid Reed, Kathleen Schenck, Teresa Scollon, Bradford A. Smith, and Annette Wannamaker. We also thank our colleague and friend Sally Gorenflo for sharing ideas about self-assessment.

Thanks to our reviewers, whose thoughtful comments helped us shape this edition:

Forrest Anderson, Catawba College

Aaron Clark, Brookhaven College

Linsey Cuti, Kankakee Community College

Heather Dorn, Binghamton University

Joseph Duemer, Clarkson University

Anthony Dykema-VanderArk, Grand Rapids Community College

Benjamin Fischer, Northwest Nazarene University

Hannah Furrow, University of Michigan, Flint

Jeanne Guerin, Sacramento State University

Brooke Horvath, Kent State University

Robert Hurd, Anne Arundel Community College

Geri Jacobs, Jackson Community College

Lynn Kilpatrick, Salt Lake Community College

David LaPierre, Central Connecticut State University

Eric Leuschner, Fort Hays State University

Linda Moore, University of West Florida

Tiffany Morin, University of North Carolina, Charlotte

David Mulry, Schreiner University

Matthew Newcomb, SUNY New Paltz

Anne-Marie Obilade, Alcorn State University

Don Ownsby, Arizona State University

Miri Pardo, St. John Fisher College

Velvet Pearson, Long Beach City College

Daniela Ragusa, Capital Community College

Laura Rogers, Albany College of Pharmacy and Health
Sciences

Vanessa Ruccolo, Virginia Tech

Kiki Rydell, Montana State University

Crystal Sands, Husson University

Graham Scott, Texas Woman's University

Christian Sheridan, Bridgewater College

Jimmy Smith, Union College

Dee Dee Snyder, The Ohio State University Agricultural
Technical Institute

Jonathan Sponsler, Lehigh Carbon Community College

Jason Ziebart, Central Carolina Community College

Thanks to our development editor, Steph Carpenter, for her energy and attention during this intense process. Thanks to Margaret Leslie for supporting and convening energy around the project, Leslie Taggart for bringing her expertise, and Cailin Barrett-Bressack for attending to the daily details. Thanks to Corinna Dibble and Megan Dykes for keeping production rolling. And thanks to Stacey Purviance and the marketing team at Cengage for crafting the message and going public. A special thanks goes to our colleague and friend Michael Rosenberg, who believed in the promise of this book from the beginning. A special thanks also goes to Kathleen Schenck for her impeccable research abilities, her automatic willingness to help us at critical moments, and her work on the instructor's manual for this project. And many thanks to the mighty Benjamin Busch, not only for bringing the book's pages to life with his illustrations but also for thinking along with us—even while traveling around the country on his own book tour. Finally, we dedicate this book to our nephews and nieces—Tyler, Perry, Carter, Miranda, Grace, and Annie—who are entering the world of public thinking and writing.

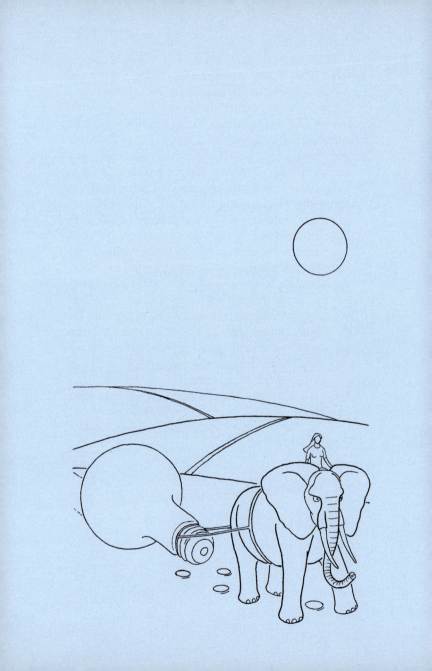

Think

Back in seventeenth-century England, Isaac Newton was sitting under a tree and minding his own business when an apple fell and knocked him on the head. As the story goes, that's how he discovered gravity. Maybe you've heard this story. There are many others like it in history and contemporary culture—stories of scientists who closed their eyes and, out of nowhere, understood the nature of reality, or writers who dreamt up an entire novel all at once. But the truth is that eureka moments are mostly, or even entirely, made up. Insights don't fall from trees. They usually come along with, or even after, some sustained intellectual activity. Good thinking happens when people's brains are in a particular gear, moving along a particular path. As it turns out, Isaac Newton was studying mathematics and the laws of motion for years before he developed his theory of gravity. He'd been learning the language of mathematics, charting out patterns, and applying concepts. His discovery was a brilliant one, but it was an extension of his prior thinking and experimenting, not a random strike of lightning. In other words, the great thinkers of history weren't wizards. And great writers aren't magicians or mystical dreamers. They do things that most of us can learn to do.

So how do insights come along? When does good thinking happen? Under what circumstances? This book tries to answer those questions. In Chapters 1 through 9, we will explain the most common intellectual skills, or what we call *moves*, in academic and professional writing projects—the moves that make things happen, that impact fields of study, and that are often most needed and celebrated. In other words, this book will teach you the moves that academic and professional writers make over and over:

1. Seek complexity

2. Seek tension

3. Apply sources

4. Apply a concept

5. Dismantle arguments

6. Justify your position

7. Change the terms

8. Escape the status quo

9. Assess your thinking

Each chapter, we hope, makes the point that good thinking is not a mystery and that it happens in tandem with learnable moves. For example, when you *examine a past assumption* (explained in Chapter 9), you are thinking hard. The very process requires a certain level of mental engagement. The same goes for all the moves explained in the book. Whether it's *transporting a concept, changing the lens*, or *unpacking a broad term*, the act itself *is* good thinking. When you make such moves, you will be doing the work of academic writing. The moves we explain can be found wherever thinking happens: on blogs, in newspapers, in speeches, and so on. But this book will concentrate on helping you master the kind of writing that happens in college and university contexts.

ABOUT EXCERPTS AND SAMPLE ESSAYS
•••

Humans learn by imitating. Even the most creative among us progress by studying and adopting what has been done before. Whether artist, musician, chemist, or engineer, we need specific models. In fact, the best practitioners in any field have always carefully studied the works, models, practices, and patterns that have been used before they came along. Einstein studied other physicists and mathematicians. Stephen Hawking did the same. And J. K. Rowling, creator of Harry Potter, closely scrutinized the work of fantasy writers before her. In short, it seems that the masters of any discipline or trade were, at some point in their lives, studious apprentices. Before they created, they read, watched, and observed—sometimes with amazing degrees of focus. The same goes for thinking and writing in college. Students at all levels (including professors and textbook writers) do well to study models and try out the critical moves in their fields. And the better the models, the better the learning.

As you read through the chapters in Part I, "Learn the Moves," you'll see short excerpts that come from a range of sources—academic journal articles, popular magazine and newspaper articles, books, speeches, and blogs. You might think of them as brief models of a featured move, passages that show how a writer is thinking, what he or she is doing intellectually. For example, in Chapter 1, "Seek Complexity," we use a passage from David Foster Wallace. It comes from a commencement speech in which he describes different kinds of freedom. The passage is included not for what he says about freedom (the content of his speech) but for his way of making distinctions (the moves he makes):

Of course there are all different kinds of freedom, and the kind that is most precious you will not hear much talked about in the great outside world of winning and achieving and displaying. The really important kind of freedom involves attention, and awareness, and discipline, and effort, and being able truly to care about other people and to sacrifice for them, over and over, in myriad petty little unsexy ways, every day. That is real freedom. That is being taught how to think. The alternative is unconsciousness, the default setting, the "rat race"—the constant, gnawing sense of having had and lost some infinite thing.

Wallace's move (what we'll call *unpacking a term*) can be modeled and applied to your own writing. In other words, *freedom* can be replaced with any number of specific concepts: responsibility, privacy, education, knowledge, power, or equality—in short, anything that you're writing about.

Part II, "Read the Moves," is a collection of longer written examples—essays, articles, book chapters, and an occasional blog. These samples work like the short excerpts in Part I, but instead of showing just one particular move (like unpacking a term), they show a number of moves working in concert. The topics range from music sampling to fashion trends, from educational technology to life after college. As with the excerpts, the purpose of the essays is to show ways of thinking—and ways to organize sophisticated ideas.

ABOUT OUTLINES

Great musicians don't just swipe at the instrument in hopes of making a good sound. They learn patterns—many

This Is Water: Some Thoughts, Delivered on a Significant Occasion, about Living a Compassionate Life, New York: Little, Brown. Copyright © 2009 by David Foster Wallace Literary Trust. All rights reserved.

patterns—and then apply them in creative ways. One difference between great musicians and novices is the number of patterns they know. Skilled musicians know a broad range of chord progressions, scales, and modes they can apply in a variety of musical situations. Novice musicians know only a few patterns, so they're more constrained. When a new progression comes their way, they have to stop playing or fumble around noisily. The same thing happens with writing. Experienced writers have learned a number of patterns through reading, direct instruction, or both. When they're in the middle of a project, they have some idea of where they might go next. And if they hit a roadblock, they have options. They don't have to stop and stare at a blank screen for hours at a time.

Maybe you've had this experience: You've taken on a big topic. You're trying to write an essay or report that gets into some complex issues. And you realize that you don't know how to structure things. You don't know what to say next. It's happened to all writers at some point. Without a form or pattern in mind, they quickly hit a wall. Even if they have sophisticated ideas, they can get confused unless they have some patterns in mind.

One common pattern is the five-paragraph essay:

- broad introduction that ends with a thesis (divided into three chunks)

- supporting paragraph 1

- supporting paragraph 2

- supporting paragraph 3

- conclusion that rewords the thesis

Plenty of college instructors despise this pattern. They urge students to avoid it, not because they hate the number five or because they want students to be uncomfortable but because *it limits what writers can do*. As a form, it is a limited intellectual tool. It invites writers to imagine topics as always having, or needing, three points. It doesn't account for the kind of complexity necessary for good academic work. But for many students, it is a handy arrangement tool. They come to college with that one tried-and-true pattern only to have it blasted away by their first-year writing professors. What they need, then, are more and better patterns for arranging complex ideas.

Part III, "Apply the Moves," addresses this need. It will help you get beyond limiting patterns like the five-paragraph essay. The section is filled with outlines—arrangement tools that you can use for structuring your own ideas. These outlines are not meant to be restrictive or limiting. Instead, they are meant to be generative: ways to get you thinking without the terrifying uncertainty of *where to go next*. Our hope is that you see these as patterns that can be transported to any number of writing projects.

ABOUT RISK

The main shift from high school to college, the one that requires the most energy and attention for most students, is the increased focus on thinking. In college, professors urge students to write with richness, depth, vitality, rigor, sophistication, complexity, inventiveness, or creativity. Whatever the name, it's the thinking that matters most. Prized above all else, the intellectual moves that lead to insights constitute the most weighty and valuable dimension of college work. In other words, an essay with perfectly tuned grammar, coherent paragraphs, and proper documentation means little without some intellectual dimension—some quality that goes beyond issues like proper formatting and correct usage.

But when writers steer toward insights—when they work toward sophistication and depth—they take on a certain level of risk. As the water deepens, the potential peril increases. Heavy ideas can slow down progress or drag a writer under. However, if you know the moves, if you know some arrangement strategies, and if you've seen how other writers handle the deep water, you're far more likely to keep on moving, to enter streams of thought, and to find the currents leading to new and better ideas.

PART I

Learn the Moves

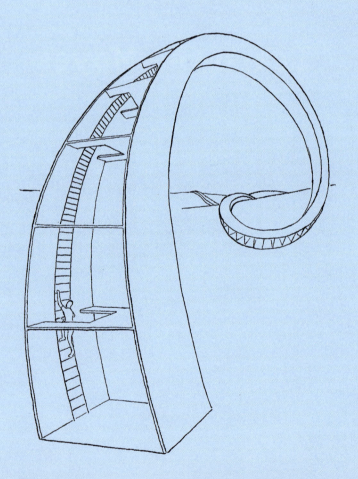

C H A P T E R

1

Seek Complexity

THINK ABOUT IT

Popular culture celebrates speedy answers. Game shows pay out big money for contestants who can buzz in quickly. Talk shows feature rapid-fire shouting matches between commercial breaks. And plenty of cop shows make it seem as though mysteries can be solved within a few days. And it's not only popular culture that wants quick solutions. The education industry sometimes supports the fast-answer regime with standardized tests that measure how quickly students conclude rather than how well they think. But thinking in college often means holding off on a fast answer and holding back a quickly formed opinion. In fact, easy answers can be dangerous when it comes to academic writing. Easy answers shut down thinking and keep us from exploring the quiet corners of thought. They short-circuit the logical powers that allow us to probe and discover.

Academic thinking requires a willingness to keep climbing beyond the normally defined steps. In short, a good part of academic thinking is about complexity. To survive in any discipline, writers have to press beyond easy answers and preformed positions. That's the task: to boldly go where brains don't normally go.

This is tricky work. We cannot wander aimlessly in a galaxy of random ideas. Instead, we have to begin thinking with the thoughts of other writers, with the shared concepts of a field, and with the usual associations of a shared language. We have to take what's given and seek complexity within, around, and sometimes in spite of it. And we don't want to unnecessarily complicate things. After all, the simple answer is sometimes the better one. But good writers and thinkers have to develop some reflexes that allow them to deal with complex issues. In the following pages, we offer four specific strategies for seeking complexity: (1) focus the questions, (2) unpack broad terms, (3) make connections, and (4) deny the usual associations.

Focus the Questions

Professional divers straighten their bodies and slice into the water. They go in like pins and plunge deep below the surface. A focused question is like a good dive: it gets you deeper into the issue. Whether you're developing a thesis statement for an essay or trying to work further into an idea, a more focused question will yield better, sharper thinking:

Broad Questions	Narrow Questions
What causes violence?	How does poverty figure into domestic violence?
How do children learn to read?	How do beginning readers use paragraphs to follow a story line?

Why are big-box stores so successful?	How do big-box stores use local resources to increase sales?
How has feminism changed society?	How did feminism help change working conditions in the 1970s?
How has computer technology changed society?	How has robotic technology impacted human interaction?

Broad questions like those above might provide some initial energy. But if we don't narrow them, we are prone to simplistic statements. Rather than probe the depths of an issue, we are more likely to stay in the shallows. For example, imagine taking the broad question about technology: How has computer technology changed society? It would be easy to list a huge range of changes—from the auto industry to politics, from social networking to classroom education. The list could go on and on. We wouldn't necessarily have to ask any probing questions. We wouldn't have to investigate, wonder, struggle to make connections, or think through any particular concepts. We would simply make a huge list and be done thinking. But a more focused question would get us somewhere. For example, if we focused on robotic technology and its influence on physical human interaction, we could begin thinking about specific concepts. We could explore how robotic arms in assembly-line manufacturing have impacted coworker relationships. Instead of listing a range of broad social changes, we would have to consider and research some specific forms of interaction: How do assembly-line coworkers share knowledge about the product? How do they signal uncertainty or concern about the product? How do they develop shared pride in the product?

A focused question, then, helps us to go further—to pursue a line of thinking into deep water. And even after a project gains focus, we can keep pursuing the ideas. We can keep asking increasingly narrow questions. In fact, the best intellectual work often generates as many questions as it answers. For example, in the following passage from *Alone Together*, Sherry Turkle offers several probing questions. Notice that her questions get increasingly narrow and more incisive:

> Overwhelmed by the volume and velocity of our lives, we turn to technology to help us find time. But technology makes us busier than ever and ever more in search of retreat. Gradually, we come to see our online life as life itself. We come to see what robots offer as relationship. The simplification of relationship is no longer a source of complaint. It becomes what we want. These seem the gathering clouds of a perfect storm.
>
> Technology reshapes the landscape of our emotional lives, but is it offering us the lives we want to lead? Many roboticists are enthusiastic about having robots tend to our children and our aging parents, for instance. Are these psychologically, socially, and ethically acceptable propositions? What are our responsibilities here? And are we comfortable with virtual environments that propose themselves not as places for recreation but as new worlds to live in? What do we have, now that we have what we say we want—now that we have what technology makes easy? This is the time to begin these conversations, together. It is too late to leave the future to the futurists.

Turkle could have stopped at the first few questions—and the usual complaint about technology taking over our lives. But that would have been the easy way out. As her

From *Alone Together: Why We Expect More from Technology and Less from Each Other*, New York: Basic, 2011.

questions progress, they become necessarily more complex; she pointedly asks about the difference between a recreational technology and a technology that takes over the worlds we live in; she wonders about our enthusiasm for ease and efficiency and how we might have entered a world with new ethical dilemmas. In this sense, Turkle's passage embodies the power of focused inquiry.

TALK ABOUT IT   More focused questions are more productive. If you keep reshaping and honing them, the resulting questions actually perform a job: they help you to generate better, more sophisticated ideas. In a small group, take a specific topic like politics, air pollution, college tuition, or space travel. Generate a short list of broad questions about the topic. And then generate a short list of more focused questions. Discuss how the more focused questions impact your thinking. To answer them, what would you have to consider, research, or understand? ■

Unpack Broad Terms

Imagine you're at a market. People are buying and selling suitcases of different sizes and brands. Each one has a word or phrase etched into the front: *People, Humanity, Femininity, Masculinity, Nature, The World, The Government, Knowledge, History, The Past, The Future, America, Religion, Liberalism, Conservatism, Christianity, Education,* and so on. You stand there watching these suitcases getting bought, traded, and sold. And then you notice something odd: none of the cases is open. People are ignoring the contents. You get the sense that the interior of each case might be important. You look down at the case in front of you. The exterior says *The Government.* You look around and unlatch it. You open it up. It's filled with thousands of little words and phrases:

township clerk
local water treatment systems
9-1-1 administrator
traffic light engineer
forest ranger
state senate voting procedure
infectious disease
outbreak policies
forest biological surveyor
firefighter
landfill engineer
civil rights law
county law enforcement officer
interstate fresh water policy
city librarian
state labor union regulations
accountants
federal copyright office administrator
graphic artist
museum curator
astronaut
Navy SEAL

You realize that all the suitcases are filled. The broad terms on the front are huge categories that contain policies, philosophies, titles, people, concepts, theories, conspiracies, facts, principles, and phenomena of every kind. In short, you realize all the stuff stowed away inside of broad terms.

In academic life, writers try not to ignore the contents of their terms. In fact, they try as often as possible to *unpack* them—to open them up and to understand the contents stowing away inside. This process is especially important with broad terms like those above (*government, history, religion,* and so on). When we rely on such terms, our brains go sailing over the top of important distinctions. For example, how often do you hear people say something about *the government*? It's a common move to complain about *the government* as though it is a singular whole—as though one group of uniformed people in an underground chamber is responsible for everything from local sewers to nuclear energy policy. But if we unpack *government*, we can see that it includes all kinds of systems, organizations, and people. And any single statement we make about *the government* would have to include everything from a 9-1-1 administrator to a forest ranger, from civil rights law to interstate fresh water policy. When we open the term and look inside, we see variety, difference, and probably a good deal of tension, which instantly makes our thinking more rich, less finite, and less dull. (Such unpacking is not meant to slow down critique or to obstruct complaining, but to make critiques and complaints more powerful. A complaint against "the government" has little impact. But a complaint against *this* politician's proposal, *that* taxation policy, *these* financial debt trends is much more exciting and specific.)

Good thinkers of all stripes find themselves unpacking terms. They explore how a common term shimmers with possibility. And the topic doesn't matter. Check out this opening passage from About.com, which urges teenagers to unpack a broad term:

> Think "sex" only means one thing? Think again! The word "sex" encompasses a lot of different types of sexual activities. The definitions of the main ones are below,[1] along with how risky they are.

---

[1] We'll let you explore those descriptions on your own.

Source: Taken from http://teenadvice.about.com/od/sex/tp/what_is_sex_info.htm, © 2012 Holly Ashworth (http://teenadvice.about.com/). Used with permission of About Inc., which can be found online at www.about.com. All rights reserved.

Or consider this more meaty passage from Alexis de Tocqueville's influential book *Democracy in America*. Here, Tocqueville (1805–1859) unpacks *patriotism*. Even though the style is a bit more ornate than modern-day writing, it's not difficult to see the move he's making. In the first paragraph below, he describes "one sort of patriotic attachment," and in the second, he describes "another species of attachment":

There is one sort of patriotic attachment which principally arises from that instinctive, disinterested, and undefinable feeling which connects the affections of man with his birthplace. This natural fondness is united to a taste for ancient customs, and to a reverence for ancestral traditions of the past; those who cherish it love their country as they love the mansions of their fathers. They enjoy the tranquillity which it affords them; they cling to the peaceful habits which they have contracted within its bosom; they are attached to the reminiscences which it awakens, and they are even pleased by the state of obedience in which they are placed. . . .

But there is another species of attachment to a country which is more rational than the one we have been describing. It is perhaps less generous and less ardent, but it is more fruitful and more lasting; it is coeval with the spread of knowledge, it is nurtured by the laws, it grows by the exercise of civil rights, and, in the end, it is confounded with the personal interest of the citizen. A man comprehends the influence which the prosperity of his country has upon his own welfare; he is aware that the laws authorize him to contribute his assistance to that prosperity, and he labors to promote it as a portion of his interest in the first place, and as a portion of his right in the second.

http://www.gutenberg.org/files/815/815-h/815-h.htm

You can probably detect some evaluation in Tocqueville's passage. He openly praises the second type of patriotism. He explains that the second is "more fruitful and more lasting." Such evaluation is sometimes unavoidable. After opening up a broad term, writers often reach conclusions about the value of one idea over another. In the following passage from a Kenyon College commencement address, David Foster Wallace unpacks *freedom*. He explains that "there are all different kinds of freedom" but that one kind is more important:

> The so-called "real world" will not discourage you from operating on your default settings, because the so-called "real world" of men and money and power hums along quite nicely on the fuel of fear and contempt and frustration and craving and the worship of self. Our own present culture has harnessed these forces in ways that have yielded extraordinary wealth and comfort and personal freedom. The freedom all to be lords of our tiny skull-sized kingdoms, alone at the center of all creation. This kind of freedom has much to recommend it. But of course there are all different kinds of freedom, and the kind that is most precious you will not hear much talked about in the great outside world of winning and achieving and displaying. The really important kind of freedom involves attention, and awareness, and discipline, and effort, and being able truly to care about other people and to sacrifice for them, over and over, in myriad petty little unsexy ways, every day. That is real freedom. That is being taught how to think. The alternative is unconsciousness, the default setting, the "rat race"—the constant, gnawing sense of having had and lost some infinite thing.

TALK ABOUT IT As a class, choose a broad term such as *technology* and then unpack it. Open it up. Rather than see it as a singular thing—with one set of effects and qualities—list as many qualities and effects as possible. Consider the good parts, the bad parts, the ugly parts. And then discuss: How do all the differences affect your thinking about the broad term? ∎

Make Connections

Humans are good at making connections. When we encounter a new idea or situation, our minds start reaching for familiar patterns so we can make sense of unfamiliar stimuli. When we get lost, we turn in all directions and try to get our intellectual hooks into something we recognize. The same thing happens when we come across an unfamiliar word: we try to find a familiar syllable or clump of letters. We grasp for meaning by grasping for stuff we already know. And we create new meaning by building on old intellectual ground. So in many respects, making connections is a basic intellectual operation. We do it naturally. But good thinkers also go looking for connections. They try to see how one situation parallels another—how one theory, debate, or text shares qualities of another.

The easiest connections we make are those between similar subjects. Consider, for example, two sports like NASCAR and Formula 1 racing. The connection is easy enough. Both sports are forms of contemporary auto racing. Whatever similarities we find will be fairly obvious, the differences relatively small. But let's broaden our scope. If we try to connect NASCAR and ancient Roman chariot races, we might discover more. Even though thousands of years (and the invention of gasoline engines) separate the two sports, they have some similarities. Juxtaposing them may prompt some good thinking:

In both sports, a crowd gathers around a circular track and watches while a few drivers risk life and limb to outpace competitors. There are no plays, quarters, half times, or breaks. It's unrelenting speed for as long as it takes. In both, the crowd can see the entire course of action, which is ongoing and constant, which means that anything can happen. The speed and force create ongoing energy and potential chaos—all completely within view. All strategies, dangers, and failures are immediately apparent. Any shortcomings or mistakes yield obvious, even disastrous, results. There is no time for the athletes or the onlookers to carefully plot out or chart the next move. In this sense, both NASCAR and chariot racing are true spectator sports. People crowd around the track and watch the spectacle. Maybe that simplicity speaks to the immense attraction and popularity through the ages.

And now consider what happens when we go looking for connections that are even less obvious. How is a NASCAR event similar to moshing? At first glance, these two phenomena seem entirely different. Moshing is a form of aggressive, usually single-sex (male), dancing at hard rock or metal concerts. NASCAR is a spectator sport that involves highly trained professionals driving souped-up cars. But beneath the obvious contrasts, these phenomena share some qualities. Both involve performance. Moshing takes place "in the pit" or the area directly in front of the stage. NASCAR events have an infield that hosts a range of notoriously rowdy behaviors. In this sense, moshing and NASCAR share something. They involve some collective public space. They both involve spectacle. And both run counter to mainstream official life. They are loud, raucous escapes from the tick-tock world of responsibility. Moshers, in this respect, aren't all that different from avid NASCAR fans.

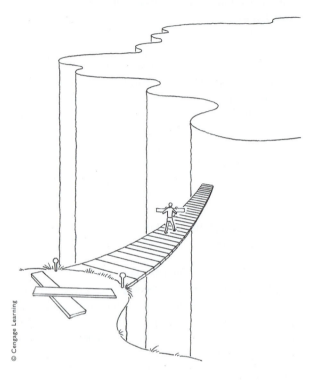

© Cengage Learning

The point here is that insights come from making connections. When we bring together similar phenomena, we can see qualities beyond the specifics and think about the general workings of, say, spectator sports through the centuries. And when we try to connect things that are usually not associated, we can generate even more powerful insights. We may even see a *pattern* of behavior—a rhythm or meaningful repetition that stretches across time and space. For example, in her essay about air (page 198), Stephanie Mills detects a pattern in human behavior (in how we look for guidance). And she connects our behavior to that of birds:

> Because we humans are always looking for guidance (or justification), usually in the form of a story, it is perennially human to try to read the metaphors in the night sky, to tell the myths associated with the constellations, and to seek the governance of the zodiac, or of fateful shooting stars, or comets as portents of millennial change.
>
> Migratory birds also consult the sky for guidance, if not of the metaphysical sort. They navigate by star patterns and the position of the sun on their journeys the length of a hemisphere, or across the trackless seas.

Mills sees a subtle but grand pattern: humans and birds both look to the sky for guidance. These quiet similarities—those that aren't obvious or easy to see—reveal a deep connection among people and between species. As her essay continues, she seeks meaning in that pattern. She tries to understand how the connection between humans and birds yields some insight:

> As the province of flying things, the air was, until only very recently, a realm beyond our powers. Now *we* claim to have conquered the sky—flight paths have become to us what sea-lanes were to our great-grandparents. Not only have airplanes become a commonplace means of transportation in the late twentieth century, in space capsules we have escaped Earth's ambit and traveled far enough away to have a look back at the home planet and take snapshots of Earth as Gaian mandala.[2]

Like Mills, good writers and thinkers explore the connections they make. They discover patterns and take the next step by asking questions like these: What's behind

---

[2] *Gaian* refers to the Gaia Hypothesis: the belief that the Earth is a self-regulating organism. A mandala is a sacred circle.

the pattern? What force or reflex creates the particular rhythm or repetition? What does the repetition help us to understand? Direct answers to such questions don't always show up in academic writing, but as we see in Mills's essay, we can often find evidence of writers working through the answers.

TALK ABOUT IT Good writers seek subtle patterns—quiet but meaningful repetition. Consider a pattern on your college campus. For instance, how does classroom layout repeat from one room to another? Are the desks and tables organized in any particular fashion? Is the organization consistent? What reflex or ideas might be responsible for the layout? What does the repetition help you to understand about college? ∎

Advanced Move: Deny the Usual Associations

Ideas don't exist in isolation. They hang around with several other ideas that have become associated with them. We see them together. If one idea is around, its associates are usually not far behind. For instance, consider a mosquito. When most people imagine a mosquito—the idea of a mosquito—they also picture itching, blood, a little swollen mark on the arm, and maybe a can of repellent. And for millions of people throughout the world, the idea of a mosquito comes along with a fear of malaria. In other words, it's almost impossible to think *mosquito* without thinking of these other things. The idea has a string of associations that go zooming through our brains almost instantaneously.

Let's get more abstract. Consider *high school*. The idea comes along with teachers, books, hallways, organized sports, maybe marching band. When someone says anything about *high school*, we probably don't think of outer space or antelopes running over a desert plain. Why? Because language is *associative*: it makes connections for us. And the most obvious associations are not random or even personal. (Granted, we all have personal associations and memories that come rolling along with particular words. When we think *high school*, we likely think of particular people, rooms, and events. But language works because so many of our associations are shared. We can communicate because we're *not* all quietly generating our own personal associations with each word. If we were, it'd be as though every single person were speaking a foreign language. We'd need dictionaries and translators for every statement.)

We can see the associative power of language at work in academic disciplines. For instance, in political science, *privacy* comes along with *individual, personal information, inalienable rights, search and seizure*. These concepts come on the coattails of *privacy*—and vice versa. They are clustered together in common thinking. Knowing these associations is part and parcel of being a political science student. One cannot unlearn them and shouldn't necessarily try. The associations, in other words, are valuable. They make thinking happen. Once *privacy* comes up, political scientists immediately understand the surrounding issues, the potential questions, and the intellectual tangles. They know, for instance, that *privacy* involves some belief in an individual's right to make personal decisions: where to live, how to worship, how not to worship, whom to marry, and so on. People who don't know these associations would have a difficult time. They'd flounder to understand even the beginnings of an article or lecture.

So common associations are important, but they can also act like blinders. They can keep us from seeing other possible connections. And so many writers explicitly deny usual associations. They spend time with unusual pairings. For instance, if we are thinking about *privacy*, we might deny the usual association with *individual*. What, then, happens to *privacy*? If it's not associated with an individual person, is it still *privacy*? Maybe. Once we separate the two concepts, things get interesting:

> Most often, privacy is not an individual phenomenon at all. In fact, very little, if anything, about human life is truly closed off from others. Our lives are shared with spouses, siblings, doctors, ministers, parents, friends, coworkers. If anything, we have a long list of co-conspirators—people who know things about us, who keep those things relatively, but not completely, quiet. More accurately, privacy is a behavior pattern whereby we choose who gets to know certain things about us. Privacy does involve choice—the decision to determine who knows what. When that decision gets taken away, or blurred in some fashion, our privacy gets compromised. In this sense, maybe privacy is not a closet where we keep secrets, but a web that we manage. If privacy is a web, then invasion of privacy is both easier to detect and harder to manage. And if this is true, it raises all kinds of questions about credit cards, corporate control of personal information, hacking, online dating, and so on.

We do not have to accept any of these statements. What's important is that we learn how to think (or even thrive) *without the usual intellectual associations*. Whenever we split up those conceptual clusters, exploratory thinking can begin. If, for instance, we tell *individual* to take a hike because we want to spend some time with *privacy*, the latter starts acting differently. It takes on new dimensions. It's those less common dimensions that academic writers seek.

In the following passage from *The Spell of the Sensuous*, David Abram calls on readers to avoid a common association. First, he describes the function of Native American shamans (holy leaders) and then cautions against a common association of that term with the "supernatural":

The shaman's ecological function, his or her role as intermediary between human society and the land, is not always obvious at first blush, even to a sensitive observer. We see the sorcerer being called upon to cure an ailing tribesman of his sleeplessness, or perhaps simply to locate some missing goods; we witness him entering into trance and sending his awareness into other dimensions in search of insight and aid. Yet we should not be so ready to interpret these dimensions as "supernatural," nor to view them as realms entirely "internal" to the personal psyche of the practitioner. . . .

In genuinely oral, indigenous cultures, the sensuous world itself remains the dwelling place of the gods, of the numinous powers that can either sustain or extinguish human life. It is not by sending his awareness out beyond the natural world that the shaman makes contact with the purveyors of life and health, nor by journeying into his personal psyche; rather, it is by propelling his awareness laterally, outward into the depths of a landscape at once both sensuous and psychological, the living dream that we share with the soaring hawk, the spider, and the stone silently sprouting lichens on its coarse surface.

Because Abram assumes that his readers are likely to link shamanism to the supernatural, he tries to separate the two concepts. In this case, the normal association diminishes complexity or even distorts the topic. It keeps readers from understanding something critical. Like a bad friend—one who drags others down—*supernatural* diminishes the complexity of *shamanism*. Only after Abram dismisses the usual association can he then go on to describe the real complexity.

TALK ABOUT IT Choose a term that consistently shows up in class reading or discussion and consider its usual

Source: *The Spell of the Sensuous* by David Abram (New York: Vintage, 1996)

associations—the other ideas that you instantly think of when you see or hear the term. In a group, discuss how those associative terms impact or even direct your thinking. What debates, positions, or events come to mind? What beliefs come to mind? ■

WRITE IT
• • • • • • • • •

Writing for complexity means cracking open our own thinking. The mission is to make our thinking less finite, less predictable, and less dull—to go looking for layers that we'd otherwise miss. Consider one of the following paths:

1. Consider a common idea that seems simple, one-dimensional, and obvious—for example, friendship, kindness, desire, or hope. Seek complexity in that idea. Apply the moves from this chapter: ask focused questions, unpack terms, make connections, and deny the usual associations. Develop a brief essay that reveals layers of your topic. After you've done some writing (developed a full draft), go back through and unpack further. Add full paragraphs that crack open your own broad terms and deny the associations that you relied on.

2. Think about your situation: In addition to being a college student, maybe you work full-time or part-time. Maybe you're a parent. Maybe you're an athlete or musician. Maybe you're studying abroad. Whatever your situation, how are you part of a pattern? Write a brief essay that explains your experience as a particular type of student. Consider the moves in this chapter: unpack broad terms (such as *people, American, college*, and *career*), ask focused questions, and deny the usual associations.

3. Take on a common idea in education, such as knowledge, science, instruction, culture, memory, or technology. Use the moves in this chapter to flesh out complexity that otherwise gets ignored or missed. Try to deny the common associations. Explain how the usual clusters of thought stop thinking. Ask focused questions. And unpack broad terms that might conceal dimensions of the concept. What insights emerge? Why is this new way of thinking important?

READ: For examples of full essays that seek complexity, check out Steven D. Krause (page 193) and Stephanie Mills (page 198).

APPLY: For specific guidance on how to structure a full essay using the moves in this chapter, see the outlines in Part III, "Apply the Moves" (pages 300–301).

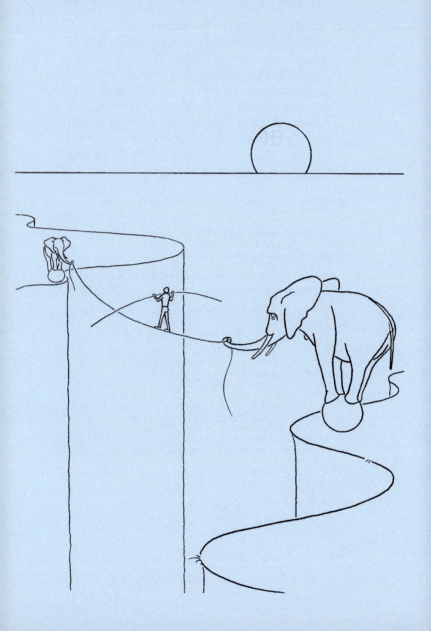

CHAPTER

Seek Tension

THINK ABOUT IT

In daily life, most people do their best to avoid conflict. By and large, we steer clear of open debate and outright tension. We don't usually jump out of our cars and accost bad drivers. We don't grab strangers' cell phones and hang them up if they're talking too loudly. We live and let live when it comes to most public situations. In fact, psychologists claim that a healthy state of mind depends, in part, on our ability to let many potential conflicts pass us by. Otherwise, we'd get caught up in nonstop friction. But when it comes to academic writing, tension is unavoidable. In fact, good writers and thinkers go looking for it. They focus on disagreement and debate. They also seek out quieter forms of tension: confusion, intellectual gaps, and cracks in meaning. In short, if there's something wrong—anything amiss—good writers seize on it.

The previous chapter focused on strategies for seeking complexity. This chapter is closely related. Tension, after all, is a kind of complexity. But it's so important that it warrants its own examination. While later chapters will deal with more direct forms of conflict and debate, this chapter focuses on how to detect subtle tension, connect to broad tensions, and bust up dualities.

Detect Subtle Tension

Open conflict is easy to see. It involves physical stand-offs, vocal debate, and obvious pressure. It's the thing that drives action movies. It's the energy that generates political debates, barroom fights, and family disputes. In open conflict, the parties usually understand the point of disagreement: the buried treasure is mine, not yours; the tax code benefits the rich, not the middle class; you spilled a beer on my boots; and so on. But subtle tension moves along quietly. It lurks in corners. And you don't have to be a credentialed scholar to know when it's there. Whenever a situation doesn't conform to your expectations, or vice versa, you experience some intellectual friction, some quiet discomfort. For example, imagine that you've walked into a college classroom on the first day and the instructor, who seems pleasant and engaged, tells about the course but does not distribute a syllabus or course calendar. Because such information is normally distributed, you and other students feel some tension.

In such moments, we wonder what's going on. We probe our thinking for possible responses—or wonder if we should be concerned in the first place. Good thinkers and writers seize on those moments of wonder. They pause and study the tension between what they've assumed and what they're witnessing. For example, in her article about Afghanistan (page 207), Virginia Postrel confronts some intellectual friction. She begins by describing the situation after US military forces took down the Taliban, the ruling political organization. In the second paragraph, she focuses on the tension between what she expected to see and what she witnessed:

As soon as the Taliban fell, Afghan men lined up at barbershops to have their beards shaved off. Women painted their nails with once-forbidden polish. Formerly clandestine beauty salons opened in prominent locations. Men traded postcards of beautiful Indian movie stars, and thronged to buy imported TVs, VCRs, and videotapes. Even burka merchants diversified their wares, adding colors like brown, peach, and green to the blue and off-white dictated by the Taliban's whip-wielding virtue police. Freed to travel to city markets, village women demanded better fabric, finer embroidery, and more variety in their traditional garments. . . .

Liberation is supposed to be about grave matters: elections, education, a free press. But Afghans acted as though superficial things were just as important. As a political commentator noted, "The right to shave may be found in no international treaty or covenant, but it has, in Afghanistan, become one of the first freedoms to which claim is being laid."

Postrel expected that Afghanis would use their newfound freedom to address governmental needs. But she witnessed them using their newfound freedom to buy beauty products and alter their appearances. The events didn't line up with her assumptions, and that *misalignment* provoked thinking. In her article, she doesn't blame or judge the Afghani citizens for not conforming to her expectations. Nor does she ignore or dismiss her own sense of wonder.

Like Postrel, good writers and thinkers capitalize on the misalignment between what they see and what they expect. They have an open mind—not open to any idea that comes rolling along, but open to investigating situations that don't immediately line up with their preconceptions. They try to understand *why* things don't conform. And perhaps most importantly, they don't lunge for a quick resolution. They don't hope to end the friction but to study it.

Sloppy thinking happens when we

- Don't see what we don't expect.
- Abandon our own wonder.
- Run from intellectual friction.

Good thinking happens when we

- See what we aren't expecting.
- Recognize the misalignment between what we expect and what we witness.
- Try to understand that misalignment.

TALK ABOUT IT In a small group, return to the classroom scenario on page 34. What expectations do you bring to college classrooms? Why do you have those particular expectations? What past experiences generated your expectations? If you walked into a classroom where no syllabus or calendar was distributed, what would you think? How would that situation rub against your expectations? ∎

Connect to a Broader Tension

As we explain in the previous chapter, good writers find patterns. They imagine how individual moments connect across time and space, even how ideas from different contexts might relate to each other. The same goes for tension. Good writers try to understand how a particular misalignment or confusion relates to something broader—to a historical, philosophical, or political friction that extends beyond the moment. For example, in the classroom scenario from the previous section, students would start by trying to understand what they were supposed to do. But as they thought through the situation, they might also consider some broader tensions related to learning, college, motivation, and uncertainty. They might, for instance, think about the difference between active and passive learning, students and consumers, or even learning and unlearning. In other words, they might connect their particular situation with a bigger and more long-standing issue.

In her article, Virginia Postrel makes such a connection. At the outset, she seizes on a specific tension between her expectations and the real events. In her own thinking, beauty products and hair salon services were superficial concerns—not "grave matters" like developing fair and free elections.

- **What She Expected:** Liberated people will use their freedom to fix their society.

- **What She Witnessed:** Liberated people will first consider their personal appearances.

If she were a sloppy thinker, she'd have ended the tension by simply condemning the Afghanis for being superficial. Instead, Postrel pursues the broader tension between "surface" and "substance." She explores why people have traditionally kept such categories in place:

> Human beings know the world, and each other, through our senses. From our earliest moments, the look and feel of our surroundings tell us who and where we are. But as we grow, we imbibe a different lesson: that appearances are not just potentially deceiving but frivolous and unimportant—that aesthetic value is not real except in those rare instances when it transcends the quotidian to become high art. We learn to contrast surface to substance, to believe that our real selves and the real world exist beyond the superficiality of sensation.

We have good cause, of course, to doubt the simple evidence of our senses. The sun does not go around the earth. Lines of the same length can look longer or shorter depending on how you place arrows on their ends. Beautiful people are not necessarily good, nor are good people necessarily beautiful. We're wise to maintain reasonable doubts.

But rejecting our sensory natures has problems of its own. When we declare that mere surface cannot possibly have legitimate value, we deny human experience and ignore human behavior. We set ourselves up to be fooled again and again, and we make ourselves a little crazy.

Postrel illustrates some common and powerful moves: First, she seizes on the tension between her expectations and real events. Second, she avoids quick judgment that would effectively end the tension. In other words, she keeps the tension alive. She studies it. Third, she connects the concrete events of the Afghan transition to broader philosophical questions about our senses (the "surface" of things).

TALK ABOUT IT In a small group, return again to the classroom scenario where no syllabus or course calendar is distributed. Connect that situation to the tension between active and passive learning. To do this, you might first try to describe active learning and passive learning. Make a list of the characteristics or behaviors you associate with each phrase, or search for each phrase online. Discuss how these characteristics relate to the classroom scenario. ■

Source: Excerpt from pp. ix–xi (697 words) from *THE SUBSTANCE OF STYLE* by VIRGINIA POSTREL. Copyright © 2003 by Virginia Postrel. Reprinted by permission of HarperCollins Publishers.

Advanced Move: Detect and Bust Up Dualities

So far, this chapter has urged you to seek tension and examine it—in short, to study intellectual friction. This final section focuses on a particular type of tension known as the *duality*, an opposing pair of ideas such as black/white, up/down, in/out, us/them, republican/democrat, hate/love, cause/effect, before/after, capitalism/socialism, tyranny/democracy, hot/cold, powerful/powerless, predator/prey, beautiful/ugly, opinion/fact, and so on. Such dualities, and many more, live in our language. They make us think in particular ways—not all of them bad. For instance, it's helpful to see that tyranny and democracy are opposites: Tyranny operates from the top down. It involves a few people, or one person, holding all political power and forcing it onto the masses. On the other hand, democracy enables the masses to determine how power will work. It's an important distinction that helps millions of people throughout the world understand their role in the social order.

However, dualities can bully our brains. They can gather in our thoughts and make us imagine two, and only two, contrary possibilities. In short, they can create *dualistic thinking*—an inability to see gray areas. When people fall prey to *dualism*, they see topics split down the middle. They see all paths as forked—one branch going left, the other going right. They fail to imagine multiple paths, many lines, or no lines at all. For example, consider the tyranny/democracy duality. At first glance, the two forms of government seem absolutely distinct. And in many ways, they are: In tyranny, the masses are controlled by a single leader. In democracy, policies are determined by a majority of voters. But if we can think beyond the duality, we might see some gray areas. Here's one example: In the early nineteenth century, Alexis de

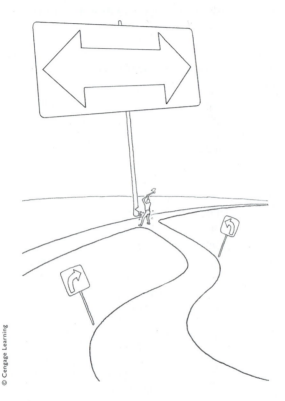

Tocqueville cautioned against the "tyranny of the majority"—the power of the masses to squash the hopes of a minority. Democracy, he explained, is not free of tyranny. If given absolute rule, a majority can enact the same degree of terror and oppression as a megalomaniacal king. If we cannot imagine this complexity (if we believe that a majority always acts democratically), we may not ask some crucial policy questions. We may even be blind to profound problems.

A LOOK AT DUALISM THROUGH TIME

Dualistic thinking is nothing new. It's as old as human civilization. Some religious traditions explicitly call on adherents to reject dualism—to inhabit a spiritual place beyond contraries. For example, the *Tao Te Ching*, from the sixth century BCE, busts up dualities. Verse 22 urges the sages to

> Yield and overcome;
> Bend and be straight;
> Empty and be full;
> Wear out and be new;
> Have little and gain;
> Have much and be confused.

Such guidance seems impossible. We expect *or* rather than *and* in each line: yield or overcome; bend or be straight; empty or be full. But the *and* collapses the opposing verbs. It says, in effect, *these two actions are not opposite*! As with some early Christians and Buddhists, Taoists believe that enlightenment lies beyond the dualistic thinking that drives so much daily life.

The point here is that we don't always have to choose A or B, tyranny or democracy, on or off, family or community, crush or be crushed. There's no overarching rule that says we must think in dualities. Often, in fact, dualities keep us from understanding the complexity of an issue. In Virginia Postrel's article, for instance, she ultimately busts up the duality that keeps her from understanding the Afghanis' behavior. Look, again, at her final two paragraphs. In the first, she admits that our senses can fool us and that we should manage our immediate response to the world. But in the last paragraph, she admits that our senses are genuine and real—as real as anything in human experience:

> *We have good cause, of course, to doubt the simple evidence of our senses*. The sun does not go around the earth. Lines of the same length can look longer or shorter depending on how you place arrows on their ends. Beautiful people are not necessarily good, nor are good people necessarily beautiful. We're wise to maintain reasonable doubts.
>
> *But rejecting our sensory natures has problems of its own*. When we declare that mere surface cannot possibly have legitimate value, we deny human experience and ignore human behavior. We set ourselves up to be fooled again and again, and we make ourselves a little crazy.

In other words, we shouldn't rely on safe dualities (such as surface/substance, sensory/real, exterior/interior). If we want to understand something as complex as human behavior, we have to think beyond those categories.

Like Postrel, many writers set up a duality by explaining the two sides and the friction between them. Then, after that explanation, they run up the middle and show the gray area in between. In her essay "Math vs. English" (page 285), Ann-Marie Paulin examines a common duality: people often classify themselves as math or language oriented—one or the other. Then, she interrogates that way of thinking. She suggests that people are capable of succeeding in both realms—that the labels ("math person" and "English person") are overly simplistic. And in the paragraphs below, she even explains some of the broader beliefs that sustain the duality:

I have been teaching college English for over twenty years, and I have often noticed that students and faculty still hold on to the old math/English duality. I notice this most often in literature classes when we discuss poetry. The students who enjoy playing with language and who are comfortable with several different meanings being possible all at once tend to catch on to working with poetry fairly quickly. Students who are math or science majors often seem alarmed and bewildered by the idea that a line of poetry can mean multiple things at once. How can three interpretations be different and all correct!?

But are things really as clear-cut as this seems? Is it really a duality? We often get the message in our culture that things are black or white, liberal or conservative, beautiful or ugly, smart or dumb. Not all cultures see things this way. Think of the yin and yang. While the symbol recognizes certain dualities, it also recognizes they are not absolute: there is a bit of the light in the dark and a bit of the dark in the light. But recognizing the subtleties requires a willingness to pay attention, to question, to stop and think. It requires time. These activities are not as popular as they once were in our moving-at-the-speed-of-technology society.

To go back to my college friend, she can do math that matters to her. She balances her checkbook, calculates appropriate tips, measures fabrics for sewing, and can measure a room to determine how many gallons of paint to buy. Same for me. (Well, my checkbook is a mess, but you get my point.) And I know there are plenty of math people who write wonderful letters and web page updates, who can tell a story that keeps everyone crying with laughter. So is the issue one of ability or desire?

In Paulin's case, the duality was already clearly spelled out. The math/English divide is entrenched in our conversations about ourselves and others. But sometimes, dualities sit quietly in our own thinking. We have to call them out. For example, in *About This Life*, Barry Lopez calls out another duality that lurks in popular thought. It is not spelled out directly in a source but hiding in people's collective assumptions or "ideologies":

> It is a tenet of certain ideologies that man is responsible for all that is ugly, that everything nature creates is beautiful. Nature's darkness goes partly unreported, of course, and human brilliance is often perversely ignored.

Here, Lopez not only points out the man/nature duality but also hints at the intellectual hijinks that constantly support and emerge from dualities. If people are to believe, and keep believing, in the humanity (bad) / nature (good) duality, they have to ignore some terrifying brutality that goes on in nature. They also have to ignore some glorious aspects of human civilization. In other words, it's not just the duality itself that creates bad thinking. There's a fog of ignorance and blindness that surrounds and supports it.

Paulin and Lopez illustrate an important point: if we are to think well, then we have to bust up dualities

---

Reprinted by permission of Ann-Marie Paulin.

Source: *About This Life: Journeys on the Threshold of Memory* by Barry Lopez (New York: Vintage, 1999).

and escape the fog of bad thinking around them. Some of our worst thinking, in fact, happens when we allow common dualities to thrive, to bully us, to make us blind to the gray areas. Consider the ways, for instance, that the conservative/liberal opposition has impacted thinking about any number of issues. Once people fall on one side or the other, they often accept a huge list of beliefs that oppose the other side. The duality, then, creates a list of other dualities. Like intellectual demons, they take over and start reproducing in our heads.

TALK ABOUT IT

1. Examine the conservative/liberal duality. As a class, list some beliefs that you think fit under each label. You might list beliefs according to specific topics such as taxes, the environment, poverty, gay rights, privacy, and gun laws. Consider one of these specific topics and try to discover a gray area. Beneath the obvious tension between liberals and conservatives, what assumptions might they share?

2. Examine the man/woman duality. What behaviors and descriptions keep the duality in place? What common phrases keep people from seeing the gray areas between men and women? ■

WRITE IT
•••••••••

Good thinkers sense subtle tension. They consider what it means, how it works, why it's there in the first place. They seek it out, seize it, and develop insights before they even begin reaching for solutions. They embrace friction, study it, and even dissolve it from the inside out. Consider one of the following paths:

1. Attend a public concert, reading, or sporting event—one that you wouldn't normally be inclined to attend. Seek tension in the situation. Carefully monitor the behavior patterns you observe. Consider any action that seems out of sync with your expectations. Avoid judging the action. Instead, focus on the misalignment between what you're seeing and what you'd expect to see. Pursue that misalignment. What forces, reflexes, or policies might cause behaviors not to conform to your expectations?

2. Return to your first day of high school, college, or work. Recall your initial impressions—what you encountered, what you witnessed. What particular intellectual friction did you experience? After you describe that friction, launch outward to a broader tension. Connect to a long-standing cultural, economic, or philosophical tension. (Remember that a broader tension doesn't have to involve something as grand as human nature. You might, for instance, find a connection between your work experience and a tension between employees and employers or between service providers and customers.)

3. Describe a specific event on your campus or in your town. Explain what makes the event important or noteworthy to fellow students or citizens. Explain the shared understanding and any different or competing opinions about the event. What are the different ways of thinking about the event? How is the meaning or significance of the event quietly disputed? Does that quiet dispute relate to a broader cultural, educational, economic, physical, emotional, or even spiritual tension?

READ: For examples of full essays that seek tension, check out Matthew Yglesias (page 203) and Virginia Postrel (page 207).

APPLY: For specific guidance on how to structure a full essay using the moves in this chapter, see the outlines in Part III, "Apply the Moves" (page 302).

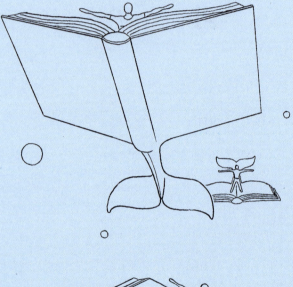
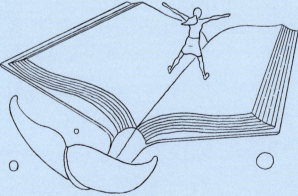

C H A P T E R

3

Apply Sources

THINK ABOUT IT

As we explain in the previous chapters, good writers seek complexity in the world around them. Sources help to make that happen. By adding dimension to our own ideas, sources clarify what we don't yet know, and they may even contradict what we think we know. In other words, sources make thinking happen. Whether it's an article, report, book, literary work, blog, wiki, or an interview, a powerful source can get us out of our own head and connect us with other currents of thought.

It's important, then, to think of sources as *sources of thought*—voices that change, flip, thicken, substantiate, and counter your own ideas. Doing so opens up all kinds of possibilities for incorporating research into your writing projects. In fact, sources can help you to make any writerly move. In other words, sources don't belong to any particular type of project or to any particular intellectual move. A source might help you bust up a duality, explain the tension surrounding a topic, dismantle someone else's argument, justify your position, change the terms of a debate, even escape the status quo. Or a source might simply provide some intellectual momentum. In this chapter, we'll focus on the following common strategies for using sources: applying a supportive source, drawing from a vital source, and synthesizing sources. And as a last step, we'll explain some of the basics for citing any sources you use directly.

Apply a Supportive Source

When it comes to dealing with sources, applying a supportive source may be the most basic and common move. Simply put, a supportive source reinforces ideas. When writers feel the need to link their own thinking with the ideas of others, they use a source to say, in effect, "It's not just me. Other people share my perspective." The source backs up the writer's point and connects the writer's ideas to a world of other people. For example, in the following passage from her book *Distracted*, Maggie Jackson describes how families are affected by cyberspace. Her supportive source is a book by the sociologist Anthony Giddens:

> In updating our definitions of family for a new age, we've traded security for freedom and swapped the group for the loose network of kin. We don't seek suffocating ideals of obligatory togetherness, day by day or over our lifetimes. Yet all this changes the nature of family ties. "Kinship relations used to be taken for granted on the basis of trust, now trust has to be negotiated and bargained for, and commitment is as much an issue as in sexual relationships," says Anthony Giddens in *The Transformation of Intimacy*.

It's important to note that the Giddens quotation does more than support Jackson's point. It thickens it. And, more importantly, it establishes a connection between one person (Jackson) and an entire field of study. Suddenly, Jackson isn't alone. She's connected. And she makes this move consistently in her book. For example, in the following passage, she refers to science fiction writer William Gibson, whose words help to make a sophisticated point about people's collective experience in cyberspace:

> Although most game developers desperately strive to make their fantasy worlds more "real," we can't and likely won't ever be able to clone our reality in fonts and pixels. That's obvious. What is not always apparent is how our time in this disembodied, alluring, liberating world changes us and especially influences our relations with each other. For this is no solo journey. Cyberspace, in science fiction writer William Gibson's words, is a "consensual hallucination," more so than any of the alternative worlds man has ever created—from Greek mythology to the layered slices of medieval heavens to film or theater.

Notice, too, that Jackson uses Gibson's voice to develop an idea that is "not always apparent." Sources often get used in this fashion. When good writers need more language, more scholarly force to establish a less obvious idea, they rely on sources. In other words, good writers like Maggie Jackson don't drop in sources for the obvious points. They rely on others *when the thinking gets harder*, when the subject matter gets more vague or foggy, and when they're in need of more precise terms.

From *Distracted: The Erosion of Attention and the Coming Dark Age*, Amherst: Prometheus, 2008. Copyright © 2008 by Maggie Jackson. All rights reserved.

TALK ABOUT IT Consider an academic subject you're interested in. Choose a topic (such as the role of children in TV advertising, intimacy in social networking, or prescription drug addiction) and do some research on it. Locate at least two sources and explain in a sentence what each contributes to your thinking about the topic. How might each be used as a supportive source in an essay? Discuss your findings in class. ■

Draw from a Vital Source

A slightly more sophisticated way to use a source is to draw ideas from it and use those ideas to build insights of your own. In other words, if you find a powerful voice (whether it's a report, essay, blog, book, or literary work), you can use it to launch and propel your own thinking and writing. In fact, using a source as a springboard is fairly typical. Millions of articles and books begin with a direct reference to a source that the writer found especially inspiring. For example, in her article "From Trickster to Heroic Savior: Jake Sully's Journey in *Avatar*" (page 224), Tiffany J. Smith draws from the famous mythographer Joseph Campbell. She uses Campbell's thinking to better understand the movie *Avatar*. In fact, she begins her essay by introducing Campbell and his relevance:

> Can mythological theories be applied to a modern day tale? The mythographer, Joseph Campbell, through his lifetime of studying myths from around the world, came to a universal conclusion: when we crack the nutshell of any myth from any part of the world, "it will always be the one, shape-shifting yet marvelously constant story that we find." In other words, all myths are basically the same story; only the characters and settings have changed. Whether intentional or not, all storytelling follows an ancient pattern

which can be understood through the "Hero Myth" or "Monomyth" concepts.

As Smith's article continues, she *comes back around* to Campbell's ideas and words. In the following passage, she explains the degree to which his ideas apply to the characters and plot of the movie:

> [*Avatar*] is a modern and dynamic adaptation of an age-old story. When the plot and characters are stripped of their flashy and charismatic exteriors, we are left with a true-to-form example of a hero's journey. Joseph Campbell maps out this journey using specific stages which director and writer James Cameron followed in the plot of the film with exceptional accuracy, even down to the archetypes represented, such as the protagonist (in this case, a trickster turned hero), mother goddess, mentor, and protector. All of them serve to follow the hero cycle.

And throughout the article, Smith keeps *coming back around* to Campbell:

> The next stage, as set by Campbell, is the "refusal of the call." During this stage, the hero ignores, or outright refuses, to accept his destiny. Campbell states, "the refusal is essentially a refusal to give up what one takes to be one's own interest." During this stage in Jake Sully's journey, he transitions from working for the military in order to control the Na'vi, to beginning to understand the importance of the land and seeing the Na'vi as more than just creatures, but as equals. Only after this understanding takes place does Jake begin the fight to protect the Na'vi, and ultimately fulfill his destiny as heroic savior.

Source: www.americanpopularculture.com/film.htm. Reprinted with permission.

In this way, the vital source propels Smith's article. Each time she *comes back around* to Campbell's ideas, her own thinking gets deeper. This is a powerful strategy for developing intellectual richness: the writer devotes an opening paragraph, or several opening paragraphs, to a vital source and then continues to return to it. Applying the source involves more than simply referencing it and then moving on. It involves several steps: (1) summarizing the source, (2) explaining how the source sheds a particular light on the issue at hand, and (3) weaving the insights from that source into one's own thinking. It's that third step, the weaving, that academic writers and readers are most interested in. The big insights often come when writers keep going back to a source—when they let it feed into each new idea they develop.

A LOOK AT SUMMARY, PARAPHRASE, AND QUOTATION

Summarizing, paraphrasing, and quoting are common practices in academic writing. They are used to portray what others have thought or said. There are many tricks, variables, and rules for each, but here are some key points about these critical practices:

The Key to Summary: It's all about precision. When you summarize, you describe someone else's ideas while also condensing them into your own words. But when we shorten something, we change it. So the trick of good summary is to hand over the most accurate version possible—to describe the heart of the work (the movie, book, article, or whatever it may be) that distinguishes it from all other similar works. It's a balancing act between brevity and accuracy. On one hand, you don't want to boil things down so that the original idea is barely distinguishable from a million other things. On the other, you don't want to drag things out too long and end up retelling a whole story or argument. Check out the differences among three summaries below:

- **Too general:** *Harry Potter* is the story of a kid with no parents.

- **Too brief:** *Harry Potter* is the story of an orphaned boy with magical powers.

- **Short but accurate:** *Harry Potter* is the story of a young wizard who must discover his own power and use it to destroy the ultimate evil force in the world.

Most often, as you'll see throughout this book, academic writers summarize an article or book in a few sentences. They don't drag things out too long because they've got other business to attend to. They're trying, after all, to *do* something with the summary. They're using it to build a point, to develop an insight of their own.

The Key to Paraphrase: Give your voice to the ideas from a source. Like summary, paraphrase involves rewording ideas from a source, but in paraphrase, the goal is not to condense or abbreviate. In other words, paraphrasing means re-explaining exactly what a source has already said without using the direct phrases from the source. It can be tricky work. If writers aren't careful, they may end up borrowing sentences and phrases without quoting them. In academic and professional situations, that's considered plagiarism. On the other hand, good paraphrase can be a powerful move—a way to thoroughly understand and give your voice to the ideas that you learned from a source. In fact, some of the best writing happens

continued

when someone carefully reads a source, understands the source at a deep level, and then articulates that understanding in a genuinely different way—with different comparisons, images, and descriptions. So don't shy away from paraphrase. Just remember the goal: to lend your own voice to the ideas in that source. (And even if you've successfully paraphrased the source in your own language, you *still* have to cite that source. See the final section of this chapter on pages 65–68.)

The Key to Quotation: Use the words that give the most insight. Writers quote for many reasons—to show what an opponent thinks, to show what supporters say, to show the exact words of an important theorist, and so on. Regardless of the purpose, quoting should highlight the most critical or the most important language from a source. We do this constantly in our daily lives. When we're describing a song to someone, we don't sing a few lines from the fourth verse. We sing the chorus—the key words and melody that make the song what it is. In academic writing, quotation works in the same way. Writers home in on the words that will carry thinking the furthest. Notice, for instance, how Shawn Burks does this (pages 216–217): he summarizes his sources' ideas and then delivers quotations that propel the thinking. The big insights come as a result of *strategic quotation*.

Finally, remember that good summary, paraphrase, and quotation rely on a deep understanding of the source. When writers *get* a book, article, or blog—*when they really get it*—summary, paraphrase, and quotation come more easily. They know the nuances, the critical insights, and the reason the source matters. So perhaps the best advice is to know your source! That means reading closely and repeatedly. It also means trying to understand the original audience for the source, the debates or tensions surrounding the source, and the underlying purpose of the writer. In short, read for context. (For more on audience, purpose, and context, see Chapter 5, "Dismantle Arguments.") As you read through this book, you'll see many examples of summary, quotation, and paraphrase. And you'll learn some strategies for getting to know sources. For instance, if you develop the skill to dismantle an argument (see Chapter 5), you'll find that articles make more sense than you might have thought—even when they're relatively difficult or dense.

TALK ABOUT IT

1. Choose one of the sources you found for the Talk About It on page 52. Then, write a brief summary of the source and choose a key quotation that characterizes the source. In a small group, describe the source you chose and then read your summary and quotation aloud. How do others in your group understand your source based on your summary and selected quotation? Do they *get* it? If not, discuss how your summary or quotation can be further refined to capture the source's main point.

2. In a small group, choose an introductory paragraph from any essay in Part II, "Read the Moves." Once you've decided, have each writer, individually, develop a paraphrase of that introduction. Then, share your paraphrases with others. How do they compare? How do they contrast? What ideas are shared? ∎

Synthesize Sources

Good writers can bring together, or *synthesize*, a range of supportive sources. They assemble several sources into one passage and integrate them to develop a point. For

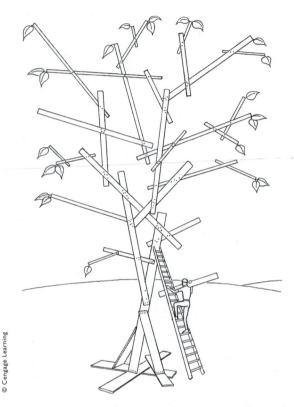

example, in their widely read book *Academically Adrift: Limited Learning on College Campuses*, Richard Arum and Josipa Roksa use a range of reports to further their investigation of higher education. In the following passage, they synthesize the ideas from three sources. Each source reinforces the others. And they all reinforce the first point of the paragraph about the aims of higher education:

Teaching students to think critically and communicate effectively are espoused as the principal goals of higher education. From the Commission on the Future of Higher Education's recent report *A Test of Leadership* to the halls of Ivy

League institutions, all corners of higher education endorse the importance of these skills. When promoting student exchange across the world, former Secretary of Education Margaret Spellings urged foreign students to take advantage of "the creativity and diversity of American higher education, *its focus on critical thinking*, and its unparalleled access to world-class research." The American Association of University Professors agrees: ". . . critical thinking . . . is the hallmark of American education—an education designed to create thinking citizens for a free society."

Here, Arum and Roksa apply sources to argue for the role of critical thinking in higher education. But the sources do more than support a point. Throughout the paragraph, they build into a crescendo—into increasingly specific ideas about *how* critical thinking functions both in and out of college.

As you get comfortable with this process, you can travel through time and assemble sources from different decades, centuries, and cultures. In other words, you don't have to keep your head in one era or one location. You can make a connection between a new bit of data and a historic insight. (See "Make Connections" in Chapter 1 for more on making connections among ideas.) Arum and Roksa make this move in the conclusion of their book. After a lengthy analysis of new information, they borrow from the past. They leave behind all the new data and focus on a historic insight—specifically, on the words of President John F. Kennedy:

Although our higher-education institutions currently are academically adrift, they can commit to a change of course that will reconnect them with their earlier design and functions. We should choose paths of purpose such as these, as Kennedy reminded us when he exhorted us to reach for the moon, "not because they are easy, but because they are hard, because that goal will serve to organize and measure the best of our energies and skills, because that challenge is one that we are willing to accept, one we are unwilling to postpone, and one which we intend to win."

As Arum and Roksa show, good writers often go searching for a way to balance new information with a historic perspective. They show the power of assembling the past and present. In his essay "Kissing Technology on the Mouth" (page 193), Steven D. Krause goes back in time even further. He makes a connection between a contemporary columnist in the *New York Times* and the ancient Greek philosopher Socrates. Krause is not deterred by the thousands of years that separate the two:

> In a *New York Times* editorial titled "You Love Your iPhone. Literally," Martin Lindstrom raises concern about the feelings of "loss" that iPhone users experience when they are without their phones. "As we embrace new technology that does everything but kiss us on the mouth," Lindstrom writes, "we risk cutting ourselves off from human interaction."
>
> Whenever I read critiques like Lindstrom's, I always remember old Socrates, 2,500 years ago, and I imagine him lecturing to a young student about the dangers of moving away from face-to-face conversation to the distancing and dehumanizing technology of reading and writing. Yet I don't think anyone would ever describe pens, papers, typewriters, newspapers, or books as "dehumanizing," nor do we think poorly of people who always have a pen at the ready.

As these passages demonstrate, vital ideas are still waiting in the past. Positions and insights that have been buried by recent trends and general forgetfulness can still fortify our thinking. The best contemporary thinkers retrieve those insights and *pull them forward* into the present.

Synthesis is more than lining up sources who agree. It also involves bringing together opposing or conflicting sources—using them, in fact, to show conflict and tension surrounding a topic. As we explain in Chapter 2, any given topic resounds with conflicting opinions, even outright debate. Often, the tension is spelled out for all to see. The parties involved argue openly over a single point of disagreement. For example, in her article for *Diabetes Forecast* magazine, Tracey Neithercott describes a new tension in the field of nutrition. In this case, the debate is narrowed down to a particular question: is high-fructose corn syrup bad for our health or not? Some groups say no. Others say yes. Neithercott clearly distinguishes the point of disagreement:

> High-fructose corn syrup is a thick, sweet liquid derived from corn. During processing, the glucose in cornstarch is converted into fructose. The final product contains either 42 percent fructose and 53 percent glucose or 55 percent fructose and 42 percent glucose. Compared with sucrose (sugar), which is half fructose and half glucose, high-fructose corn syrup isn't too different. That's the main argument made by scientists who say the hullabaloo over the sweetener is unfounded. A 2008 review of data on high-fructose corn syrup and sugar, published in the *American Journal of Clinical Nutrition*, said it was unlikely that high-fructose corn syrup caused the current obesity epidemic. The American Medical Association's Council on Science and Public Health came to the same conclusion in a report last year. Both reviews suggest the obesity epidemic has instead stemmed from an increase in total food consumption. In other words, supersized soda has done more for Americans' burgeoning waistlines than the type of sugar it contains.

Critics of the liquid sweetener, pointing to the 2004 *American Journal of Clinical Nutrition* article that spurred the high-fructose corn syrup debate, say there's an association between the rise in consumption of sugar-sweetened beverages (most of which contain high-fructose corn syrup) and the rise in obesity in the United States.

Here, the writer synthesizes two sources that clearly disagree. But sometimes the tension among sources isn't as obvious. In fact, scholarship is full of gray areas. People agree, disagree, agree a little, and disagree a little. It's not simply a matter of black and white. There is a sliding range of positions:

Outright Disagreement (*Why They Are So Very Wrong*): Disagreement is sometimes dressed up in highly formal terms. Other times, it is as brazen as a political debate on cable news. Of course, it depends on the context: whether the disagreement takes place in an academic journal, a professor's personal blog, or a conference presentation. (See "Consider the Context" in Chapter 5 for more on context.) Regardless of the context, academic writers usually do not target or condemn a particular person. Instead, they disagree with an intellectual trend or theory:[1]

- The progressive approach misses the nature of the key problem.

- The department's position on brainstorming sends the conversation backward several hundred years.

- Mid-twentieth-century learning theory was mired in overly simplistic notions about human

---

[1] That trend or theory might be characterized by a particular person, but it's the theory, not the individual human, under examination.

memory—primarily that it's absolutely separate from "higher order" thinking.

Qualified Disagreement (*Why They Are a Little Off*): Even when they find a flaw with a position, theory, or trend, academic thinkers often find some value in it. In other words, they find a reason for not trashing it outright:

- While Keynesian economics helped governments weather the crises of the twentieth century, the theory missed, and continues to miss, the impact of foreign currencies.

- Although Lanham takes into account the growth of Indian cinema, he overlooks the financial realities of the Indian economy.

- The proposed policy for genome research only goes so far.

Qualified Agreement (*Why They Almost Have It Right*): Even when academic writers find value, they may still find some flaw—a shortcoming in the data, a misstep in the reasoning, a slight error in judgment. For example, physicists today openly acknowledge some flaws in Einstein's theories, but they also acknowledge his immense contributions to the field. In other words, it's okay to support, even to celebrate, a position and still point out a minor flaw:

- Smith is correct in one important aspect of the argument.

- Despite its minor problems, the expressionist position does draw out important layers of the writing process.

- The new media theorists, especially those tuned into streaming technologies, have begun to consider an important dimension: the physical limitations of the human eyeball and brain.

Outright Agreement (*Why They Are So Very Right*): Despite all the suspicious minds and serious doubts, academic thinkers sometimes agree entirely. In fact, they may even celebrate their peers' positions with absolute enthusiasm. They have conferences and journals devoted to particular theorists in their fields. Sometimes, they decide that a particular way of thinking contributes so much to the collective work that it should be openly applauded:

- Kenneth Burke's take on human motive moved the entire field of study into decades of sophisticated questions.

- The third-wave feminists generated the most powerful sociological insights of the era.

Good thinkers and writers acknowledge the range of positions in any debate and seek the nuances within those positions. As you make sense of the sources you find and synthesize their ideas, consider how they relate to one another within this continuum of agreement.

TALK ABOUT IT One powerful strategy for understanding an article, book, or blog is to ask some basic questions about the underlying tension: Is there a debate about the issue? What is the nature of the debate? What are the positions? What names are associated with each position? Where does the author of this particular work come down? With whom does he or she agree and disagree? What is the nature of the agreement or disagreement? Is the agreement or disagreement qualified? In a group, examine the following passage from a *Chronicle of Higher Education* article by William Deresiewicz. At what point do you sense a tension? What words or phrases clue you in to the tension? How would you characterize the author's concern?

With the social-networking sites of the new century—Friendster and MySpace were launched in 2003, Facebook in 2004—the friendship circle has expanded to engulf the whole of the social world, and in so doing, destroyed both its own nature and that of the individual friendship itself. Facebook's very premise—and promise—is that it makes our friendship circles visible. There they are, my friends, all in the same place. Except, of course, they're not in the same place, or, rather, they're not my friends. They're simulacra of my friends, little dehydrated packets of images and information, no more my friends than a set of baseball cards is the New York Mets. ■

Cite Your Sources

Once you've started using sources, you enter an important and long-standing tradition of citing those sources. The process involves attributing information to specific sources and telling your readers how to track down those sources if they choose. Depending on the audience and situation, this process can range from informal (giving a name in a sentence) to formal (documenting the author, date of publication, publication type, permanent URL). The important point is to identify the particular source in a way that corresponds to your readers' expectations and feels appropriate for your project.

The Long Buildup: Sometimes, writers take several sentences to introduce and contextualize a source. They explain the source's credentials, background, or influence in the field before they integrate relevant ideas. This is usually the case when writers are drawing from a vital source—one that has big impact on the project's ideas. For example, in his essay (page 214), Shawn Burks draws several important points from Alice Waters. When he introduces Waters, he explains her influence in the field (culinary arts) and her relevance to the topic:

Source: http://chronicle.com/article/Faux-Friendship/49308/

Where I live, the current trend lending itself to these pit-falls is the push for local meats. The region has always been agrarian and has an extensive and devout local food community, whose connection to the local food movement has followed national trends. A restaurateur-philosopher and a leading voice in the local food movement, Alice Waters has changed the way Americans buy and consume food over the last forty years through her business Chez Panisse as well as her community education programs. In her book *In the Green Kitchen: Techniques to Learn by Heart,* Waters defines the role of cooking in daily life: "Cooking creates a sense of well-being for yourself and the people you love and brings beauty and meaning to everyday life" (2).

Burks's strategy here is appropriate because he relies on Waters for a range of ideas. As his essay continues, he *comes back around* to Waters—and even describes the particular way she figures into some tension within the field. For those reasons, he gives her a relatively thorough introduction.

The Quick Tag: If a source doesn't have as much signifi-cance—if it's simply providing support or representing a position in a debate—writers often give a quick attribu-tion or tag. In other words, they don't give background information about that source. They simply set up the idea, relay the information (in a summary, paraphrase, or quotation), and then cite it. For example, in his essay (page 219), Bradford A. Smith moves quickly along with his ideas. When he borrows information from a source, he cites the source with a superscript number and then continues with the point:

Superconductivity—creating a zero-resistance path for electrons to flow—depends on specific factors, including a very low temperature and a limited magnetic field environment. By nature, electrons repel one another, but in extremely cold conditions (in the range of −300 degrees Fahrenheit in some materials), electrons actually "pair" up and move together unhindered.[2] With their potential for reducing wasted energy, superconductors have been generating interest and excitement within and beyond the scientific community since their discovery.

In magazines, newspapers, and blogs, writers credit their sources using one of the two strategies above. In other words, they give a name and a title if appropriate. Occasionally, they may also tell when the source was published. But in academic work and longer book-length projects, writers must always give complete information: page numbers, publisher information, and publication dates. And that's where specific formatting comes in—where formal documentation styles are used so that readers can trace the information if they choose. The documentation styles differ depending on the academic field and the publication.

In the Burks as well as the Smith passages, you'll notice numerical references. In Burks, the (2) at the end of his passage refers to the page number in Waters's book that contains the quotation. Because Burks follows the rules established by the Modern Language Association (MLA), he references the page number in his text and then later, at the end of his essay (page 219), gives all the publication information. Smith, however, uses a different style that's common in the scientific disciplines.

Reprinted by permission of Bradford A. Smith.

The [2] in his passage refers to the second source that he cites. He includes all the publication information for the source in a list of references at the end of his essay (page 223).

ASK ABOUT IT If you're writing a formal project for a college course, don't just guess at the process of citing sources. As you may know, not all disciplines (not even all professors in each discipline) follow the same rules for citing sources. Most college writing-intensive courses slot time for learning the rules of a particular documentation style, such as Modern Language Association (MLA) or American Psychological Association (APA) style. Before you get too involved in citation, it may be valuable to ask which style is most preferred. ■

WRITE IT
• • • • • • • • •

Sources help to complicate our ideas and get us thinking in new ways. But it takes some work to find sources that are useful and to weave the ideas from those sources into your writing. As you consider your own project, take one of the following paths:

1. Think about the present condition or state of a particular practice like Facebooking or a public trend like voting among college students. Do some online research on your topic and find out what others are saying about it. Try to find the thoughts of both average people and scholars in the most relevant discipline (communications or culture studies). In an essay, describe the trend and use the moves from this chapter: apply a supportive source, draw from a vital source, and synthesize. Develop a thesis about your topic that takes various viewpoints into account. Keep going back to your sources, letting

them inform each new idea you develop. Search for insights in your sources and apply them, in the form of summary, quotation, or paraphrase, as you develop your points. (Cite sources according to the documentation style your instructor specifies.)

2. Choose a current tension or conflict in your field of study. For example, if you're a nursing major, you might consider the debate surrounding hospital versus hospice care. Or if you're studying economics, you might focus on arguments about the future of the euro. In an essay, detail the nature of the tension and the positions that have developed around it. How many positions can you identify? Who represents each position? When did the debate begin, and how has it changed over time? Do the different sides agree about anything? What insights emerge from examining these different voices alongside one another?

READ: For examples of full essays that apply sources, check out Charlene Li and Josh Bernoff (page 210), Shawn Burks (page 214), and Barbara Ehrenreich (page 274).

APPLY: For specific guidance on how to structure a full essay using the moves in this chapter, see the outlines in Part III, "Apply the Moves" (pages 300, 303, and 315).

Apply a Concept

THINK ABOUT IT

In 1752, Ben Franklin flew a kite during a rainstorm and, as the story goes, "discovered electricity." But he wasn't caught in the rain by accident. He'd already been thinking through some concepts. He understood a little something about current and charge. And when the famous lightning bolt hit his kite, Franklin developed some insights—that is, after he woke up from the initial blast. The point here is that ideas come when concepts meet up with specific situations.

A concept is an idea that moves through time, across situations, from one person to another. Concepts are part of the world. They determine how we live, what we do, and, of course, how we think. And in academic life, concepts rule. They drive the daily work, long-term studies, experiments, and the written scholarship. Every discipline functions on some basic and not-so-basic concepts. Psychology includes self, id, ego, memory, adaptation, decompensation, abnormality, extrinsic motivation, and so on. Physics includes force, mass, acceleration, motion, velocity, and time. Such concepts make up the basic ingredients of scholarly work. Without them, thinking and writing would cease. There'd be no new experiments, no new hypotheses, no new theories, no new ideas, nothing.

We can harness the power of concepts when we apply them to specific texts, cases, or situations. And that is the focus of this chapter: how to apply a general concept to something specific. We don't mean physical application—as in standing in a field with a kite. We mean an intellectual process, one that involves choosing a concept, adopting language for the concept, and applying that language to a specific text or situation.

Adopt Specific Language

To illustrate the process, we'll use a concept from literary studies: the protagonist, or main character of a story. Next, we need some specific language to apply, so we'll borrow a definition from the English department at the University of Victoria:

> The protagonist in a work of fiction is the character with whom the reader is meant to be chiefly concerned; she or he is the main character, who, whether sympathetic or not, is the focus of the plot. A work of narrative or drama may have more than one protagonist.

Armed with such a definition, we can apply this language to anything with a protagonist: a film, television show, play, short story, or a popular novel such as J. R. R. Tolkien's *Lord of the Rings*. Notice that the following passage explains different ways in which we are "chiefly

---

concerned" with Tolkien's protagonist, Frodo Baggins. In other words, we don't simply say that Frodo *is* the protagonist because we are chiefly concerned with him. Instead, we try to explain *how* we are concerned:

> We care about Frodo and his mission. We follow him from the moment he inherits the ring of power, so we watch him go from an innocent bystander to an active player in the battle for Middle Earth. Of course, we hope that Frodo and his companion, Sam, survive—that they don't end up as spider food or Orc victims, but we also hope that Frodo does not give in to the ring. We want him to survive, save the world, and not crave power. We want him to stay uncorrupted, and this is maybe our most consistent but quiet concern throughout the story.

Even by explaining how we are "chiefly concerned" with this protagonist, we're still not done. We've only begun thinking. We can continue by applying the concept to specific scenes or actions. The following passage does the same thing as the first: it applies the general concept (protagonist) to the specific character (Frodo), but it goes even further by focusing on a specific scene. As we narrow in, we discover more about the character and the concept:

> At the climax of the final book, just as Frodo prepares to destroy the ring by throwing it into the fires of Mt. Doom, he hesitates. He decides he will keep it. "It is precious to me," he says. Our concern now has reached its peak. We realize, after hundreds of pages and many scenes following Frodo through hardship, that he is falling prey to the ring. His selflessness has withered away. We fear that Middle Earth and all of the characters who have come to matter to us will be destroyed because Frodo has, in the end, given in to greed.

Notice that we're not simply describing the character. Instead, we're *applying a concept* that allows us to think about him in a particular way—how, and for what reasons, a reader cares about Frodo. If the definition we had chosen to apply had been about how the protagonist relates to the other characters or about how the protagonist relates to the setting or to the arc of the plot, then we would have come up with a different path for thinking. Our point here is that thinking happens—almost instantaneously—when a concept gets applied to a specific situation or text. The general interacts with the particulars, and ideas begin to form. After the initial thinking gets under way, we can tread onward and examine smaller passages, scenes, or dimensions. And this move works not only for literary criticism. We can apply *any* concept to *any* situation and let thinking happen.

TALK ABOUT IT

1. Living in a society means adopting, and probably wrestling with, some basic concepts, such as freedom, responsibility, patriotism, justice, nature, childhood, adulthood, and terrorism, and more specific concepts, such as religious freedom, free market capitalism, corporate responsibility, and social justice. Consider one of these concepts and discuss how it influences your thinking or daily life.

2. In a class discussion, consider critical literacy as a concept. Look it up online. Borrow some language from a source and then apply it to your classroom. Ask how a specific assignment or activity functions as critical literacy. Remember that you're not evaluating but using a concept to understand how the assignment or activity works. ■

Take on the Big Concepts

In the original *Jaws* movie (1975), three men set out to find and kill a notorious great white shark. On a tiny fishing vessel, they make their way into open water. They are emboldened, in good cheer, and ready for victory. As the police chief, Martin Brody, is throwing bait off the back of the boat, he encounters the shark for the first time. As the huge animal surfaces, Brody sees with his own eyes the trouble ahead of them. His face goes flat. He realizes that they are outmatched. The shark is simply too big, the situation too intense for the tools available. He backs slowly into the cabin and tells the captain, "You're gonna need a bigger boat." The same goes for thinking. As we go along through school, we encounter increasingly complex situations and texts. We encounter bigger animals, bigger problems, and more confusing phenomena, so we need bigger concepts to deal with them. In short, we need bigger boats.

As students, we've all had to deal with increasingly bigger concepts. Consider, for example, how science courses evolve as we go through school. Early on, we learn some basic concepts: friction, mass, speed, and so on. We watch balls rolling down planes and balloons bursting. Then, we learn about gases, liquids, and solids. In the next course, we study the interaction of elements—the forming of compounds, the intermingling of atomic parts. If we go all the way to physics, we start learning about the movement and patterns of atomic parts. As with all the academic disciplines, the further we go, the more complex concepts we encounter. Complex concepts are generally more complicated, and require more explanation, than simple concepts. Consider the following examples:

- **Simple Concepts:** conflict, character, protagonist, freedom, technology, cost, force

- **Complex Concepts:** existential angst, antihero, post-modern dislocation, cyborgism, cost/benefit ratio, thermodynamics, particulate radiation

So what does this all mean for academic writing? It means that we sometimes have to *slow down*. Before we can begin applying a complex concept, we have to make sense of it. We have to explain it for ourselves and others. For that reason, academic writers often take a full paragraph (or several) to flesh out a concept. For example, in the following passage from his essay (page 219), Bradford A. Smith slowly explains a complex concept in physics. He compares superconductivity—a complex and abstract concept—to the humble task of moving furniture around a room:

Superconductivity might be called an "experimental fact," the existence of which has been proven but the exact workings of which are still being explored and developed. Conducting materials have little electrical resistance, while superconducting materials have zero electrical resistance. Superconductors help to reduce wasted energy. To understand why this is important, consider the problem of moving heavy furniture: hauling a couch from one room to another becomes a far easier task when furniture rollers arrive on the scene. The rollers serve as a conduit, guiding the cumbersome furniture into place. Similarly, electrons require certain conditions in order to move smoothly and freely. Superconductivity—creating a zero-resistance path for electrons to flow—depends on specific factors, including a very low temperature and a limited magnetic field environment. By nature, electrons repel one another, but in extremely cold conditions (in the range of −300 degrees

Fahrenheit in some materials), electrons actually "pair" up and move together unhindered.[2]

Developing a comparison, as Smith does, can help writers to test out their understanding. (In other words, if you can create an effective comparison, you're probably getting nicely acquainted with the concept.) But we can also rely on outside sources to help explain a complex concept. Notice, for instance, how we used the definition of protagonist at the opening of this chapter: We gave a direct quotation from a reliable source as part of our explanation, and we used a key phrase from that quotation ("chiefly concerned") as we applied the concept. The source kept working for us, and we *came back around* to it as we explained the concept.

Let's examine one more example: in the following passage, Charles Q. Choi, writing in *Scientific American*, uses a source to explain the concept of hypercorrection. In the first paragraph, Choi references and quotes from a source, Janet Metcalfe, to flesh out the concept. Choi then *comes back around* to the source in the third paragraph:

To understand hypercorrection, says cognitive psychologist Janet Metcalfe at Columbia University, "suppose I ask you, 'What is the capital of Canada?' and you say 'Toronto.' I say, 'How confident are you?' and you say, 'Very highly confident.' When I then tell you that actually the capital is Ottawa, you're very likely to remember it—not just a few minutes later but weeks later, and maybe for much longer, we think."

Scientists reason that in hypercorrection, after people discover that ideas they felt very sure about were not in fact correct, the surprise and embarrassment they feel makes them pay special attention to alternative responses about which they felt less confident. People then go on to take the corrected information to heart, learning from their errors.

"In contrast, if I asked you a question to which you gave a not-very-confident answer, like, perhaps, 'What color does amethyst turn when it is heated?' and you say, 'blue' with low confidence, when I tell you that it's actually yellow, you're not very likely to remember it," Metcalfe says.

As you research issues and develop writing projects, you will encounter a number of complex concepts. Don't shy away from them. But don't get mired in them either. Consider these two common moves for walking slowly through big concepts: (1) Like Choi, borrow from a plain-speaking source. Return to it for key ideas. (2) Like Smith, who compares superconductivity to furniture rollers, develop a comparison or a metaphor.

TALK ABOUT IT In a discussion group, take on a complex concept such as environmental justice. Look it up online and consult at least two different sources. Then, try to draft a paragraph that thoroughly explains what environmental justice is, how it works, why it matters to some people more than others. ∎

Advanced Move: Transport a Concept

Concepts are portable. They get carried over mountains, across oceans, and through time. Democracy, for example, was transported from ancient Greece to

© Cengage Learning

sixteenth-century England and then to the American colonies. In other words, the founding fathers of the United States didn't invent the concept of democracy. They imported and adapted it. Later, as colonists moved west across the Great Plains and over the Rocky Mountains, they carried along their concepts of private land, squatters' rights, statehood, and individual wealth.

Transporting concepts is common work in academic life. Psychology borrows from sociology. Literary studies borrow from philosophy. Education borrows from psychology. Engineering borrows from physics. Business borrows from everyone and anyone. And, as we explain above, concepts are *generative*. They make thinking happen. So borrowing concepts from another discipline means borrowing a way of thinking. Imported concepts can solve old problems and generate new insights. Velcro, rock and roll, electricity, even the World Wide Web all came along because people borrowed concepts from one field and applied them to another. Transporting even relatively simple concepts, like teamwork and collaboration, can change the way people think, and the way they implement policies. For example, in his article from *Arts Education Policy Review*, Ryan Fisher examines operational challenges in the field of arts education. Right out of the gate, he brings business management concepts to his aid:

> To better understand the true importance of teamwork and collaboration, it is important to reach outside the field of education and examine a field in which teamwork has been implemented and proven effective. The business world has focused on creating and improving teams, teamwork, and collaboration for the past twenty years. . . .
>
> The first team concept that can be derived from our business models is that fine arts team leaders must realize that there is a more effective way to use the team. Although many fine arts teams have had success and provide quality programs in their schools through the arts, there is a need to have a greater vision. Each individual program has become solely focused on what gains can be made in its respective division while neglecting the goals of the entire arts team. This is not conducive to the overall effectiveness of the broader field of arts education.

Source: Fisher, R. (2007). "Putting the 'Team' in the Fine Arts Team: An Application of Business Management Team Concepts." *Arts Education Policy Review*, 108(4), 25–32.

While Fisher acknowledges that teamwork already exists in arts education, he calls for "a greater vision" in the way fine arts teams borrow from the successful practices of business management. It is this particular business perspective, or way of seeing, that Fisher hopes to transport into his field.

Sometimes, writers transport a concept that seems impossibly out of sync with the discipline at hand. Imagine, for example, someone in religious studies borrowing concepts from business marketing. The two fields seem planets away from one another. But the following passage from the *Journal for the Study of Religions and Ideologies* describes a study that blends the fields:

> Marketing is a concept that the general public associates with the business world, with monetary exchange (buying and selling). It seems hard to accept and to understand that marketing can be used in order to support social causes, not to mention religion, a domain focused on spiritual values. Nevertheless, practice has proved that the connections between marketing and religion can be multiple and profound, and academics have begun to deepen the study of these relationships.

This kind of blending happens constantly in academic work. Sometimes, writers set out deliberately to see how concepts from across the hall or across campus can rejuvenate their daily work. But the process also happens quietly—even unconsciously. Sometimes, writers don't even realize what they are doing. The foreign concept hitches a ride and shows up in their thoughts.

Regardless of how it happens—deliberately or accidentally—the process of transporting a concept makes thinking happen. Ideas that may never meet are suddenly

Journal for the Study of Religions and Ideologies. 8.22 (Spring 2009): p171.

sharing mental space. And when that happens, two intellectual traditions converge. All of the assumptions, terminology, and research methods start interacting. In the following passage from her book *Alone Together,* Sherry Turkle describes how a recent concept "migrated" from science fiction to engineering. She makes a sophisticated but common move. She is standing at the intersection of two academic fields and letting the ideas blend in her thinking:

> In a television news story about a Japanese robot designed in the form of a sexy woman, a reporter explains that although this robot currently performs only as a receptionist, its designers hope it will someday serve as a teacher and companion. Far from skeptical, the reporter bridges the gap between the awkward robot before him and the idea of something akin to a robot wife by referring to the "singularity." He asks the robot's inventor, "When the singularity comes, no one can imagine where she [the robot] could go. Isn't that right? . . . What about these robots after the singularity? Isn't it the singularity that will bring us the robots that will surpass us?"
>
> The singularity? This notion has migrated from science fiction to engineering. The *singularity* is the movement—it is mythic; you have to believe in it—when machine intelligence crosses a tipping point. Past this point, say those who believe, artificial intelligence will go beyond anything we can currently conceive. No matter if today's robots are not ready for prime time as receptionists. At the singularity, everything will become technically possible, including robots that love. Indeed, at the singularity, we may merge with the robotic and achieve immortality. The singularity is technological rapture.

From *Alone Together: Why We Expect More from Technology and Less from Each Other*, New York: Basic, 2011.

This final insight comes from the blending of science fiction and engineering—the mythic and the technological. The passage shows how new ideas spark into being when a concept from one discipline meets up with the logic of another. Like Turkle, you can go looking around in other disciplines. Something you read about psychology or sociology can be imported to your English course. Imagine, for instance, that you're writing about video-game violence. How might the id, a psychological concept, shed light on the attraction to certain games? Or how might ethnocentrism, a concept from sociology, help you to understand typical video game characters?

TALK ABOUT IT In a small group, list several concepts central to a course you are taking. Choose one of those concepts and discuss how it could be applied to another discipline. How would you describe the concept to others not familiar with your field? What insights would come from transporting the concept to another discipline? ∎

WRITE IT

Thinking happens when concepts get applied to specific situations or texts. Insights develop when we examine the general idea interacting with specifics. Remember, for instance, how we come to understand Frodo Baggins (from *The Lord of the Rings*) when we apply the protagonist concept. Consider one of the following paths for your own writing project:

1. Consider one of the following complex concepts: existential angst, antihero, postmodern dislocation, or cyborgism. Consult a variety of sources to find out how experts define the phrase. Apply language from one of those sources to a specific habit, pattern,

or decision in your life. How does the concept help you to understand your behavior?

2. Apply the concept you chose for option 1 to a fictional character—to someone in film or literature. Remember to narrow in on specific scenes and events. Apply the concept to specific decisions, actions, and even emotions.

3. Take a common concept from this book and apply it to a situation in your daily life. At first, you might wonder how these concepts (such as complexity, subtle tension, dualistic thinking) relate at all to your life. But try borrowing specific language. For example, consider the following passage from Chapter 2:

> Dualities can bully our brains. They can gather in our thoughts and make us imagine two, and only two, contrary possibilities. In short, they can create *dualistic thinking*—an inability to see gray areas.

How might an "inability to see gray areas" work in your life? How does this language help to make sense of a specific decision that you had to make?

4. Examine a scientific concept (particulate radiation, gravitational pull, molecular diffusion) or a legal concept (fraud, material witness, habeas corpus). Consult a variety of sources until you think you understand the concept. And then apply the concept to an artistic or literary work. Remember to use specific terminology and come back around to specific phrases as you apply the concept.

READ: For examples of full essays that apply a concept, check out Bradford A. Smith (page 219) and Tiffany J. Smith (page 224). Also see Annette Wannamaker (page 231), who both applies a concept and dismantles an argument.

APPLY: For specific guidance on how to structure a full essay using the moves in this chapter, see the outlines in Part III, "Apply the Moves" (pages 305–306).

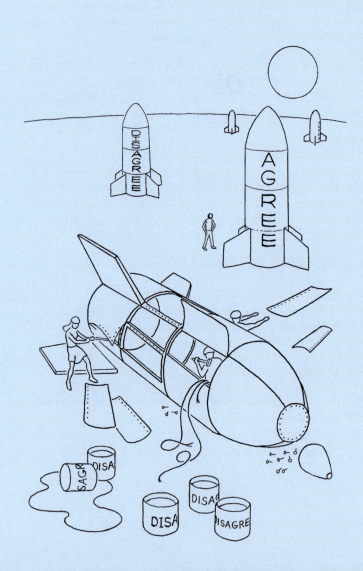

CHAPTER

Dismantle Arguments

THINK ABOUT IT

Arguments come at us constantly. From passionate diatribes to calm treatises, arguments move us to feel and act. We take positions, go to college, take jobs, leave jobs, declare a major, buy a new gadget, and sign on various dotted lines all because someone along the way provoked our thinking. In short, arguments are powerful forces. They shape lives. They start countries. They get people thrown in jail and freed from tyranny. And in academic life, arguments make disciplines come alive. In fact, most of the scholarly work published in academia is argumentative in nature. Scholars at all levels and in all fields study one another's arguments—their assertions about what's true, what's false, what should be done, ignored, funded, or emphasized in further study.

Being a good reader of arguments means holding off on the rush to judge or respond. This can be tricky because arguments incite judgment and response. The more powerful the argument, the more powerful the drive to agree, disagree, or holler back. But we comprehend more about an argument when we consider it rather than automatically react to it.

Sloppy thinking happens when we

- Ignore an argument's complexity.

- Judge it, dismiss it, accept it, or respond to it before we've fully understood it.

Good thinking happens when we

- Work to understand the argument.

- Articulate how the argument works before responding.

The best way to understand an argument is to take it apart, examine the innards, and explain how the elements function. This chapter focuses on that process. For now, we will ignore the acts of judging and responding to arguments. We want, instead, to isolate the move of dismantling—of carefully taking apart and inspecting what has been asserted. To that end, we will analyze the following elements: the context, the reasoning, the writer/speaker, and the audience.

Consider the Context

First, we should understand the situation surrounding the argument—when and where the argument was written or made public. If we get a sense of cultural surroundings (shared concerns, attitudes, or even the political climate), we can better determine the function of the other elements. We can better understand references, terminology, audience, and reasoning. And we can better understand why the writer may have focused on some issues and ignored others. For instance, if we

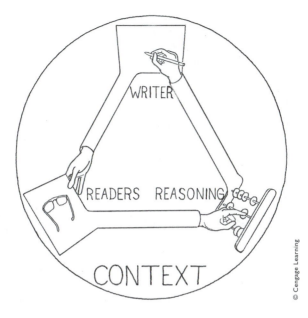

© Cengage Learning

were examining the Declaration of Independence (a written argument from the late eighteenth century), it would be valuable to know that royalty was a widely accepted idea then—that most people in Europe and the American colonies believed in the power of some unelected people over the masses, that equality between a royal person and a nonroyal person was a relatively radical idea. If we know that about the context, we would read the Declaration in a particular light. (For more on the Declaration and its context, see Chapter 6, pages 117–119.)

The same goes for any topic in any era. If we were examining an argument on student loans from 2012, we would do well to understand some trends: that the American economy through the first eight years of the twenty-first century steadily declined, that middle-class families were most damaged by the financial collapse of 2007, that fewer traditional-aged college students tended to vote than older citizens, that state and federal funding for colleges had been consistently declining for at least two decades, that tuition rates were increasing throughout the country, and that federal grants had been diminishing. Understanding such trends would help us to dismantle any given argument about loans. We would know from the start why the subject mattered to people, why arguments were being made, and who cared.

Examining context requires some research, and it's often hard to know where to begin. After all, nearly any social trend might factor into your topic. How much of the surrounding culture should you consider? Where should you begin looking? One key strategy is to start reading contemporary articles from newspapers, monthly magazines, or in more recent years, blogs. We can glean a good deal about public opinion from these sources because they tap into day-to-day events and people's responses to them. For example, the following passages are introductory paragraphs from three articles on student loans. Together, they tell us something about people's attitudes and concerns regarding the topic:

> For many ambitious Americans from modest backgrounds, college debt has helped transform their 20s and early 30s from an age in which to explore the world, establish themselves, or pursue idealistic or artistic goals into a time of oddly limited career options and scaled-down dreams. "It colors every little decision you make," says 26-year-old Gabriel Schnitzler, who graduated from Yale Law School in 2001 with $106,000 in loans. (Franke-Ruta, Garance. "The Indentured Generation." *The American Prospect*, September/October 2003.)

Source: http://www.utne.com/2003-09-01/The-Indentured-Generation .aspx

With the country's national debt flying higher than a bald eagle, the Deficit Reduction Act of 2005 should have come as welcome news. Students and educators, however, worry that some of the bill's provisions will only exacerbate an already massive problem: individual student loan debt. The bill, reports Aaron Block from the *San Antonio Current*, raises interest rates on both parent and student loans from 7.9 percent to 8.5 percent, which will ultimately add almost $5,000 to the average recipient's debt load. (Rose, Nick. "'Till Debt Do Us Part." Utne.com, June 1, 2006.)

The Project on Student Debt estimates that the average college senior in 2009 graduated with $24,000 in outstanding loans. Last August [2010], student loans surpassed credit cards as the nation's single largest source of debt, edging ever closer to $1 trillion. Yet for all the moralizing about American consumer debt by both parties, no one dares call higher education a bad investment. The nearly axiomatic good of a university degree in American society has allowed a higher education bubble to expand to the point of bursting. (Harris, Malcolm. "Bad Education." nplusonemag.com, April 25, 2011.)

From these brief passages, we can quickly discern that student debt is part of a national conversation about household debt, that Americans are generally aware of the bigger debt problem, that politicians discuss it openly, that interest rates on debt are part of the crisis, and that little is being done to address the scale of the crisis. Of course, these three introductions could very well lead us astray. We have to admit that possibility. But it doesn't take long to find another three or thirty articles that echo these broad points. In short, armed with a good search engine, it's not difficult to get a sense of the prevailing cultural attitudes about a given issue.

So learning about context might begin with finding patterns among sources. This can give you a broad view of the cultural landscape. But you should also consider the *publication* itself—the magazine, website, or book publisher that first made the argument public. If you are examining a written argument, for example, you can find out a good deal by quickly inspecting the publisher. For example, Nick Rose's article (excerpted above) was published by *Utne Reader*, which describes itself in the following way:

> *Utne Reader* and Utne.com are digests of independent ideas and alternative culture. Not right, not left, but forward thinking. We're most interested in creating a conversation about everything from the environment to the economy, politics to pop culture.

A quick look at Utne's website can tell us much. It publishes articles about labor issues, student concerns, the environment, personal well-being, and community activism. In other words, it seems largely sympathetic to student debt. Someone like Nick Rose, then, isn't arguing against the grain of the magazine or its readers. He doesn't have to convince readers that huge amounts of student debt are bad. As we'll explain in the latter sections of this chapter, a sympathetic audience impacts the nature of an argument—what it has to do, what it has to include, what it might exclude.

TALK ABOUT IT When we consider context, we're bound to deal with tension—disagreements, debates, subtle confusions, or anxieties among people. Many arguments, of course, directly state the tension: they describe

Source: http://www.utne.com/about.aspx

the positions involved, the nature of related debates, and the particular points of disagreement. You can often encounter these elements directly. But you can also probe for quieter, less obvious tension. You can sense the long-standing debates and disagreements even if they are not explained directly. In a small group, examine the three preceding passages on student loans (pages 90–91). What specific sentences, phrases, or words clue you in to points of disagreement? ■

Analyze the Reasoning

Arguments depend on a *claim* (an assertion that expresses someone's position) and *reasoning* (the *why*, or justification for someone's claim). These two elements make arguments go. For example, let's return to the topic of student loans. Of course, any number of claims can be made about the topic, but we'll make the claim that loans should be interest-free. In the following passage, the reasoning builds to and supports that claim:

> Most students today simply cannot pay for college, nor can their parents. In fact, paying for a full four-year degree is now far beyond the ability of nearly all American families. Only the very wealthy can pay for an entire college education, which means that nearly all college students graduate with some form of debt—debt that stretches into decades or over lifetimes. Because a generation of debtors is bad for the overall economy, student loans should, at the least, be interest-free.

As with many written arguments, the reasons in this passage are strewn together with the claim. If we were to list them out, the elements might look like this:

Claim: Student loans should be interest-free.

Reasons: Most college students cannot pay for college and, therefore, must get loans.

Most college students will graduate with loan debt.

A majority of college students shouldn't graduate with growing debt.

A generation of debtors is bad for the economy.

Dismantling an argument requires that we pull apart the reasons—that we detect and carefully untangle each reason from the others. Most arguers don't call out their reasons as directly as we have here. They weave their reasons together with testimony, facts, and information from sources, which means the reasons might be separated by many paragraphs or pages. So when you're dismantling an argument, you have to look for statements that justify the main claim by asking *why* (and *why else*) the writer/speaker holds that particular position.

This process can be especially tricky because not all reasons are stated. Many reasons, in fact, go unstated because the speaker/writer assumes that readers will automatically accept them. For example, if someone tells you to run from the building because it's on fire, that's all the reasoning you need. One reason is enough. But here's the interesting twist. That one reason relies on other *unstated* reasons (or assumptions):

The building is on fire!

Burning buildings aren't safe.

They contain flames and smoke.

Flames and smoke are deadly.

Deadly things should be avoided.

After someone makes the claim (that we should leave the building) and gives a reason (because it's on fire), we don't stand around considering the unstated reasons. Our brains fill in the rest as we're moving to the nearest exit. In this respect, we can be glad that the speaker and the audience share some assumptions. But most situations aren't so straightforward. Those subtle reasons aren't always obvious. For example, some unstated reasons operate in our argument about student loans:

> **Unstated Reasons:** Anything bad for the economy should be changed.
>
> Graduating college students make up a significant force in the overall economy.

Even though we do not express these reasons, they are part of the argument—part of the quiet intellectual matter swirling around in the argument. That's how reasoning works: while some points are expressed, other points often hover quietly in the background. And this is not necessarily bad or wrong. But if we're dismantling an argument (or writing one), we should try to understand all the elements—the unstated and the stated.

Let's more carefully examine the two unstated reasons. The first ("Anything bad for the economy should be changed") is so obvious that it doesn't need to be expressed. When something is bad, people generally assume that it should be changed. An arguer doesn't usually have to convince others of that point. So we can safely leave it unstated. We can assume that readers won't get hung up on it. But the second unstated reason ("Graduating college students make up a significant force in the overall economy") is different. It's arguable. Someone might wonder about it: Are graduating college students *really* a significant force in the overall economy? How significant? Because someone might ask these questions, we may decide that the reason cannot go unstated—that it must be expressed, explained further, and supported.

As this example shows, reasoning depends to some degree on the context, on what has been said, on what the audience believes, on what arguer and audience collectively assume. In other words, those attitudes and concerns that surround any given argument figure into and give shape to the reasoning. As we'll show in the following sections, the writer/speaker and audience are always interacting in subtle ways. The nature of that interaction determines what gets said or left unsaid.

Analyze the Writer/Speaker

The writer or speaker is the identity attached to the argument. When we analyze the writer, we're not concerned about the biological human who wrote the text. Instead, we're interested in the person who is *implied by the text*, what some critics call the *persona*. If it is hard to imagine how a writer is implied by a text, think of the difference between the persona you create when you write a thank-you note to a relative versus the one you create when you text a friend ironically threatening to do him violence if he's late again. You're the same person who wrote both texts, but you've adopted two very different roles.

When we analyze speakers and writers, we examine the way they figure into their arguments. This is a relatively easy task when writers talk openly about themselves. When they mention their own experiences or offer personal reflections on the issue, they make clear how they figure into the argument. When writers don't draw attention to themselves, we have to work a little harder. We have to detect the writers and flush them out. We have to determine something about them based on *how they've presented their argument*. For example, consider the following two passages. While the first writer draws attention to himself, the second does not, but both writers can be analyzed:

Matthew: I am a college student, a single father, and a part-time salesperson. I have two loans from two different lending institutions. I'll likely graduate with more than $20,000 worth of debt. I'll immediately start looking for a job in my field and hopefully start climbing out of this financial hole. If I'm lucky enough to get a job, I'll cling to it and hope that I can get out of the red within a decade, but I know that I might pay on that debt for the rest of my life.

Kelli: Student loan debt is crushing an entire generation. It's not only the staggering totals that loom after graduation but the interest that keeps those totals bearing down for years to come. Millions of college students enter the workforce indebted and beaten down before they can even imagine participating in the American dream.

It's not difficult to detect Matthew. He's there in black and white. His personal experiences connect him to the topic and establish his authority to make claims about student loans. On the other hand, Kelli does not draw attention to her own experiences. We might, then, wonder about her connection to the issue. But we don't necessarily need her personal story. We can, instead, inspect her words and sentences. For instance, notice Kelli's use of *crushing, staggering, loom,* and *bearing down*. These terms tell us something about her persona and relationship to the topic. We know that she sees the topic from a student's perspective. We also know, from the last sentence of her passage, that she has a broad understanding of the issue. "Millions of college students," she tells us, are currently faced with the problem. If we were to keep reading Kelli's argument, we would look for more clues about her persona—for ways that she can support or ground her understanding of the issue.

Analyzing a writer or speaker, then, is a process of tracing words and phrases that tell us something about the persona. Each word choice, each sentence, and each point can shed some light—not simply where the writer stands but what he or she values, what he or she assumes. However, we should be careful. If we're not attentive to our own reading, we might be inclined to conjure biases about the writer. This can take an ugly turn if we allow those suspicions to steer our thinking. We might characterize the writer in the worst possible terms: "He just wants to come off smarter than everyone else." "She's just knocking everyone who disagrees with her." "He wants everyone to join his cause without even asking hard questions." Such statements often say more about the dismantler than the writer or speaker in question.

A LOOK AT PURPOSE

Understanding an argument depends largely on understanding the *purpose*—or the motivating drive—of the argument. Is the writer out to condemn something, to fix a shared way of thinking, to propose a new way of thinking? While there are many purposes, the following general types show up regularly in academic projects:

- **Supporting or Condemning (*This Is . . . or Isn't . . . a Good Idea*):** In this type of project, writers support or condemn a specific practice, idea, or policy. They argue, for instance, that some new research misses the mark, that conventional logic is perfectly sound, or that a new perspective is worth close attention. In such arguments, scholars call on their colleagues to *recognize a flaw in* or to *see the value of* the subject matter. They denounce something or celebrate its worth—or, as is the case most often, do a little of both.

- **Fixing (*It's Not Quite What We Thought*):** As new recruits join academic life, as new technology gets implemented or tossed aside, scholars often find a way of tweaking a shared perspective. They are not out to change the fundamentals or to call for a different direction but merely to *amend some prior approach or shared thinking*. For instance, in their work on climate change, a number of scientists have explained that deforestation rates have as much, if not more, impact as fossil fuels on the overall greenhouse effect. These scientists are not out to dismiss thousands of experiments and conclusions about climate change. Instead, they are explaining a slight misunderstanding in the field. They are fixing, not dismissing.

- **Choosing a Side (*I'm Weighing In on This Debate*):** As we explain in Chapter 2, academia is full of debate. There are small, polite skirmishes as well as long-term feuds in which scholars line up and try to outmaneuver the opposition—or, in the best of all worlds, change their minds. Individual scholars, at some point, have to decide where they stand on the big unresolved conflicts. And quite often, they do so in a public manner. Usually, these arguments begin with a careful explanation of the debate. Then, the writer *comes down on one side and breaks down her reasons*.

continued

- **Warning** (*There's Danger Ahead!*): Because authors examine trends, they are often the first to see how things might (or will) play out. And so many projects are driven by the need to *warn others of whatever is coming*. Many articles and books deal with the impending crises that face the disciplines and their subject matter. Economists, for instance, warn of future hits to financial institutions or international currency problems. Biologists warn of bacterial adaptation. Psychologists warn of seclusion.

- **Proposing** (*Here's a Better Way of Doing It*): While most academic writing focuses on how people think, much of it also calls for action. Writers in all fields make a case that something needs to change, so they *describe the need and the specific way to address it*. Sometimes, they even chart out particular steps for addressing a problem. They may establish the precise methods for making things better or they might call for new thinking—a proposal to adopt a new mental framework—which is a critical move in academic writing.

- **Transforming** (*Let's Escape the Status Quo*): If disciplines are to move forward, or in any direction, they have to occasionally snap free from standard methods and conventional beliefs. And as usual with human behavior, disciplines do not change easily. They have to be nudged, shouldered, and shoved out of their usual habits. Scholars, then, often become the voices of dissent in their own disciplines. They call on their colleagues to *recognize a flaw in the usual way of doing things*. And if that flaw is buried deep in the workings of the field, then the call for change can become insistent. (Chapter 8, "Escape the Status Quo," examines this process closely—as both a purpose in writing and a fundamental intellectual move.)

Of course, there are many more purposes. But these represent a big chunk of the argumentative writing in academic life. And sometimes, the purposes converge. Someone might, for instance, weigh in on a debate while also warning of danger ahead. The important point here is that a position can take many forms and that it always depends on a specific purpose.

Analyze the Audience

When we say *audience*, we don't mean the specific people reading an argument at a given time. We mean the people who would most likely sit through, listen to, or read the argument—the people who have certain values, attitudes, knowledge, and expectations that would make them most apt to tune in. Of course, we usually don't have direct access to the audience of an argument. We can't look at them as though they were all seated in a theater. We can't ask them what they believe, what they value, what they know. But we can discover a good deal about an audience by considering the publication and language of the argument.

As we explain in the earlier section on context, the publication refers to the journal, publisher, or website that brought the text into public view. And each publication has its particular style and tendencies. *Family Circle*, a moderately conservative magazine for women with families, is not likely to publish an argument on the glories of nipple piercing. On the other hand, the *Body Piercing* journal will likely not publish a puff piece about nicely shaded back porches where families can assemble in the evenings. In short, we can conclude a great deal about the audience—its values, interests, and expectations—by looking at the publisher of an argument. We can sense the kinds of attitudes and values circulating within that audience.

The publication can also tell us something about the expertise level of the audience. An audience for a scholarly journal has a high degree of expertise and disciplinary knowledge. For example, an article in the *Journal of Chemical Physics* targets physicists—and physicists only. Consider the following passage from an article titled "Self-Consistent, Constrained Linear-Combination-of-Atomic-Potentials Approach to Quantum Mechanics." If you're a physicist, you'll have little problem comprehending the point:

> The simplest perturbation, moving electrons around in HF leads to Koopmans' theorem,[47] as the first difference, and the coupled perturbed equations,[45, 48] as the second difference. Corresponding to Koopmans' theorem in HF is Janak's theorem that the derivative of the energy with respect to occupation number is the orbital eigenvalue in DFT.[49]

The writers in the *Journal of Chemical Physics* assume that their readers will zoom along at high speeds while recalling all the principles, experiments, and theories that are quietly referenced. They don't worry about explaining big terms or principles. Contrarily, here's a passage from Danah Zohar's *The Quantum Self*, a book about quantum mechanics written for a nonspecialized audience. As you can see, Zohar's audience needs more assistance with the ideas. Readers are guided carefully through some fundamental points about physics:

> In classical physics, movement seems a simple enough concept, familiar to us in our everyday perception of the way that things get about. An object, say a ball, travels continuously from point A to point B, takes a given amount of time to make its transition from one to the other, and makes its journey in the first place because someone threw it. Thus it

moves smoothly through space and time as a result of cause and effect. We all know that this is the basic way events in our world are constructed.

Yet at the quantum level of reality, the whole picture of continuous movement through space and time breaks down. Quantum physics is, as one Oxford physicist puts it, a physics of "lumps" and "jumps."

And beyond the publication type, we can inspect the way the messages interact with a primary audience. Even if we didn't know the publication type of the two passages above, we could probably determine the type of audience each is targeting. We could determine the type of reader (expert or novice, scientist or philosopher) and even whether that reader is potentially suspicious or accepting of the ideas.

TALK ABOUT IT In a small group, discuss the following argumentative passage about student loans. Even if you don't know where the argument was published, you can probably determine something about the primary audience. Describe the primary audience—their values, hopes, or needs:

Elected officials in government have essentially abandoned college students. They have abdicated their duty to represent all the electorate—not simply the seniors who tend to vote in much greater numbers than traditional college students. While they listen to banks and financial institution lobbyists, members of Congress and the state legislature have lost touch with the citizens working to enter the shrinking middle class. ■

Source: *The Quantum Self: Human Nature and Consciousness Defined by the New Physics*, New York: Quill/William Morrow, 1990. Copyright © 1990 by Danah Zohar.

Advanced Move:
Call Out the Quiet Argument

Arguments don't always look like arguments. In fact, they can stow away in other things—questions, jokes, stories, songs, films, and pieces of fine art. We don't mean that everything you encounter is arguing a point. We mean that all kinds of things besides written and spoken arguments *assert something about the world*. For example, a movie like *Juno* (2007) asserts something about the emotional and social struggles of teen pregnancy. The *Harry Potter* series asserts something about the power of fellowship to undermine evil. And the new World Trade Center, being erected to replace the towers destroyed on 9/11, will most likely assert something about American endurance.

If we can develop our radar, we can detect and dismantle the quiet arguments around us. The process is a bit different from the process of dismantling a written argument. You're not looking for stated and unstated reasons but elements that build up to a claim—details that accumulate and express something. For example, in the *Harry Potter* series, there's no single scene that states, unequivocally, how fellowship can undermine evil. Instead, many scenes and situations are built around that claim. The same can be said about other films, literary works, pieces of art, and even architecture. In her essay about the Sydney Opera House (page 239), Astrid Reed explains that the building asserts something about art. Of course, the Opera House itself does not "speak," but all the details in it add up to a message. In the following passage, Reed explains what that message is:

> The exterior sections of the complex soar like yacht sails filled with wind. For some, the building evokes seashells or the white tips of waves on a choppy sea. The million

ceramic tiles encasing the exterior glow with heat each day at sunset as the sky turns pink and orange. Each year, on New Year's Eve, fireworks reflect a spectacular lightshow onto the spans of the white exterior shells.

The purpose of the building is, of course, to offer a striking venue for the performing arts. The Opera House provides a home not only for Opera Australia, but also for the Australian Ballet, the Sydney Symphony and Philharmonic Orchestras, and several theater companies. Each week, the building hosts an average of forty performances that are enjoyed by thousands of visitors. Each interior element of the building serves to heighten and enhance the audience's experience. A cascade of low, sweeping stairs creates a dramatic approach into the main doors, but the building can also be accessed from many different levels and balconies on all sides. Inside, the warmth of the pink granite and wooden beams contrasts and intersects with cool glass and slabs of grey concrete. Striking dashes of blue sky, water, boats, ferries, and the Sydney Harbour Bridge are framed like precious snapshots by tall lengths of glass. There are more than a thousand rooms within the complex including concert halls and theaters of various sizes and purposes. Mirroring the geometrical pattern of tiles outside, all these rooms fit together inside like the chambers of a beehive. Acoustical engineering elements like huge glass disks and birch wood panels descend from the ceilings of the main concert hall like abstract sculpture.

Over the last half century, Sydney has developed into a cultural mecca. Museums, galleries, music, theater, and dance in Sydney rival the offerings of any large European or American city. The Opera House has served a real purpose for cultural enthusiasts from around the world by offering a spectacular venue for people to enjoy the arts. But the building's influence as a great architectural wonder has reached far beyond its walls, inspiring and encouraging a range of arts in Australia and throughout the world. Its very existence seems to have fostered a high bar of creative achievement. Such a place could never suffer the mediocre.

The Opera House does not claim, in written language, that mediocre art is not allowed, but Reed draws out the details, the exterior and interior elements that accumulate or add up to an undeniable claim. Her careful analysis of the place generates a conclusion: that the Opera House "seems to have fostered a high bar of creative achievement." Writers in all fields make this three-part move: (1) they closely inspect the details of a building, film, literary work, even something as big and ill-defined as a city; (2) they find a pattern in those details that suggests an argument; and (3) they express that argument in writing.

TALK ABOUT IT Architecture on college campuses makes claims. The structures and geography indirectly assert ideas about learning, education, enlightenment, freedom, and so on. The paved roads winding their way through a commuter campus might say, "Thanks for coming. See you next time." The immense stone columns on a library might say something about the immensity of an intellectual tradition. Or the flashing lights of a student union might assert something about an institution's timeliness or trendiness. In a small group, consider a piece of architecture (a statue or building) on your campus. Closely inspect the details and find a pattern that suggests an argument. Do the details add up to some point about education, freedom, learning,

---

Reprinted by permission of Astrid Reed.

hardship? Also consider the context. What is the relationship between the subject and the surroundings? Do they complement one another or oppose one another? Try to express that argument in writing. ■

WRITE IT

1. Take on a specific written argument—an article, blog post, even the transcript of a speech. Use the following steps to help you dismantle the argument. You need not take on every step or question here. A detailed explanation of one of these points may launch your examination and provide sufficient momentum.

Context
- Why is this topic or particular argument important? How do you know?
- What is the tension?
- How does this writer or speaker claim to resolve or address the issue more comprehensively or accurately than others?

Reasoning
- Identify the topic, main claim, and supporting reasons.
- Take some aspect of the argument (either a major claim or some supporting reason) and show its relationship to some other part of the argument.
- Identify the boundaries of the argument—what it seeks to do, what it doesn't.

Writer/Speaker
- Who is writing? How does the writer construct his or her authority to argue on this topic?

- Is the persona serious, formal, comedic, or something in between? How does the persona influence or shape the message? How is the persona crafted or chosen to fit an audience's expectations or needs?

Audience
- Who is being targeted? What are their expectations and assumptions?
- How does the publication figure in? What does it tell you about the audience?
- Is the audience hostile or friendly? Already knowledgeable about the issue or in need of being taught? Does the volatility of the topic require treading lightly around the audience's attitudes? Or can the writer go forward and not worry about offending readers or encountering resistance?

2. Choose a nontextual work, such as a work of art or architecture. Examine the quiet argument that the work is making. In an essay, analyze the message of the work. How does the message relate to the work's purpose? Consider how people use the work. For instance, is its function practical or purely aesthetic? How, if at all, has the work's purpose changed over time? Here, also think about the context surrounding the work. Where is the work, and how does its physical setting affect its purpose? Its message? How might the surrounding cultural atmosphere or political climate affect the argument that the work is making?

READ: For examples of full essays that dismantle an argument, check out William J. Carpenter (page 235), Astrid Reed (page 239), and Barbara Ehrenreich (page 274). Also see Annette Wannamaker (page 231), who both dismantles an argument and applies a concept.

APPLY: For specific guidance on how to structure a full essay using the moves in this chapter, see the outlines in Part III, "Apply the Moves" (pages 305, 307–308, and 315).

Justify
Your Position

THINK ABOUT IT

Imagine this: You win a ticket for a week-long cruise in the Caribbean. And because the cruise coincides with your spring break, you take the opportunity. But things go wrong. In the midst of a storm, your ship begins to sink. After a terrifying swim in churning waters, you find your way to a lifeboat. You and a dozen others on board are disoriented but alive. In the distance, you can see a small island. If everyone can paddle together, you might make it to land. But there are countless people still in the water—maybe in life jackets, maybe not. And they seem to be drifting farther from your lifeboat and farther out to sea. You could paddle toward them in hopes of pulling another few people on board, or you could head straight for the island. To make matters worse, the rain is coming down hard. The lifeboat is filling up. The quicker you get to the island, the better. What do you do? What argument do you make to the others?

If you're lucky, you'll never be in this situation. But if you're like most humans through history, you'll have to make tough calls. And you'll have to adopt difficult positions. You'll have to weigh in on topics that have no obvious answer—situations in which every position has pitfalls, potential value, and clear shortcomings. These situations will require you not only to have an opinion but also to break down your reasons.

When you take a position, you privilege one way of thinking above others. You say, in effect, "This is the best path." Despite all the other paths, you deem one more worthy of your thinking and maybe your action. But how is it best? Is it more sophisticated, clearheaded, logical, compassionate, practical, relevant, productive, or inclusive? Is the position more responsive to the facts? Is it more in line with surrounding trends? Is it more in sync with the probabilities? Will acting on it hurt the fewest people? Save the most? This chapter focuses on the moves that build to thoughtful positions. While there are many and varied strategies for developing and delivering arguments, this chapter stays focused on the intellectual moves that generate reasonable positions: adopt a position and purpose, line up the evidence, break down your reasons, support your reasons, dismantle and deny the opposition, and seek reasons inside reasons.[1]

---

[1] Are we talking about persuasive writing? Yes. This chapter focuses on the process of putting forward your opinion on a topic. But it's not all that different from other chapters. When you seek complexity or apply a concept, you make a range of decisions. You decide on the focus, you determine what idea to pursue, and you find a duality to bust apart. In other words, your opinions are very much involved. But in this chapter, you're putting all your energy into supporting and defending your position on a topic.

Adopt a Position and Purpose

The *position* is the stance of the writer—the single idea that you will establish and justify with sound reasons. And that position depends on your *purpose*—the overall motivation of the argument. Are you out to condemn something? Fix something? Propose a new way of thinking? You might begin with the overall purpose to argue a point, but your thinking will get more focused and rich if you can define your purpose more narrowly. Consider the list of purposes from Chapter 5:

- **Supporting or Condemning** (*This Is . . . or Isn't . . . a Good Idea*): These arguments call on readers to recognize a flaw in or to see the value of the subject matter. They denounce something or celebrate its worth—or, as is the case most often, do a little of both.

- **Fixing** (*It's Not Quite What We Thought*): In these arguments, writers are not out to change the fundamentals or to call for a different direction but to amend some prior approach or shared thinking.

- **Choosing a Side** (*I'm Weighing In on This Debate*): These arguments begin with a careful explanation of the debate. Then, the writer comes down on one side and breaks down her reasons.

- **Warning** (*There's Danger Ahead!*): In these arguments, writers set out to warn others of whatever is coming. Such arguments are often based on past and present trends.

- **Proposing** (*Here's a Better Way of Doing It*): In these arguments, writers make a case that something needs to change, so they describe the need and the specific way to address it. Sometimes, they even chart out particular steps for addressing a problem.

- **Transforming** (*Let's Escape the Status Quo*): In these arguments, writers call on their readers to recognize a flaw in the usual way of doing things. And if that flaw is buried deep in the workings of a field, then the call for change can become insistent.

Purposes often depend on the context and the audience—who's listening, who's invested in the topic, who's potentially at odds with the writer's position, what other positions have been expressed. In short, the situation matters. Writers have to ask themselves what kind of argument would work best, which would be best received, and which would have the most impact. For instance, choosing a side in a debate may be worthless if the debate itself is flawed. Instead, the writer might be better off escaping it altogether and promoting an entirely different perspective. Similarly, a writer might decide that proposing a solution can wait because the problem itself needs to be understood first—or the problem has been wrongly defined by others.

As you think about your position, consider the purpose and ask yourself what the main aim of the project is. The answer will help you to make a range of other decisions, such as what you will research, what kind of information is most important, what other positions you should consider, and what concepts are most relevant.

Line Up the Evidence

Justifying a position often requires *evidence*—facts, data, testimonials. Evidence is information from the world beyond the argument. It is out there in studies, experiments, and reports. It is part of history, part of the record beyond anyone's particular position. Of course, evidence can be disputed. Data can be interrogated and thrown out. Testimony can be dismissed. In fact, disputing evidence is its own kind of argument—the kind in which people inspect the soundness of information or the methods that generate it. See, for example, Barbara Ehrenreich's argument about the "science of cheer" (page 274). However, we don't have to abandon evidence simply because it can be questioned. Even though facts and data are disputable, they are still necessary for justifying positions. Some positions, in fact, rely exclusively on evidence. For example, in his article about current college graduates (page 244), Joel Kotkin argues that an entire generation is "screwed." Such a claim needs help. It needs specific instances that lead to the claim. Throughout his article, Kotkin lines up evidence:

> How has this generation been screwed? Let's count the ways, starting with the economy. No generation has suffered more from the Great Recession than the young. Median net worth of people under 35, according to the U.S. Census, fell 37 percent between 2005 and 2010; those over 65 took only a 13 percent hit.
>
> The wealth gap today between younger and older Americans now stands as the widest on record. The median net worth of households headed by someone 65 or older is $170,494, 42 percent higher than in 1984, while the median net worth for younger-age households is $3,662, down 68 percent from a quarter century ago, according to an analysis by the Pew Research Center.

As the article continues, Kotkin describes trends in housing, health care, technology, debt, and employment. The trends come from a range of sources, such as the US Census Bureau, Pew Research Center polls, the Bureau of Labor Statistics, and even recent college graduates. The evidence builds throughout the article and justifies Kotkin's position that an entire generation has been dealt a bad hand. With that idea established, he takes another step in his concluding paragraph and makes a claim about the whole country:

> Wanting the next generation to succeed is in everyone's long-term interest. Eventually they will constitute the majority of parents, potential homeowners, and workers. This year they will comprise 24 percent of voting-age adults, up from 18 percent in 2008; by 2020 they will amount to a third of all eligible voters. And if, by then, they are still a screwed generation, they won't be the only ones suffering. America will be screwed, too.

Such a broad claim simply wouldn't work if Kotkin hadn't carefully lined up evidence throughout his argument. Without the evidence, his position would seem highly suspicious at the least. But with his careful presentation of evidence, we can acknowledge the seriousness of his main claim.

TALK ABOUT IT Daniel Patrick Moynihan, a four-term US senator, famously said, "You are entitled to your own opinions but not your own facts." He was responding to the reflex in public life to choose some facts and ignore others, or to simply rewrite history so that it corresponds to one's own worldview. Have you witnessed that reflex? Have you seen or heard people selecting and fashioning facts so that they can maintain their position? Discuss your experiences in small groups. ■

Break Down Your Reasons

Positions need *reasons*—statements that express why you believe in your position. And it always pays to break down and articulate your reasons, which can be a challenge if you are deeply committed to a position. It can be like untangling a ball of rope or trying to find the beginning of a tape spool. You have to scratch away until you find some beginning point—some basic understanding of your own thinking. So how do we begin? How do we discover the *why* behind our positions? We can take a cue from the Declaration of Independence, which is famous not simply for starting a revolution but also for breaking down the reasons for that revolution. It begins with something that the founding fathers believed to be "self-evident" or beyond question:

> We hold these truths to be self-evident, that all men are created equal, that they are endowed by their Creator with certain unalienable Rights, that among these are Life, Liberty and the pursuit of Happiness.—That to secure these rights, Governments are instituted among Men, deriving their just powers from the consent of the governed, —That whenever any Form of Government becomes destructive of these ends, it is the Right of the People to alter or to abolish it, and to institute new Government, laying its foundation on such principles and organizing its powers in such form, as to them shall seem most likely to effect their Safety and Happiness.

So the American Revolution gets launched with a general statement about equality and the role of governments to secure and protect it. That, according to the Declaration, is the first justification for American independence. To argue that the colonists should be free from tyranny,

Source: http://www.archives.gov/exhibits/charters/declaration_transcript.html.

Thomas Jefferson (the primary author of the Declaration) needed the principle that "all men," not just the colonial men, should be free from tyranny. Once that principle is established, Jefferson goes on to list specific situations that oppose it. The King of England, Jefferson explains, kept colonists from making decisions about their own communities, kept British soldiers in the colonial towns, and forced colonists to pay for their own harassment. After listing the specifics, Jefferson concludes:

> We, therefore, the Representatives of the united States of America, in General Congress, Assembled, appealing to the Supreme Judge of the world for the rectitude of our intentions, do, in the Name, and by Authority of the good People of these Colonies, solemnly publish and declare, That these united Colonies are, and of Right ought to be Free and Independent States, that they are Absolved from all Allegiance to the British Crown, and that all political connection between them and the State of Great Britain, is and ought to be totally dissolved; . . .

Analyzing the Declaration as an example, we can see that argumentative reasoning is often driven along by some principle of right and wrong, some general belief about what should or shouldn't happen, or some general understanding of behavior. This is not to say that reasoning *must* begin at such a sweeping or universal level. In fact, if every position on every topic were connected to statements as broad as "all men are created equal," it'd get wildly difficult to express our reasons. But much reasoning in academic life (and in our daily lives) relies on some principle. To justify our positions, we often need an idea that *not only applies to but also extends beyond* the specific situation.

Here's another way to think about it: in some respects, reasoning is an audience issue. Since the

Declaration of Independence was written for a big audience (people throughout the colonies, aristocrats in England, and government officials throughout Europe), it had to do more than express the American colonists' concerns. It had to connect those concerns to a broader principle, one that people in England, France, and Spain could consider and understand. Reasoning, in this sense, is *the acknowledgement that other people's brains are involved*.

TALK ABOUT IT

1. The founding fathers understood that "all men" of European descent were equal. It took nearly two centuries before women and non-European men were acknowledged equally under American law. As a class, try to break down the reasons behind the idea that all people (regardless of wealth, race, sex, or sexual orientation) should be treated equally under the law. Consider instances in which the law does not treat individuals equally, such as age (children who may not vote, teenagers who commit violent crimes), status (citizens vs. noncitizens), or sexual orientation (same-sex couples who may not marry).

2. Discuss the context of the Declaration of Independence. What can you determine about the situation? Remember that the Declaration was written at the end of the eighteenth century. The audience included American colonists, English aristocrats, and heads of state throughout Europe. Jefferson (the primary author) and his colleagues were seeking freedom from King George's control. Beyond the obvious tensions, what can you sense? What ideas may have been heated, new, or potentially unacceptable? How do you know? ∎

Let's take a more recent example. In her book *Distracted: The Erosion of Attention and the Coming Dark Age*, Maggie Jackson argues that America is descending into a time of cultural and educational decay. That is her position. Her purpose is to warn us of this impending "dark age." In the first paragraph below, she gives the warning. And in the second, she begins breaking down her reasons. As you'll notice, her reasoning includes some general principles about attention and society:

> We should be concerned when we sense that short-term thinking in the workplace eclipses intellectual pattern making, and when we're staking our cultural memory largely on digital data that is disappearing at astounding rates. We should worry when attention slips through our fingers.
>
> For nothing is more central to a flourishing society built upon learning, contentment, caring, morality, reflection, and spirit than attention. As humans, we are formed to pay attention. Without it, we simply would not survive. Just as our respiratory systems are made of multiple parts, so attention encompasses three "networks" related to different aspects of awareness, focus, and planning.

Even though Jackson doesn't ask the question explicitly, we can almost imagine the second paragraph beginning with "Why should we worry?" In other words, the second paragraph launches her reasoning. It's where she begins explaining the whys of her position. Throughout her chapters, then, she builds reason on top of reason until the whole argument looks something like this:

From *Distracted: The Erosion of Attention and the Coming Dark Age*, Amherst: Prometheus, 2008.

Position: We should be alarmed at our inability to pay attention.

Reasons: Because attention allows people to focus

Because attention allows people to make sound judgments

Because attention allows people to remember and reason

Because all these reflexes are crucial to a thriving society

And because all these reflexes are diminishing in the population

Support Your Reasons

In daily arguments, in the quick back-and-forths that we might have with a coworker or friend, we often don't need to support our reasons. We need only express the *why* behind our thinking. But in more formal arguments, our reasons need support. And that's where information comes in—where evidence, facts, data, and testimony are most helpful. For example, let's go back to Jackson's book. She does not merely announce each reason and then move on. She supports each with information from a range of sources. In the following paragraph, she explains a crucial function of attention and then backs it up with information:

Attention also tames our inner beast. Primates that receive training in attention become less aggressive.[29] One of the highest forms is "effortful control," which involves the ability to shift focus deliberately, engage in planning, and regulate one's impulses. Six- and seven-year-olds who score high in tests of this skill are more empathetic, better able to feel guilt and shame, and less aggressive. Moreover, effortful control is integral to developing a conscience, researchers are discovering.[30] In order to put back the stolen cookie, you must attend to your uneasy feelings, the action itself, and the abstract moral principles—then make the right response. All in all, attention is key to both our free will as individuals and our ability to subordinate ourselves to a greater good. . . . Attention is not always effortful, but it carries us toward our highest goals, however we define them. A culture that settles for numb distraction cannot shape its future.

This is how Jackson's book proceeds. She gives a reason and then provides information to support that reason. It's a double layer of justification: here's a reason; here's some information that supports that reason.

Position: We should be alarmed at our inability to pay attention.

Reason: Attention makes people less aggressive ("tames our inner beast").

Supporting Info: Research about "effortful control"

In fact, even Jackson's paragraph structure is fairly typical (and helpful). First, she states the reason and then gets into the supporting information. The paragraph has a sense of uniformity or coherence because we understand, from the first sentence, why we need the information she gives us—why it's there and what it's doing.

Dismantle and Deny the Opposition

Whenever you're justifying a position, there are likely other positions swirling around. And you can't just ignore them. Consider again the shipwreck scenario at the start

From *Distracted: The Erosion of Attention and the Coming Dark Age*, Amherst: Prometheus, 2008 of this chapter: If you were to propose saving others in the water, you couldn't ignore the others on your raft who had already decided to rush for the island. You'd have to explain why they're wrong, why your position is better. The same goes for academic writing. It's not enough to say "You're wrong" and then row in whatever direction you see fit. You have to break down other positions and explain why they're wrong—less practical, less accurate, less humane, and so on. And that's where all the steps from Chapter 5 come in. Before you can deny opposing positions, you have to take them apart. The more thoroughly you break down and explain the logic of the opposition, the more intact and sound your position becomes.

Consider this example: In 2007, the *New York Times* sponsored a blog quorum on the "economics of street charity." The blog's author, Stephen J. Dubner, is a popular author on economics, and he thought it would be interesting to pose the following hypothesis to various people who have thought long and hard about economics:

> You are walking down the street in New York City with $10 of disposable income in your pocket. You come to a corner with a hot dog vendor on one side and a beggar on the other. The beggar looks like he's been drinking; the hot dog vendor looks like an upstanding citizen. How, if at all, do you distribute the $10 in your pocket, and why?

With this question as a springboard, various respondents offered opinions. But one respondent, Barbara Ehrenreich, took on the question by dismantling it. In the following passage, Ehrenreich breaks down the very structure of the question. She senses that the elements involved (the drunk beggar, $10, and the hot dog vendor) add up to an obvious answer: give the beggar a hot dog and you can congratulate yourself for helping him without contributing to his addiction. She continues by denying (even condemning) that idea:

> Could we first dispense with the smarmy connect-the-dots answer this question seems to cry out for? That is, that I'd use the $10 to buy a hot dog for the beggar and perhaps give the change to the vendor as a tip, thus rewarding a hardworking citizen while assuring that the shiftless beggar does not get the wherewithal for another drink—while of course giving me a nice little hit of middle class self-righteousness. . . .
>
> Although I'm atheist, I defer to Jesus on beggar-related matters. He said, if a man asks for your coat, give him your cloak too. (Actually, he said if a man "sue thee at the law" for the coat, but most beggars skip the legal process.) Jesus did not say: First, administer a breathalyzer test to the supplicant, or, first, sit him down for a pep talk on "focus" and "goal-setting." He said: Give him the damn coat.
>
> As a matter of religious observance, if a beggar importunes me directly, I must fork over some money. How do I know whether he's been drinking or suffers from a neurological disorder anyway? Unless I'm his parole officer, what do I care? And before anyone virtuously offers him a hot dog, they should reflect on the possibility that the beggar is a vegetarian or only eats kosher or Hallal meat.
>
> So if the beggar approaches me and puts out his hand, and if I only have a $10 bill, I have to give it to him. It's none of my business whether he plans to spend it on infant formula for his starving baby or a pint of Thunderbird.

In these paragraphs, Ehrenreich dismantles and denies the entire argument. She shows that the writer behind

Source: http://www.freakonomics.com/2007/08/09/freakonomics-quorum-the-economics-of-street-charity/. Copyright © 2007 Stephen J. Dubner.

the question is an economist who believes that human motivation and ethical obligation can be boiled down to questions of money and usefulness. She also explains the subtle reasoning that operates within the question. Finally, she reveals the attitudes and expectations of its readers: they want to be congratulated for their ethical care of a beggar, when in fact that "care" is merely paternalistic or condescending.

Advanced Move: Seek Reasons Inside Reasons

Sometimes, a position can be justified for a single but powerful reason. Remember the example from Chapter 5: If someone tells you to run from the building because it's on fire, you don't need a second or third reason. One is enough. But when it comes to thinking in academic life, the topics usually call for us to crack open the reasons and seek out the more subtle thinking inside them. In fact, the best thinking often comes along when we get beyond the obvious, established reasons—the ones that we automatically conjure, the ones we've heard over and over in other arguments. For example, in his article "Charlotte's Webpage" (*Orion Magazine*), Lowell Monke explains his position against educational software for young children. He describes familiar reasons people have offered before: that too much time on a computer makes children reliant on calculators, too cut off from exercise, too unaware of the world outside. Those are good reasons, but watch where Monke goes. In the second paragraph below, he breaks down a reason to discover a more subtle reason inside it—one that we might not expect:

> This [clicking answers on a computer screen] is a very different way of engaging the world than hitting a ball, building a fort, setting a table, climbing a tree, sorting coins, speaking

and listening to another person, acting in a play. In an important sense, the child gains control over a vast array of complex abstract activities by giving up or eroding her capacity to actually do them herself. We bemoan the student who uses a spell-checker instead of learning to spell, or a calculator instead of learning to add. But the sacrifice of internal growth for external power generally operates at a more subtle level, as when a child assembles a PowerPoint slideshow using little if any material that she actually created herself.

Perhaps more importantly, however, this emphasis on external power teaches children a manipulative way of engaging the world. The computer does an unprecedented job of facilitating the manipulation of symbols. Every object within the virtual environment is not only an abstract representation of something tangible, but is also discrete, floating freely in a digital sea, ready at hand for the user to do with as she pleases. . . . A picture of a face can be distorted, a recording of a musical performance remixed, someone else's text altered and inserted into an essay. The very idea of the dignity of a subject evaporates when everything becomes an object to be taken apart, reassembled, or deleted.

Monke explains why, beyond the obvious, children might suffer from educational software. He doesn't just say that computer learning makes a child less active. He explores the subtle harm of digital interaction. It's not simply inactivity but a particular kind of inactivity. In other words, he looks inside the common reasoning to find something more specific—something *more specifically harmful* about computer learning.

This is a difficult move because our initial reasons are often common reasons—those that seem obvious, big, and undeniable. We have to get beyond the automatic power of those reasons and imagine the many possible

Source: *Orion* (Sept./Oct. 2005)

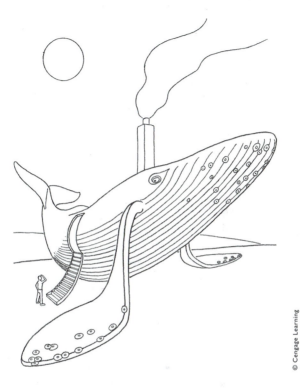

© Cengage Learning

ideas within them. Like Monke, we might then see how something works, how something might be specifically harmful or helpful. We might even see some subtle layer of thinking that others have missed altogether.

WRITE IT
• • • • • • • • •

When good questions can be raised, positions have to be justified. When there's more than one obvious answer, we have to work through the ideas and chart them out. As you consider your own project, take one of the following paths:

1. Many argumentative positions depend on some principle of fairness. Consider a situation in which someone or some group of people was not treated fairly. Write an essay that condemns the unfair policy or action. As you develop reasoning for your position, seek out a source that offers an explanation of fairness. Apply specific language from that source to the specific situation.

2. Try a "fixing" argument. Go back to a previous era in your life—to early adolescence or high school—and describe a way of thinking that you were taught or that you accepted simply by virtue of living in a time and place. Explain how that thinking was flawed, shortsighted, even infected with some subtle misunderstanding. Without dismissing the entire way of thinking, fix that shortsightedness.

3. Try a "proposing" argument. Take on a specific practice in education (such as using standard print textbooks or attending a physical classroom several times per week). Explain what's wrong with that practice—the thinking behind it, the practical shortcomings of it. And then propose a better way. Make a case for that better way. Explain why it's more agile, helpful, practical, efficient, or even humane.

4. Often, arguments in academic writing are not full-scale wars or even skirmishes. They are drawn-out examinations of an issue that involve different, and sometimes opposing, perspectives. Consider a practice that is widely accepted in mainstream education (such as online writing courses or housing academic disciplines in different buildings) and develop a position about the value of that practice—why it is worth continuing or why colleges might want to

reconsider it. Rather than dismiss potential opposition, include other perspectives in your reasoning.

READ: For examples of full essays that justify a position, check out Joel Kotkin (page 244) and Christine Overall (page 252).

APPLY: For specific guidance on how to structure a full essay using the moves in this chapter, see the outlines in Part III, "Apply the Moves" (pages 310–311).

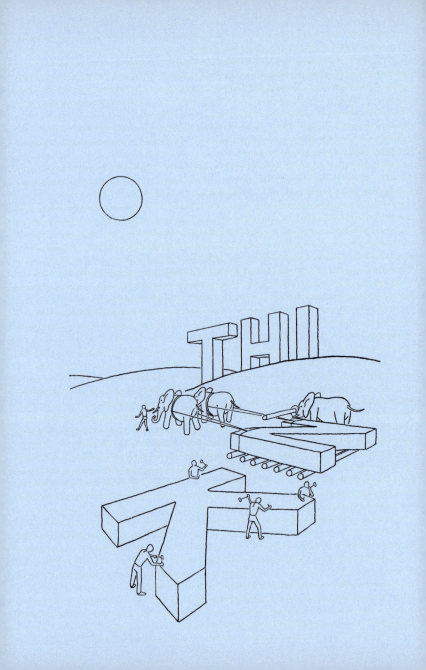

CHAPTER

7

Change the Terms

THINK ABOUT IT

Language is alive. It morphs over time. New terms and phrases are constantly coming along while plenty of others fall out of favor or fade from common use. Consider these gems from the past: *knickers, house shoes, chap, cocksure, davenport, galoshes, hullaballoo, scally-wag, scurryfunge*. Terms like these have gone—or are going—the way of the dodo. Social and cultural forces are nudging them out of common use. This is not a new phenomenon. It's how language works. New products, new sensitivities, new trends, and new groups of people come along and influence the mainstream conversation. Slowly, and sometimes quickly, common terms fade away. Not long ago, women were *dames*, men were *dudes*, money was *jack*, bling was an *orchid*, detectives were *dicks*, and *great* was *ducky*. Anyone who's lived more than a couple of decades can probably recall a number of such substitutions. Language moves along at the speed of social life.

Academic language changes too. Terms fade because new tools replace old ones, new people enter the conversation, and new ideas become attractive. And in academic life, the process is often public and formal. Terms and phrases get examined in professional journals and at disciplinary conferences. They get inspected, interrogated, analyzed, and sometimes kicked to the sidelines. In fact, we might even say: Academic terms don't simply fall out of fashion. They get kicked out of fashion. It all begins when someone detects something wrong:

- A term or phrase suggests an old prejudice, one not in keeping with prevailing values.

- A term or phrase ignores complexity that should be considered.

- A term or phrase suggests something different from the normal activity or concept that academic writers want to engage.

- A term or phrase has gathered some negative, and therefore distracting, connotations.

For academic writers, this is all serious business because the disciplines rely on key terms—those that show up in experiments, articles, books, and studies. The terms frame debates, make issues, and actually define the nature of college study. Consider, for instance, the role of *consciousness* in psychology, *divine* in religion, *institution* in political science, or *voice* in literary studies. Academic writers rely on such terms to make thinking happen. And if those terms get questioned or pushed aside, then the intellectual fabric of the discipline can change—maybe drastically. The hope, however, is that changes in the common terminology make for better thinking, better study, better research. Academic writers see this process as crucial— as part of their responsibility. They often set out to find gaps, old biases, or subtle inaccuracies in the language of the discipline.

This chapter focuses on that process: detecting an inaccuracy or a flawed association and then proposing a new term—one that's more accurate, less flawed. In other words, the moves in this chapter are argumentative in nature. They require you to see a need for change, propose a change in terminology, and justify that change. Along the way, you might borrow some moves from Chapter 5, "Dismantle Arguments," or Chapter 6, "Justify Your Position."

Detect and Describe Inaccuracy

When it comes to describing or explaining something, accuracy might not seem like a big deal. After all, an airplane will not fall from the sky if we use the wrong term. But the wrong term can do plenty of damage. It might hamper thinking. It might conceal the complexity of a situation or blur subtleties. And when academic writers are blind to subtleties, entire intellectual traditions can get bogged down or even travel along deeply flawed paths for decades. So it's often up to individuals to make a case against terms—to call them out and describe the intellectual error that they generate. For example, in the following passage from her essay (page 262), Kathleen Schenck explains how the title of a college course mischaracterizes the students who take it. The title English for Speakers of Other Languages, or its acronym ESOL, blurs away important distinctions. In Schenck's words, it "fails to differentiate" the students who take the class:

> Another issue is again the inaccuracy of the term ESOL. At my high school, students chose Spanish, French, German, or Latin classes to fulfill the foreign language requirement.

The token "dead" language of Latin aside, we teenagers at a Midwestern public high school qualified as "speakers of other languages" who were also, of course, taking English classes. The term ESOL fails to differentiate between those learning English as a language and those studying Shakespeare in order to gain AP status for a lighter first-year college course load.

Joan M. Herbers, a biologist, calls out a similar problem with the phrase *slave ants*. In the following passage from "The Loaded Language of Science," she explains how the widely used phrase misses something critical about the real behavior of the species:

> I now call for biologists to discard the use of slave metaphors to describe insect behavior. Not only are the terms damaging, but in fact they are not particularly accurate. Unlike human slaves, captive worker ants cannot breed, nor are they sold to other captors. Instead, the predatory species must repeatedly raid colonies to replenish its work force; indeed, voracious colonies can overexploit their captives and engender their own demise when there is no one left to do the work.

Herbers and Schenck illustrate a common move among academic writers: they explain how a term distorts or misses something. In this sense, they are discovering more than a language problem. They are pointing out an intellectual flaw, a crisis in the shared thinking of the discipline.

Reprinted by permission of Kathleen Schenck.

Source: *The Chronicle of Higher Education* (Mar. 24, 2006). © 2005 Chronicle of Higher Education, Inc. Reprinted with permission.

TALK ABOUT IT Consider a common term or phrase related to college courses, such as *higher education, standardized test, unit, chapter test, midterm review,* or *knowledge retention.* How does the term or phrase miss something critical? ■

Detect and Describe the Quiet Associations

In Chapter 1, we describe the way words come along with a string of quiet associations. For example, when most people see the phrase *high school*, they think of teachers, hallways, books, maybe a sport or marching band. Language works because people share in these associations. But sometimes, it's this layer—the unspoken layer—that creates problems. For example, in the following passage from her book *A Way of Seeing*, Margaret Mead detects something amiss with *superstition* and the way the term gets used in cultural anthropology:

> In a religious context, where truths cannot be demonstrated, we accept them as a matter of faith. Superstitions, however, belong to the category of beliefs, practices and ways of thinking that have been discarded because they are inconsistent with scientific knowledge. It is easy to say that other people are superstitious because they believe what we regard to be untrue. "Superstition" used in that sense is a derogatory term for the beliefs of other people that we do not share. But there is more to it than that. For superstitions lead a kind of half life in a twilight world where, sometimes, we partly suspend our disbelief and act as if magic worked.

Source: *A Way of Seeing* by Margaret Mead and Rhoda Metraux, New York: McCall, 1970. Copyright © 1971 by Margaret Mead and Rhoda Metraux.

When researchers refer to a culture's beliefs as *super-stitious*, according to Mead, they unknowingly dismiss those beliefs as less worthy of study, less worthy of serious examination. Mead is not saying that research-ers deliberately use *superstition* to insult the beliefs of other people. Instead, she is explaining that the term has some quiet associations that work against anthropo-logical research. It's the quiet thinking—the intellectual stuff that rolls in on the coattails of the term—that Mead wants readers to consider.

Let's look a bit more closely at the term *superstition*: why might the term pose problems for anthropolo-gists—researchers who seek to understand civilization and human relations? To answer this, we should con-sider the way people commonly use the term. In main-stream American culture, superstition includes fear of broken mirrors, the number 13, Friday the 13th, black cats crossing one's path, and so on. Imagine that an office manager, let's call him Chad, refuses to leave home on Friday the 13th. Despite important meetings and dead-lines, he insists that going out for any reason on that particular day poses serious danger. Although he can't prove it, Chad believes in some cause/effect relationship between the designation of the day and the potential for harm. His coworkers would probably wonder about his mental stability. They would call him superstitious. Let's say that another office manager, Leah, decides to stay home and crouched in her basement because a tornado is bearing down on the city. We wouldn't call her super-stitious. We'd call her sane, normal, even responsible.

So people assign the term *superstition* to Chads of the world, not Leahs of the world. In its most common use, *superstition* refers to beliefs that are commonly dismissed as quaint or exotic—as less in touch with cause and effect, less reasonable, less scientific, less enlightened.

So if anthropologists refer to another culture's beliefs as *superstition*, they automatically (but quietly) portray that culture as less reasonable, less in touch with cause and effect. In short, they make a subtle judgment about the culture by simply assigning the term. Mead, then, draws attention to that subtle judgment and explains how it infects anthropologists' thinking.

Mead's move is not unique. Many academic writers deal with quiet associations. They probe the realm of attitudes, beliefs, and sentiments that linger around terms. In the following passage from "Overcoming White Supremacy: A Comment," bell hooks,[1] a widely read cultural theorist, explores the terms *racism, white supremacy, internalized racism*, and *Uncle Tom*. Of these related terms, hooks explains that *white supremacy* best expresses the nature of racial tension:

> As I write, I try to remember when the word racism ceased to be the term which best expressed for me exploitation of black people and other people of color in this society and when I began to understand that the most useful term was white supremacy. It was certainly a necessary term when confronted with the liberal attitudes of white women active in feminist movement who were unlike their racist ancestors—white women in the early woman's rights movement who did not wish to be caught dead in fellowship with black women. In fact, these women often requested and longed for the presence of black women. Yet when present, what we saw was that they wished to exercise control over our bodies and thoughts as their racist ancestors had—that this need to exercise power over us expressed how much they had internalized the values and attitudes of white supremacy. . . .

---

[1] hooks does not capitalize her first or last name.

Likewise, "white supremacy" is a much more useful term for understanding the complicity of people of color in upholding and maintaining racial hierarchies that do not involve force (i.e., slavery, apartheid) than the term "internalized racism"—a term most often used to suggest that black people have absorbed negative feelings and attitudes about blackness held by white people. The term "white supremacy" enables us to recognize not only that black people are socialized to embody the values and attitudes of white supremacy, but that we can exercise "white-supremacist control" over other black people. This is important, for unlike the term "uncle tom," which carried with it the recognition of complicity and internalized racism, a new terminology must accurately name the way we as black people directly exercise power over one another when we perpetuate white-supremacist beliefs. Speaking about changing perspectives on black identity, writer Toni Morrison said in a recent interview: "Now people choose their identities. Now people choose to be Black." At this historical moment, when a few black people no longer experience the racial apartheid and brutal racism that still determine the lot of many black people, it is easier for that few to ally themselves politically with the dominant racist white group.

Herbers, Schenck, Mead, and hooks all call out the automatic associations and inaccuracies that come along with words and phrases. The terms they target (*slave ant*, *ESOL*, *superstition*, *racism*) can be obstacles to better thinking or distractions to better questions. And it's those obstacles and distractions that academic writers want to omit.

Source: "Overcoming White Supremacy: A Comment" by bell hooks.

As a class or group, examine another term and consider its quiet associations, the automatic ideas that come with the term itself. Consider, for instance, one of the following: *ethnic, third world, mature, punk, book-smart, hot.* List the associations that come to mind. Also discuss how the situation, or context, might affect the associations of the term. ■

Propose a Different Term

Once an old term is shown to be insufficient or flawed, there's room to offer something different. Sometimes, writers propose a substitution—something more accurate or something with less cultural baggage. For example, in the following passage, Joan M. Herbers proposes a new term (and metaphor) to replace the old *slave ant* metaphor. She also begins making the case for the new term. That is, she describes how the new term more appropriately fits with ant behavior:

> I propose, then, that we adopt a pirate metaphor to replace the slavery jargon. Human pirates engage in behavior much like the ants I study: They attack ships to steal cargo, usually inflicting considerable mortality among the defending crew. We can therefore write about pirate ants, captive ants, raiding parties, and booty. Since we scientists love jargon, I further propose that we call this "leistic" behavior, from the Greek leistos for "pirate."

Likewise, Kathleen Schenck throws her support behind a newer acronym—one that has already been offered but hasn't been widely received in her field. Notice how the following paragraph explains the value

Source: *The Chronicle of Higher Education* (Mar. 24, 2006). © 2005 Chronicle of Higher Education, Inc. Reprinted with permission.

of the new acronym. In other words, the paragraph *gives reasons for* shifting to ELL:

> A new term is needed. In fact, one already exists: ELL. ELL stands for English Language Learner. This term subtracts the numbers from the equation altogether and focuses on the positive as well as the present: currently, this person is learning English. The level of proficiency is not brought into question, nor is the native language or dialect of English being learned. The logic behind the term ELL acknowledges that English is a subject to be studied, like geology or math. I did not, for example, sign up for High School Geometry for Those Who Have Never Done Well in Math, or HSGTWHNDWM. ELL acknowledges that the English language contains a multitude of dialects—many of which are found in the United States. A non-native English speaker showcases just another dialect. This dialect is not secondary to any other dialect, nor is it indicative of the speaker being less intelligent, more of an outsider, or unfinished in some way. Furthermore, learning English is not synonymous with a promise to use only English. If the speaker knows two languages or seven, she may enjoy a more culturally and linguistically diverse life in many of America's metropolitan areas than most monolingual speakers of American English currently enjoy. With a wider acceptance into varied cultural groups comes a wider understanding of the same groups, increasing one's intercultural competence, employability, and, one could argue, compassion.

Reprinted by permission of Kathleen Schenck.

A LOOK AT WORDS AND WORLDVIEW

Sometimes, the change in terms is a shift away from an entire worldview. The writer introduces a new intellectual species, a new linguistic creature that roams around in the culture and eventually takes up residence in everyday talk. We see such creation all the time when it comes to technology. Years ago, *Facebook* had no meaning whatsoever—nor did *blog*, *Wi-Fi*, or *nanotechnology*. New situations also generate new terms. In the following passage from "Occupy Wall Street's 'Political Disobedience,'" Bernard E. Harcourt proposes a new phrase to characterize the Occupy movement. In the past, such protests were characterized as *civil disobedience*. As Harcourt explains, the phrase needs updating:

> Our language has not yet caught up with the political phenomenon that is emerging in Zuccotti Park and spreading across the nation, though it is clear that a political paradigm shift is taking place before our very eyes. It's time to begin to name and in naming, to better understand this moment. So let me propose some words: "political disobedience."

Harcourt, then, is calling for a new term to accompany and cultivate a new way of thinking. He's calling on people in the Occupy movement and its critics to imagine something beyond the status quo—or the usual ways of thinking. The next chapter, "Escape the Status Quo," will explore this move in depth.

Source: Bernard E. Harcourt, "Occupy Wall Street's 'Political Disobedience'", October 13, 2011, *The New York Times*. http://opinionator.blogs.nytimes.com/2011/10/13/occupy-wall-streets-political-disobedience/?scp=1&sq=apply%20concept&st=cse

Flip the Terms

Sometimes, the most powerful way to change terms is to flip them upside down, to invert the logic that lurks within them so that *doing* becomes *undoing*, *destruction* becomes *creation*, *seeing* becomes *blindness*, *multiplying* becomes *dividing*, and on and on. One famous version of this is the statement: "A way of seeing is also a way of not seeing." In other words, developing a perspective means developing a blindness to things outside of that perspective. A less formal version of this has been popularized and spread around on bumper stickers: "Don't Believe Everything You Think."

The process is not simply a thought experiment; it is an intellectual maneuver to open up possibilities. It may sound difficult—and it can be—but it happens all the time in daily life, even in informal conversations. As we're talking, we suddenly understand that the opposite of what we've said, or were going to say, makes more sense. In other words, the opposite of our normal intellectual path can sometimes create insights. For instance, in his book *Everywhere Being Is Dancing*, Robert Bringhurst flips some common logic about poetry:

> Poetry, I'm often told, is something made of words. I think it really goes the other way around: words are made of poetry (and so is a good deal else).

From there, Bringhurst explores how this idea (the inverse of what people normally think) might be true,

---

Everywhere Being Is Dancing: Twenty Pieces of Thinking, Berkeley: Counterpoint, 2008. Copyright © 2008 by Robert Bringhurst. All rights reserved under International and Pan-American Copyright Conventions.

how it might enrich people's understanding of language. Like Herbers and Mead, Bringhurst shows how thinking gets caged in a common and uninspected phrase. In fact, plenty of academic writers have put their brains in a kind of inverse relationship with common ways of thinking. They've imagined the opposite, the inside/out or the upside/down of the usual. In the following passage, Adam Gopnik describes recent research about dogs. As it turns out, Gopnik explains, early humans didn't choose dogs as their closest animal companions. The dogs chose humans:

> Dogs, we are now told, by a sequence of scientists and speculators . . . domesticated themselves. They chose us. A marginally calmer canid came close to the circle of human warmth—and, more important, human refuse—and was tolerated by the humans inside: let him eat the garbage. Then this scavenging wolf mated with another calm wolf, and soon a family of calmer wolves proliferated just outside the firelight. It wasn't cub-snatching on the part of humans, but breaking and entering on the part of wolves, that gave us dogs.

Once Gopnik expresses the opposite of how people normally think about dog/human relationships, he ventures further. In other words, after the logic has been turned on its head, everything starts looking different. Next, he explains how our language creates and reinforces an illusion:

> Certainly, the qualities inherent in breeds—nobility, haughtiness, solidity, even the smiling happiness of the Havanese—are tricks of our mind, where we project primate expressions of inner mood into canine masks. The Havanese isn't happy and the Shih Tzu isn't angry and the

bulldog isn't especially stolid or stubborn; they are just stuck with the faces, smiling or snarling, we've pinned on them through breeding. And the virtues we credit them with—whether the big ones of bravery, loyalty, and love or the smaller ones of happiness, honesty, and guilt—are just as illusory. . . .

Yet . . . dogs have found a shortcut into our minds. They live . . . within our circle without belonging to it: they speak our language without actually speaking any, and share our concerns without really being able to understand them. The verbs tell some of the story: the dog shares, feels, engages, without being able to speak, plan, or (in some human sense) think. We may not be able to know what it's like to be a dog; but, over all those thousands of years, Butterscotch [Gopnik's dog] has figured out, in some instrumental way, what it's like to be a person. Without language, concepts, long-term causal thinking, she can still enter into the large part of our mind made up of appetites, longings, and loyalties. She does a better impersonation of a person than we do an approximation of a dog.

TALK ABOUT IT In a small group, take on a common term related to college writing, such as *inspire, express, convince, develop*, or *edit*. After you choose a term, imagine its opposite. How might the opposite term say something about the process of writing? Might the opposite reveal something important? Can you imagine if the opposite term were constantly applied in writing courses? What would happen? ∎

Source: http://www.newyorker.com/reporting/2011/08/08/110808fa _fact_gopnik

Advanced Move: Change the Lens

No matter how hard we try to see things for what they are, we're always seeing the world through a lens. Our comprehension is colored by our culture, upbringing, and our place in history. Consider, for example, how someone born in the late 1800s might respond to a rap music video or the latest television show about zombies. Even some basic reflexes such as amazement or fear are shaped largely by the culture around and within us. In academic life, scholars admit this influence. They acknowledge that their intellectual reflexes are shaped by their backgrounds and by the disciplines they've entered. In other words, someone studying psychology learns not simply lists of terms and concepts but also ways of interpreting data, texts, and situations. A psychology major may look at something such as bullying one way, while a sociologist may see it another.

- *Psychologist*: Bullying is an expression of personal struggle often created by a difficult home life.

- *Sociologist*: Bullying is cultivated by a society that constantly celebrates outward strength, force, and aggression.

These are not simply different definitions but different *ways of seeing*. However, the differences are not fixed or exclusive. A sociologist is allowed to think in terms of psychology—and vice versa. In other words, people can change their perspectives and change back again. We are not stuck with one lens. With some effort and know-how, we can shift the lenses we've learned (or have been given) and see differently. The result can generate big insights. For example, in his essay "Thirteen Ways of Looking at a Crack House," Jayme Stayer explores a range of lenses. He begins his essay by explaining his own reaction to first seeing abandoned houses in Detroit, Michigan—what he calls *shitholes*. And in the following passage, he describes another perspective, that of a visiting bishop from Africa who sees the crack houses of Detroit weren't a sign of urban blight or abandonment. They were shelter:

> A bishop from Africa was once driven around Detroit and shown the poorest sections of the city. When his host pointed out that the city was eager to tear down the abandoned homes in order to clear away the blight, the African bishop responded that his people would be lucky to live in such houses. From his perspective, those houses weren't miserable hovels or dangerous bonfire-starters. They were shelters from the blazing sun and torrential downpours. Poor Africans who live in shanty towns or refugee camps, the bishop was suggesting, would be happy to have 2,000 square feet per family, hard floors to sleep and walk on, and shelter from the heat and rain. . . .
>
> The bishop didn't see the cultural context of those abandoned houses. Unfamiliar with the urban riots, or the cycles of poverty, gang wars, and drug violence of the American scene, he didn't know why or how the houses had come to be abandoned. The only thing he saw riding past in his car was shabby, if potentially usable, structures.

Stayer's insight is not simply that abandoned houses can look different to different people. His point is more involved. As he explains below, the different lenses make us ask different questions and come to a better understanding of the subject itself:

> Which lens is right cannot be decided until those terms start duking it out inside of a rhetorical argument: Historically, how did this neighborhood come to be abandoned and why? Politically, what should we now do with the houses?

Artistically, how do we portray poverty and for what reasons do we do so?

TALK ABOUT IT Using Google Maps, Google Earth, or MapQuest, you can select different ways to view an area—either with a digital map or from a satellite image. In a small group, access Google Maps, Google Earth, or MapQuest and enter your city or town. Once your area comes up, narrow the focus so that you can see the college campus or a surrounding neighborhood. Then, switch the viewer from Map to Satellite. Discuss how the change affects your thinking. How does a satellite image impact your reaction? How is it different from the digital map? And what happens to your thinking if you omit the road and highway labels? How does the world change without them? ■

WRITE IT
• • • • • • • • •

Sometimes, terms simply wear out because a culture moves beyond them. But in academic life, what often happens is this: a scholar senses a problem with common terminology and then convinces others of that problem. The change in terminology kicks up the intellectual dust. It makes new ideas possible. As you consider your own project, take one of the following paths:

1. Some of the writers quoted in this chapter reveal the problems inherent in certain terminology. They chart out how they've rethought these terms and the specific insights that come from analyzing accepted language. Choose a term in an academic discipline or in a field of interest that you think deserves closer scrutiny, such as *poetry, art, artistic, patient, file sharing, social networking, piracy*, and so

on. In an essay, explain the term as people typically use and understand it. Then, explain the problems inherent in that term. What does the term overlook or miss? How does it misdirect thinking? Then, consider what new term would allow new ideas to percolate. Propose this new term to replace the old one and explain the insights gained from shifting to the proposed term.

2. One way to generate fresh thinking on a topic is to consider the opposite—a term or phrase that represents the inverse of established thinking. Choose a term or phrase that you see as limiting or problematic. Then, list some terms or phrases that convey the opposite of the established idea. Select one of these opposites and write an essay that analyzes the new term in light of the old one. What insights emerge from examining the inverse of the original term? Why is this new way of thinking valuable or important for others to consider?

3. Take on a familiar and physical subject (such as a dorm, neighborhood, street, or statue) or a subject from popular culture (such as a film, song, or video). Describe it from your perspective—in the way that you have typically understood it. What has it meant? What is its significance or value? And then shift the lens. Try to see the subject with a totally different perspective. For example, how might someone from another culture see the subject? Think of an entirely different person. If you are native-born, try out the perspective of an immigrant. Or if you are liberal, try out the perspective of a conservative. To help you understand the other perspective, apply at least two sources. Bring them in to help explain some basic assumptions and values associated with the other perspective. As you re-see the subject,

what aspects become important? What new tensions come to the surface? What tensions diminish?

READ: For examples of full essays that change the terms, check out John McCormick (page 258) and Kathleen Schenck (page 262).

APPLY: For specific guidance on how to structure a full essay using the moves in this chapter, see the outlines in Part III, "Apply the Moves" (pages 312–313).

Escape the Status Quo

THINK ABOUT IT

Consider the infrastructure of your community: the buildings, roads, traffic lights, drainage ditches, gutters, electrical grid, fences, and so on. All of those structural features are designed to keep daily life working with a degree of regularity. Without a sound infrastructure, people would find it difficult, or impossible, to implement a schedule—to have regular meetings, get products to stores, ship crops, buy food, meet with clients, talk with students, answer emails, or post blogs. In other words, the infrastructure maintains a *status quo*, or usual state of affairs.

And it's not only the physical structures that maintain the status quo. People do as well. We all help to re-create normal modes of living: Most of us talk rather than sing our way through the day. Most of us don't wear leotards and helmets in public. We shop at stores rather than perform wrestling matches in them. We use restrooms rather than open sewer grates for our personal business.

We sit on the subway rather than stand on our heads, answer the phone rather than fling it at strangers whenever it rings. In short, most of us spend our days using the given infrastructure and reinforcing the usual state of affairs. From office managers to senators, from police officers to presidents, from teachers to border agents, from students to opera singers, most spend their days reinforcing normality.

Now consider the infrastructure of your intellectual life. What is the intellectual status quo? What are the usual ways of thinking? These are difficult questions because we normally don't think about the way we think. And it might be easy to imagine that everyone has his or her own separate thoughts, that we all have our own unique and personalized interior lives. But consider the following passage. It contains statements that are most likely shared by many college students and instructors:

> Other people matter. Tardiness is not a communicable disease. Cows are food; people are not. Fire is not one of my ancestors. Grass does not care to see me. I have an inalienable right to drink water. The past is behind us, the future in front. Falling down can hurt. No matter how hard I flap, I cannot fly without the help of technology. The tooth fairy is a fictional character. Tomorrow, the staircases will lead to the same floors as today. A squirrel will not answer my questions even if I ask nicely. Other people are thinking right now. The moon is real, but it is not out to get me. No one owns Tuesday. Cats are animals rather than plants. Time does not have an opinion, self-esteem problems, or family reunions. The wind is not trying to steal my soul. The sun will rise again.

If you are part of mainstream contemporary life, you probably accept most or all of the preceding statements.

And we could list thousands (or millions) more statements like these and thereby prove a certain degree of shared thought. This is not to say that we are all automatons—robots or puppets enslaved by a hive mind. But if we are participating in daily life (going to school, going to work, buying products, eating food from grocery store shelves, and so on), we are automatically accepting some shared notions about ourselves, other people, and the world around us. These shared notions help to constitute the status quo. They keep things normal.

But the status quo is not simply a list of quiet assumptions. It also involves the way ideas flow along without contest or debate. The statements in the preceding passage, for instance, usually stay below people's radar. They are camouflaged by broad acceptance. This is how the status quo works: it rolls along with quiet agreement or compliance. In other words, people generally do not keep redeciding to believe in shared assumptions. Instead, they go about their work, their days, and their leisure time not even wondering about them.

TALK ABOUT IT Reread the statements on page 152. What would happen if we assumed the opposite of many or all of them? Life would quickly get weird. We might not be very helpful to those around us. We'd likely feel alienated. We'd have a hard time interacting with others. Some version of WTF! would always be rolling around in our thinking. Imagine, for instance, how your nights would change if you believed that the moon was out to get you. Imagine how you would respond to night classes, weather reports, songs, or advertisements about nightlife. Getting along in everyday life would be a challenge. You'd have to duck out of commitments. You'd have to carefully choose dates, jobs, classes, and friends.

In a small group, take one of the other statements from page 152 and imagine how life might look if you all believed the opposite. What practical matters might you have to consider? What other ideas might you accept or dismiss? ■

Although it's ultra quiet, the status quo shapes our daily lives. All the assumptions we have about the world around us (the wind, the moon, time, cats, Tuesdays, and so on) give shape to the society we inhabit. For instance, we don't have moon protectors in major urban

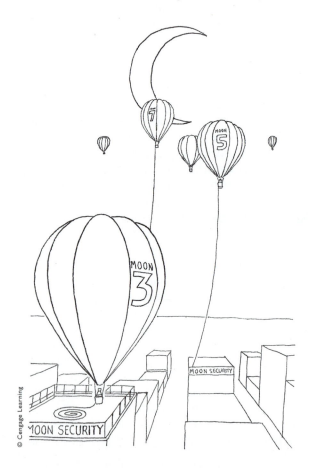

environments. Why? Because most people in our civilization don't see the moon as a threat. And because we don't have moon protectors, most people never think to ask if we should consider them. In other words, widely shared assumptions help to shape the human environment, and that environment, in turn, helps to reinforce widely shared assumptions. It's circular and regenerating. The usual way of thinking re-creates itself over and over again in part because it's easier to live within the established patterns.

However, the status quo does change. Despite the immense power of normality, people sometimes come along and challenge a quietly shared assumption. People in our daily lives sometimes call out and then push against the normal intellectual flow. And they do this because the normal way of doing things has become stale, inefficient, bogged down, undermining, or just plain bad. For instance, consider the shift in college instruction: Several decades ago, nearly all classrooms were structured to facilitate lecture. All desks or seats faced forward. Now, classrooms are often structured to support group work, discussion, and interaction. At some point, enough people understood the need for drastic change.

Sometimes, the status quo conceals an ongoing mistake—a profound error in judgment or practice that comes to light only after someone recognizes it as such. In fact, academic work often attempts to do just that: to recognize the intellectual and practical errors that people keep missing. Scholars in all academic disciplines try, as best they can, to understand the power of the status quo—to realize when the usual way of doing things (the usual measures, assumptions, and practices) becomes a problem or an impediment. And that scholar, whoever introduces change, might at first seem strange or awkward to everyone else.

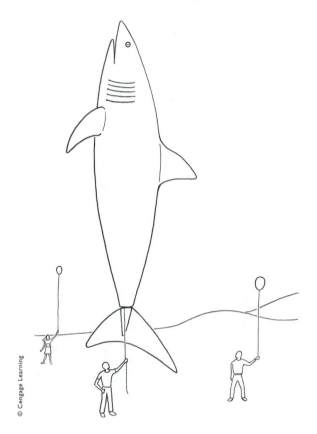

So when it comes to academic life, we are talking about intellectual norms—about the ability to recognize the norms within a given context and to question whether those norms are worthy of being normal. It's not easy. It requires some powerful moves—but these moves are learnable, applicable, and very doable. For the rest of this chapter, we will outline and describe those moves: (1) call out quiet assumptions, (2) question the maxims, (3) question the reasoning, and (4) bust up common comparisons.

Call Out Quiet Assumptions

As we explain at the outset of this chapter, much of what and how we think is automatic and unstated. In most situations, we move along over the top of our assumptions—and in much of daily life, that's okay. But good thinkers learn to hear those murmuring beliefs and interrogate at least some of them. They root out assumptions, put them under the intellectual microscope, and evaluate their worth. For example, in his essay (page 267), Michael Anderson looks into his own past and calls out widely held beliefs about race. In the following passage, he explains how his childhood in Northern Michigan was defined by a collective understanding of racial progress:

> Like many students at the time, we talked about the "N-word." Our class studied the word's entry in an old school dictionary, and as we weighed the pseudo-scientific language against its known cultural obsolescence, we felt secure that time had done its job. We felt sad for the ignorance of the past and happy that things had changed. And these were some of our easiest lessons, because they jibed with other, larger stories about national progress that presented the ideal America as race-blind, which again subtly confirmed our lack of experience.

And later in the essay, Anderson explains how those quiet assumptions worked—how they got tangled up in daily life and common thinking. In the following passage, he describes the unstated thoughts and shared beliefs that maintained the status quo. He even gives voice to the unthinkable—to the ideas that he couldn't have imagined before:

What we didn't see was our own way of processing, our own collective blindness, our own intellectual habits: we were dealing with race by accepting another way to ignore it. It didn't occur to us to challenge the broad, gaping generalization represented by the collective pronoun *they* because it seemed so very obvious: black people. The label was unexamined, incontrovertible, totalizing. Maybe we needed to hear a deep and perhaps menacing voice inquire, "Who do you mean by *they*?" Or perhaps we needed a black friend who was good at radio-controlled cars, racing bikes, and chess, which were other things we enjoyed.

Of course, not all quiet assumptions harm people and society. Some, as we explain at the outset of the chapter, simply keep things running along. They maintain the infrastructure so that we can communicate and carry on with public life. But as Anderson shows, when quiet and "normal" assumptions work against people, when they limit how we think, good writers and thinkers call them out.

Recognizing the status quo and judging it come easy when we look to the past. We can look back at any decade, year, or recent month and judge what was deemed "normal" thinking with the clarity of hindsight. For example, in her book *The Score: How the Quest for Sex Has Shaped the Modern Man,* Faye Flam describes how European societies in previous centuries responded to the discovery of sperm:

> At first, the world being rather sexist, people thought sperm contained the entire makings for a new person. Little people actually existed inside the sperm, they thought, and some scientists claimed to have seen them. . . . Embedded in sperm, those "preformed" people faced many hazards,

---

Reprinted by permission of Michael Anderson.

and the sexual mores of the eighteenth and nineteenth centuries were aimed in part to protect them. . . .

Any illusion that our own puritanical Western society victimizes only women is quickly dispelled in reading about all the ways boys were prevented from masturbating in the 1800s. Some were confined in straightjackets or wrapped in cold, wet sheets while sleeping. Doctors applied leeches to boys' penises to remove blood, or "congestion"; male genitals were burned with electric currents, hot irons, and caustic chemicals. Or a boy's penis was stuck in a metal "cage" that sounded an alarm if he had an erection.

Many of these treatments were applied to girls, too, and a few got surgery to remove the clitoris. According to some sources, preventing masturbation was the main impetus behind the standard American medical practice of circumcising boys from the nineteenth century to today. Doctors continued to believe in the dangers of masturbation well into the twentieth century, and solo sex wasn't pronounced safe by the American Medical Association until 1972.

From our current position in the twenty-first century, much of the past seems painfully ignorant. But we should be cautious. We shouldn't assume that new or current thinking is automatically more correct than past thinking. We shouldn't join the cult of new information—those who automatically revere the latest data at the expense of everything that came before. Let's not forget that engineers still cannot fathom how the Great Pyramids were built or how Roman aqueducts were conceived. In fact, plenty of scholars find that ancient viewpoints offer more insight than anything in recent times. The philosopher Friedrich Nietzsche even declared that philosophy *started* to go downhill more than 2,000 years ago. In other words, the really powerhouse thinking, according to Nietzsche, came before what most people consider the beginning of Western civilization. In short, the passage of time does not automatically generate better thinking. Despite our technological prowess (cell phones that arrange our days and GPS units that tell us where to turn), humans may be increasingly more confused about plenty of things. Good thinkers have to consider the past and the present with both reverence and healthy doubt.

Question the Maxims

Maxims are repeated, familiar statements. They are asserted in all walks of life, and their repetition makes them seem true. Consider some of the conversational maxims that creep into all forms of public discussion and debate:

Opposites attract.
Actions speak louder than words.
No pain, no gain.
Whatever doesn't kill you only makes you stronger.
A picture is worth a thousand words.
Beauty is only skin deep.
Beggars can't be choosers.
Blood is thicker than water.
Experience is the best teacher.
The bigger they are, the harder they fall.
The eyes are the window to the soul.
Time is money.
Honesty is the best policy.

Such statements rarely get challenged. In fact, they often settle discussions, stop thinking, and make everyone involved nod in agreement. But good thinkers are not swayed by the easy comfort of maxims. They often stand against the current and question the prevailing wisdom. They take on entrenched ideas and show how they might, in fact, crumble under the weight of scrutiny. They explain, for instance, that experience might be a costly, inefficient, and dim-witted teacher, that a thousand words might be far more valuable than one picture, that opposites might repulse one another, or that plenty of things that don't kill you might diminish your spirit or sap your energy.

Any given topic likely comes along with maxims—statements that reinforce common wisdom. Whether it's politics ("You can't trust government"), work ("Another day, another dollar"), domestic life ("Home is where the heart is"), even kids ("Boys will be boys"), any topic seems to attract a certain number of familiar sentiments that keep the same old thinking in place. But good writers go after the maxims. They call them out and challenge the thinking. In her book *Bright-Sided: How the Relentless Promotion of Positive Thinking Has Undermined America* (excerpted on page 274), Barbara Ehrenreich calls out a maxim related to cancer:

> There was, I learned, an urgent medical reason to embrace cancer with a smile: a "positive attitude" is supposedly essential to recovery. During the months when I was undergoing chemotherapy, I encountered this assertion over and over—on Web sites, in books, from oncology nurses and fellow sufferers. Eight years later, it remains almost axiomatic, with the breast cancer culture, that survival hinges on "attitude."

From here, Ehrenreich interrogates the belief behind the maxim. She brings forward a range of studies that disprove the relationship between positive attitudes and cancer survival. In the process, she roots out other maxims related to cancer, such as the sentiment that cancer can be a "gift" or an "opportunity to grow." She concludes,

> Breast cancer, I can now report, did not make me prettier or stronger, more feminine or spiritual. What it gave me, if you want to call this a "gift," was a very personal, agonizing encounter with an ideological force in American culture that I had not been aware of before—one that encourages us to deny reality, submit cheerfully to misfortune, and blame only ourselves for our fate.

Ehrenreich interrogates the soundness of such widely expressed statements and thereby questions the entire intellectual culture that accepts and repeats these statements. This is the power of questioning maxims: the process ultimately brings you face-to-face with widely shared truths—which might, in fact, be widely shared illusions. The process, however, takes some time. Because the maxims are so familiar, so normal-sounding, they have to be extracted. Plenty of information (facts, evidence, testimony) has to counter the familiarity of the maxim.

TALK ABOUT IT Education is full of maxims—claims that show up repeatedly and without debate or discussion. Consider one of the following statements. Explain why it might, despite its ring of truth, be suspicious:

• Everyone learns differently.

- You have to learn the rules before you can break them.

- You have to believe in yourself.

- When the student is ready, the teacher appears. ■

Question the Reasoning

The status quo does not drift along free of reason. It does have logic. The problem, as we've explained, is that the reasoning often resides quietly away from conscious and explicit scrutiny. If the status quo is to be questioned, its logic must be brought out into the light of day. For example, in the following passage from *How Children Succeed*, Paul Tough explains the usual logic about brain development—or what's called the *cognitive hypothesis*. Then, in the second paragraph below, he argues that the usual logic could be wrong, or at least oversimplified:

There is something undeniably compelling about the cognitive hypothesis. The world it describes is so neat, so reassuringly linear, such a clear case of inputs *here* leading to outputs *there*. Fewer books in the home means less reading ability; fewer words spoken by parents means a smaller vocabulary for their kids; more math worksheets at Junior Kumon [a tutoring center] means better math scores. The correlations at times seemed almost comically exact: Hart and Risley [child psychologists] calculated that a child who grew up on welfare would need precisely forty-one hours of language-intensive intervention each week in order to close the vocabulary gap with a working-class child.

But in the past decade, and especially in the past few years, a disparate congregation of economists, educators, psychologists, and neuroscientists have begun to produce evidence that calls into question many of the assumptions behind the cognitive hypothesis. What matters most in a child's development, they say, is not how much information we can stuff into her brain in the first few years. What matters, instead, is whether we are able to help her develop a very different set of qualities, a list that includes persistence, self-control, curiosity, conscientiousness, grit, and self-confidence.

Tough goes on to explain the exact problem with the usual reasoning: people who believe in the cognitive hypothesis believe that practicing any skill more often will result in better learning. This belief, he explains, is flawed:

For certain skills, the stark calculus behind the cognitive hypothesis—that what matters in developing a skill is starting *earlier* and practicing *more*—is entirely valid. If you want to perfect your foul shot, shooting two hundred free throws every afternoon is indeed going to be more helpful than shooting twenty free throws every afternoon. If you're in fourth grade, reading forty books over the summer is going to improve your reading ability more than reading four books. Some skills really are pretty mechanical. But when it comes to developing the more subtle elements of the human personality, things aren't so simple. We can't get better at overcoming disappointment just by working harder at it for more hours. And children don't lag behind in curiosity simply because they didn't start doing curiosity drills at an early enough age. The pathways through which we acquire and lose these skills are certainly not random— psychologists and neuroscientists have learned a lot in the past few decades about where these skills come from and how they are developed—but they are complex, unfamiliar, and often quite mysterious.

Source: *How Children Succeed: Grit, Curiosity, and the Hidden Power of Character* by Paul Tough (Boston: Houghton, 2012).

Like many scholars, Tough is pointing to some logical problems or fallacies. While there are many such logical problems—with a range of names—the following three tend to haunt common wisdom persistently:

The Wrong Cause: Sometimes called faulty cause/effect, this problem involves seeing a causal relation where one may not exist. In recent years, for instance, thousands of parents in the United States have blamed vaccinations for autism. They cite a range of studies that show a correlation between vaccinations and the first signs of autistic behavior. But they may be confusing correlation with causation since autistic behavior often becomes apparent at roughly the same time children get immunization shots. The scientists who have fought this faulty cause/effect reasoning have argued that autism may, in fact, have many causes (both genetic and environmental) and may lie deep in early embryonic brain development.

The Wrong Name: This may also be called the wrong category or the wrong identifier. The problem here is one of definition. When we give something a name, we define it and then act according to that definition. Names create a way of thinking. (We live this out every moment of our waking lives—even in the way we think about ourselves. It is why boys get *boy names* and girls get *girl names*. If parents decided to name their baby boy Sue, he would consistently struggle with the established gender categories.) In short, names matter. The wrong name can have dramatic consequences. For example, during the past several decades, the US government has been waging a war on drugs. In some ways, the phrase seems to fit the situation: soldiers are sometimes involved, arms are traded and sold, people get killed. But as many sociologists, and a few politicians, have pointed out, *war on drugs* is simply the wrong phrase because the soldier/enemy metaphor ignores how drug addiction is an internal enemy, requiring counseling rather than hand grenades and tanks.

The Wrong Conclusion: We often leap to conclusions. Something happens, then something else happens, and we generate a finalizing statement: "Even though I tried, I failed my first English course, so I'm just not good at writing." The logical problem here is that the conclusion doesn't necessarily follow from what is known. A huge range of conditions may have resulted in someone failing an English course. But those conditions do not figure into the conclusion "I'm not good at writing." The problem lies not in the truth or falsehood of the conclusion but in the way a conclusion gets developed: too many logical steps get skipped over. Sometimes called a non sequitur, this logical problem haunts our daily lives, and it lurks in formal academic work as well.

The bigger problem with all of these logical flaws is that they can result in ideas that get widely accepted and then established in the status quo. Once something becomes finalized, published, and widely accepted, it's often hard to question. But calling out the problematic logic can change everything. Simply calling attention to the logical flaw in a common phrase or stated conclusion can disrupt the status quo. Like pulling a single brick from the bottom of a tower, good thinkers sometimes bring down a whole intellectual contraption that would otherwise have stood with its flaws.

© Cengage Learning

Advanced Move:
Bust Up Common Comparisons

Sometimes, common wisdom comes packaged in a nice comparison.[1] For example, many people accept the claim that a household budget is like a national economy. If we accept this comparison, then we can build various ideas

---

[1] This section relates to the logical problems (pages 165–166). Faulty comparisons, sometimes called false analogies, are yet another consistent logical flaw.

on top of it. We can imagine that controlling wealth is simply a matter of balancing cost and income. But the comparison blinds us to how currencies function—that the dollar's value, for instance, depends on fluctuating values of other currencies. If we try to make national economic policy correspond to the practicalities of running a household budget, we'd quickly create a disaster.

Or consider the widely accepted comparison between a human brain and a computer. Teachers, parents, even doctors rely on the comparison as a way to understand how learning works. But the comparison may create a kind of blindness—a misunderstanding of the brain's functions. In the following passage, Danah Zohar first questions the logic of that comparison. Notice that she begins her analysis by calling out a quiet (or underlying) assumption. Then, she shows the limitations of that assumption:

All the computer models of the brain share an underlying assumption that the brain itself functions according to the same laws and principles as a vast computing machine— that is, that its separate parts (its neurons) cooperate in an ordered mechanistic way, following all the determinist laws of classical physics. In such a model, one brain state follows necessarily from another. All we have is one group of static, predictable neurons "looking at" and reacting to other groups. Nowhere in the brain do all of these separate groups get integrated. There is no "central committee" of neurons overseeing the whole process, giving it unity and making free, spontaneous decisions. Where, then, in all of these deterministic neural connections and events, is the person we experience ourselves to be? What accounts for the "I" who experiences hunger, decides to eat an apple, and feels the pleasure of doing so? How do we even have "an experience" of eating an apple rather than so many scattered impressions of a million different sensory inputs?

The questions she poses in the latter part of the passage reveal the limitations of the computer model. And once she has posed the questions, she sets herself up to answer them—to explore ideas that are not constrained by the usual computer/brain comparison. In the following passage, she opens the door to something else—the "holographic paradigm":

> And if the physics of the computer model cannot, in principle, give us the physics of consciousness, then it can't be a wholly adequate model of how the brain works, nor, in turn, a very accurate reflection of ourselves and how we function as human beings.
>
> Motivated by the inadequacies of the computer model, some people have proposed a quite different model for thinking about consciousness and the brain, one that is intended to pick up on the theme of unity and account for it in physical terms, and that makes very different suggestions about consciousness and the self. This is the holographic model, or the "holographic paradigm" as it is sometimes rather grandly described.

Zohar illustrates an important consequence of the moves described in this chapter: When scholars take on the status quo and nudge something out of place, they leave a hole in common thinking. In many respects, they leave a hole in reality. The comfortable conclusions, the nicely smoothed-over walls of normality, are suddenly gone. Not always, but often, scholars try to fill the hole they've created. They turn away from the comfortable and consider something different—a new idea, a new conclusion, a new comparison. But this is hard work because new ideas, generally speaking, do not fit as well as old ones, which have had time to settle in and become

Source: *The Quantum Self: Human Nature and Consciousness Defined by the New Physics*, New York: Quill/William Morrow, 1990.

normal. Foreign ideas are harder to process, harder to digest.

TALK ABOUT IT Consider the comparison we reference at the beginning of this section: a national economy and a household budget. In a small group, list the ways these two phenomena are different. What factors show up in one and not the other? ∎

WRITE IT

Much academic work may seem strange or out of touch with common sense. By design, many scholarly projects set out to move thinking away from the limitations, inaccuracies, or plain old plainness of established thought. Consider one of the following paths for developing your own project that escapes the status quo:

1. Examine a common practice in education, one that is widely and quietly accepted. (Avoid practices such as standardized tests, school uniforms, or attendance policies. Such practices are openly debated. People have already brought them into the light of day and scrutinized them. Instead, consider some practice that is so widely accepted that your peers and your teachers *wouldn't even think* to question it.) Apply the moves in this chapter: Call out quiet assumptions related to the practice—for instance, assumptions about learning, success, or knowledge. Question related maxims and the logic that keeps the practice in place. Bust up any comparisons that come along with the practice.

2. Examine a popular form of entertainment such as basketball or NASCAR. Write an essay that explains how that form of entertainment reinforces the status quo. How does it support common ways of thinking

about people, success, men, women, individuality? Even if it appears, to most people, like a break in the routine—like something that pushes against the mainstream—consider how it might *actually* uphold widely accepted modes of living. Consider the common images, celebrities, behaviors associated with the form of entertainment. How do they reinforce the status quo?

3. How are you stuck in the status quo? Write a reflective essay that describes your own complicity in the normal infrastructure of society. What quiet assumptions about your community, your neighbors, or your schools do you accept? What keeps you believing? What keeps you from rejecting the norm? What hopes or fears are built into your acceptance of the status quo? What lessons, messages, or maxims maintain those hopes or fears?

READ: For examples of full essays that escape the status quo, check out Michael Anderson (page 267) and Barbara Ehrenreich (page 274).

APPLY: For specific guidance on how to structure a full essay using the moves in this chapter, see the outlines in Part III, "Apply the Moves" (pages 314–315).

Assess Your Thinking

THINK ABOUT IT

Professionals in all fields devote countless hours to examining and judging their own performance: football players watch recorded games and inspect each play, dancers practice in front of mirrors, engineers inspect their methods at every step, actors study their gestures on camera, and even comedians record their acts and carefully analyze their timing. Whether we're talking about writers, artists, musicians, engineers, or athletes, people get better at their crafts when they self-assess. To improve, they have to do more than practice. They have to examine past behavior, analyze what did or didn't work, and then readjust.

When it comes to thinking, we can't necessarily shine a light at our own thoughts. We can't watch a video for an intellectual play-by-play. And so far, there's no neurological scanning device that shows how we develop ideas. However, we can inspect our writing. In fact, there may be no better way to get inside our own brains than to analyze what we've written. In that process, we can look at how we've formulated ideas, how we've pursued some thoughts and ignored others. We can see our own reasoning at work. We can dismantle our own arguments. We can see how we supported or escaped the status quo. In short, when we go back to our own writing, we can study our own moves.

To improve, writers of all kinds have to get over themselves and see their own work from a distance. It's difficult but necessary. In fact, it's so important that college courses often contain formal assignments (reflection letters, portfolios, self-critique essays) that invite students to assess their own progress over the academic term. In this brief chapter, we offer two strategies for self-assessment: (1) examine past assumptions and (2) describe new thinking.

Examine Past Assumptions

As we explain in Chapter 2, a real event can sometimes crash against our thinking and force us to rethink. And sometimes, the force is enough to make us reconsider our own quiet thoughts—our own assumptions about what is good, bad, real, or unreal. In these moments, we are thrown into a kind of frenzied self-assessment. We interrogate not only what we think but *what we didn't even know we thought*. For example, in the following passage from her book *If You Want to Write: A Book About Art, Independence and Spirit*, Brenda Ueland examines her past assumptions about art and then comes to a new realization. She starts by describing the situation that made her insight possible:

When van Gogh was a young man in his early twenties, he was in London studying to be a clergyman. He had no thought of being an artist at all. He sat in his cheap little room writing a letter to his younger brother in Holland, whom he loved very much. He looked out his window at a watery twilight, a thin lamppost, a star, and he said in his letter something like: "It is so beautiful I must show you how it looks." And then on his ruled notepaper he made the most beautiful, tender little drawing of it.

When I read this letter of van Gogh's it comforted me very much and seemed to throw clear light on the whole road of Art. Before, I had thought that to produce a work of painting or literature you scowled and thought long and ponderously and weighed everything solemnly and learned everything that all artists had ever done aforetime, what their influences and schools were, and you were extremely careful about *design* and *balance* and getting *interesting planes* into your painting; and you avoided, with the most stringent severity, showing the faintest *academic* tendency, and were strictly modern. And so on and so on.

But the moment I read van Gogh's letter I knew what the creative impulse was. It is a feeling of love and enthusiasm for something, and in a direct, simple, passionate and true way you try to show this beauty to others by drawing it.

For Ueland, a specific thing (van Gogh's drawing) and the event that prompted it (writing a letter) get her thinking differently about art. At first, van Gogh's drawing doesn't support Ueland's definition of art, and so she is forced to reconsider her ideas. Notice how Ueland slowly walks through the misconceptions she had, using specific terminology (in italics) that she mistakenly applied to art. She sets up her final insight by returning to the thing that prompted her thinking in the first place—the tiny sketch that changed her conception of art and the creative process.

Source: *If You Want to Write: A Book About Art, Independence and Spirit*, Saint Paul: Graywolf, 2008. © Copyright – Brenda Ueland. © Copyright 2008 – BN Publishing.

Examining past assumptions often means evaluating old prejudices that were passed along to us, biases that infiltrate thinking and become routine ways of responding to the world. For example, in his book *Living Buddha, Living Christ*, Thich Nhat Hanh examines an old prejudice:

> Many years ago, I recognized that by understanding your own tradition better, you also develop increased respect, consideration, and understanding for others. I had had a naïve thought, a kind of prejudice inherited from my ancestors. I thought that because Buddha had taught for forty-five years and Jesus for only two or three, that Buddha must have been a more accomplished teacher. I had that thought because I did not know the teachings of the Buddha well enough.
>
> One day when he was thirty-eight years old the Buddha met King Prasenajit of Kosala. The king said, "Reverend, you are young, yet people call you 'The Highest Enlightened One.' There are holy men in our country eighty and ninety years old, venerated by many people, yet none of them claims to be the highest enlightened one. How can a young man like you make such a claim?"
>
> The Buddha replied, "Your majesty, enlightenment is not a matter of age. A tiny spark of fire has the power to burn down a whole city. A small poisonous snake can kill you in an instant. A baby prince has the potentiality of a king. And a young monk has the capacity of becoming enlightened and changing the world." We can learn about others by studying ourselves.

Here, Nhat Hanh uses a parable to examine his past assumptions about enlightenment and spiritual leadership. The knowledge he builds through reading and study allows him to realize his misconceptions, the false beliefs that were passed along to him and that crept into his thinking over time. Nhat Hanh steps outside his limited worldview and recalibrates his thinking.

A LOOK AT REFLECTION ASSIGNMENTS

In a range of college courses, students are asked to self-assess in formal assignments. These *reflective* assignments give students a chance to record their thoughts and judge their own progress—to explain, in their own words, how they understand course goals and the extent to which they've achieved them. In a reflection essay or letter, students refer to specific intellectual tasks they performed. They seek complexity and tension in their own past selves. They call out and examine past assumptions. They try to understand their own quiet operations.

Reflective assignments often have stated criteria—or standards of judgment for examining performance. Here are some sample criteria for a reflective assignment:

- The main idea of the reflection is appropriately focused and readily accessible to the reader.

- The main idea is sufficiently supported and well-developed throughout the reflection.

- The reflection thoroughly explains how your ideas evolved or changed over the course of the assignment.

- The reflection clearly shows how you developed a new insight.

continued

In such criteria, words like *appropriately*, *readily*, *sufficiently*, *thoroughly*, and *clearly* point to the evaluation taking place. Student work is assessed based on how well it meets each of the established criteria. An essay might achieve one goal well, another moderately well, and another not so well. But despite the individual criteria, the goal of these assignments usually involves intensive and detailed examination of the student's own thinking. The most successful writing, then, provides thorough and focused explanations of changes, stumbles, small steps, and leaps forward in one's own thinking.

TALK ABOUT IT

1. As a class or group, reflect on your assumptions about writing: its relationship to thinking, its role in education, and its connection to the world beyond college. List the assumptions that come to mind. Which assumptions are beneficial? Which need to be rethought?

2. In a discussion group, recall your early educational experiences. Make a list of criteria that teachers used to assess your performance. Even if they weren't stated directly (as they often are in assignment prompts or syllabi), how did you know about them? How did you know what to shoot for, what to avoid, or what to fix? How did you know about the difference between excellent work and satisfactory work—or between passing and failing? ∎

Describe New Thinking

Good thinkers are usually good at describing their own thinking. In other words, they're good at detailing the intellectual changes they experience. They try, as best they can, to sense moments of separation from a past assumption toward a new intellectual reflex. For example, in the following excerpt from a reflective essay, a

literature student explains a flaw in her past approach and a different way going forward:

> In preparing to write an analysis of *Othello*, I was lost on where to begin. The greatest breakthrough for me was when I reflected on my earlier self-assessments and feedback. I realized I should first choose passages and analyze them, gradually moving to the creation of a thesis, as opposed to creating a thesis and searching desperately for evidence to support it. I should let a work reveal itself to me first.

Source: http://lakeland.edu/Assessment/pdfs/SelfAssessment25Aug03.pdf.

In the past, this writer had begun assignments with a thesis statement and then hunted for passages to prove that thesis. But after reflecting on the approach and considering feedback from instructors, she realized a more fruitful strategy: letting ideas gradually develop into a thesis. In this case, the writer stepped outside her own practice, saw herself from a distance, and, as a result, shifted her approach.

Sometimes, self-assessment results in a seismic shift. Writers change their minds, literally, and disavow a previous perspective or behavior. An English professor at Abraham Baldwin Agricultural College, Sandra L. Giles experienced a major shift in thinking as a doctoral writing student. In her essay "Reflective Writing and the Revision Process: What Were You Thinking?" Giles highlights that shift as she describes a common misconception about self-assessment: it's a farce, a "waste of time," since, in the end, the only thing that matters is what instructors think and what grade they assign. Here, she explains how reflecting on her writing (through what she calls "process notes") changed her perspective and helped her to adopt a new intellectual habit:

> My first process note for the class was a misguided attempt at good-student-gives-the-teacher-what-she-wants. Our assignment had been to attend an event in town and write about it. I had seen an email announcement about a medium visiting from England who would perform a "reading" at the Unity Church in town. So I went and took notes. And wrote two consecutive drafts. After peer workshop, a third. And then I had to write the process note, the likes of which I had never done before. It felt awkward, senseless. Worse than writing a scholarship application or some other mundane writing task. Like a waste of time, and like it wasn't real writing at all. But it was required. . . .

As the semester progressed and I continued to have to write those darned process notes, I dropped the attitude. In a conference about my writing, . . . [my instructor] responded to my note by asking questions focused entirely on helping me refine my intentions for the piece, and I realized my task wasn't to please or try to dazzle her. I stopped worrying about how awkward the reflection was, stopped worrying about how to please the teacher, and started actually reflecting and thinking. New habits and ways of thinking formed. And unexpectedly, all the hard decisions about revising for the next draft began to come more easily.

Here, Giles describes an important change of gears. She once attempted to perform for the instructor (which felt empty and useless), but then began reflecting on her own work. Giles explains not merely the difference in her actions ("I did this and then I did that") but the thinking responsible for that difference. And, most importantly, she explains how she was able to pull her insight forward and apply it to future writing situations.

Assessing our thinking doesn't always produce major "aha" moments. Sometimes, our insights are more subtle, less defined. We've come around to some new way of thinking, but we haven't yet reached any firm conclusions or clear solutions. In her essay "A Hard Look at Parking Lots" (page 290), Teresa Scollon rethinks her attitude toward American car culture and the parking wars we find ourselves embroiled in:

Source: *Writing spaces: readings on writing*. Volume 1 / edited by Charles Lowe and Pavel Zemliansky. Copyright © 2010 by Parlor Press.

It's hard to look at how I'm tied to all of this. I don't like to think that parking, or driving, is really that important to me. Apparently, I'm both subject and attuned, at a deep level, to stresses and conflicts imposed on me from without. And my response is no more noble than anyone else's. Like it or not, I can get competitive. I may refrain from honking or obscene gestures or fisticuffs, but the truth is, tomorrow morning, if I can ease into a parking spot before you do, I'll feel fine.

Scollon acknowledges the complexity of her thinking—the ambivalent feelings that she has toward car culture. On one hand, she wants to free herself from it, but on the other, she realizes the hold it has on her, and the benefits she experiences from it. She may not make a major shift in thinking or behavior, but she may rethink her response the next time someone cuts her off and swoops into the last available parking spot.

TALK ABOUT IT

1. In a small group, discuss experiences you've had with writer's block. What did you do to overcome it? What specific strategies did you use to start writing? Which of these strategies could you pull forward to a current situation you're experiencing?

2. Consider common knee-jerk reactions like road rage or impatience at the checkout line. As a group, talk about experiences you've had in which you snapped out of some patterned way of thinking. What prompted you to rethink the situation, your behavior, or your own thinking? ■

Reprinted by permission of Teresa Scollon.

WRITE IT
• • • • • • • • • •

Rethinking our thinking sounds like hard work. And it is. But with clear intellectual maneuvers, self-assessment can become routine, a reflex that helps us in all of our intellectual pursuits. As you assess your own thinking, consider one of the following paths:

1. Think about something you understand well, like a particular academic subject or a personal interest. Reflect on your knowledge. How did you come to understand it? What specific behaviors or ways of thinking did you adopt to hone your expertise? Consider if you denied any past assumptions in order to become better at this task. As your understanding developed, did you find yourself having to change your perspective or dismiss old prejudices? What happened? Consider how you know you're good at this activity in the first place. What criteria do you apply to measure your success? Did you develop your own criteria, or were they established for you? Describe the process of becoming an expert to readers who might not be familiar with your interests.

2. Consider an error in thinking you've made in the past—not a simple mistake but a bad judgment or flawed position. Maybe you misjudged someone or refused to acknowledge something about a situation. Maybe you overestimated your own abilities or didn't fully appreciate your own naiveté. Concentrate not only on your actions but also on the assumptions behind them. Also consider the ways you talked yourself into believing yourself. What reasoning did you use? What did you actively ignore? Write an essay that explains the intellectual

operations behind your flawed thinking. (You might also try to explain how you came through to some better, richer way of thinking.)

3. If you're like most people, you judge yourself. You judge your behavior in social settings, your skill level in academics or sports, maybe even your reflex to be kind or cruel. But all forms of judging depend on some criteria—on certain standards of behavior beyond the specific situation. In an essay, explain what criteria you use to assess your own behavior. Where did those criteria come from? Did someone teach them to you? Did you pick them up from watching someone else? What, if anything, would you change about the way you assess yourself?

READ: For examples of full essays in which writers assess their thinking, check out Ann-Marie Paulin (page 285) and Teresa Scollon (page 290).

APPLY: For specific guidance on how to structure a full essay using the moves in this chapter, see the outlines in Part III, "Apply the Moves" (pages 317–318).

Read the Moves

THIS SECTION includes a range of texts that illustrate the moves described in Part I. As you read, you'll see a range of styles and topics. But more importantly, you'll see writers *seeking complexity, applying sources, applying concepts, dismantling arguments*, and so on. In other words, you'll be able to identify the intellectual moves described in Chapters 1–9. Sometimes, the writers rely exclusively on a small number of moves. For instance, Stephanie Mills (page 198) consistently *unpacks terms* while Joel Kotkin (page 244) primarily *lines up evidence*. In other cases, the writers apply a variety of moves—everything from *seeking tension* to *escaping the status quo*. In all cases, the writers are enacting moves and building insights. Despite the fact that the writers come from different disciplines, different parts of the country, and even different worldviews, they share some moves—ones that you, too, can borrow for your own projects.

RECOGNIZE GENRE

You are probably familiar with pop music. You know that most songs on mainstream rock and country radio stations have verses, repeating choruses, a bridge, and maybe some lead instrument solo. When you hear the chorus repeat, you probably don't think that the musicians are taking the easy way out. You don't holler, "Hey! I already heard this part!" Instead, you know that a repeating chorus is part of the pop music *genre*, or category, and you relax into the overall structure of the song. You accept the instrumental section and get ready for a final chorus. Your familiarity makes you a good listener. You're not surprised. You're not grappling to understand the order of sounds.

That's how genres work: they establish and reestablish expectations. People listening to a new country music hit do not expect to hear a tuba solo in the middle of the song. Instead, they expect to hear twangy guitars, steady drums, bass, slide guitar, a low male voice, a high female voice—and a range of more subtle elements related to lyrical content, song length, melodies, harmonies, and so on. If a music producer proposed a tuba solo in the next Carrie Underwood song, he'd likely get some weird looks. Carrie Underwood is a country music star. A tuba just wouldn't fit. And the weird looks would prove the point: *genres establish what people expect.*

This is not to say that individual songs or groups can't stray from the norm. Genres are not laws. They are categories that hold on over time and maintain certain expectations. They establish how audiences approach the subject matter. This happens in all media. When we're watching a television crime drama, for instance, we don't expect the characters to break into a choreographed song and dance. When we watch *Glee*, we don't expect the episode to begin with a dead body. Genre matters in writing as well. There are certain expectations for certain types of work:

- **Report:** a detailed summary of events or gathered information. A report is primarily a means of conveying information. It tells what happened or what has already been concluded.

- **Essay:** an expression or demonstration of a complex idea. Essays walk through and portray sophisticated thinking. Their job in academia, and in public life, is to help writers and readers to think through an issue—not necessarily to conclude an issue or even to determine an action, but to understand it better. This is why the essay dominates so much college work— why writers in all disciplines publish essays.

- **Proposal:** a call to act on a specific situation. Proposals are often solutions to public problems or detailed suggestions for addressing a specific need. They take various forms depending on the audience—whether corporate, governmental, or academic readers are involved.

- **Memoir:** a personal account of one's own life. Memoir is like autobiography but more selective. Rather than cover all layers and dimensions of one's life, memoir homes in on a particular element or time in the writer's life and borrows selectively from other parts. For instance, a presidential memoir would recount school memories only if they ultimately shed some light on the presidential years.

- **Profile:** an examination of someone else's public role. Profiles are like memoirs, but they focus on someone other than the writer. They look selectively at a particular part of someone's life—usually the public part. A profile of a social worker would focus on his work with clients. A profile of a CEO would focus on her duties or actions in corporate life. Profiles can be short (written like an academic essay) or long (written in book format).

- **Review:** a summary and critique of a specific text or service. Reviews come in a huge range, the most popular or well-established being the book review and the movie review. Reviews are openly evaluative, which means the writer is making an argument about the worth of the book, movie, text, proposal, product, or venue. Reviewers, in a sense, make a case for others to read, see, use, or visit the thing in question.

Of course, there are many more genres: manifestos, mission statements, press releases, elegies, and so on. And you're probably familiar with some of the common literary genres such as sonnets, detective novels, romance novels, and crime novels. By virtue of living in a complex and highly networked society, you encounter many genres on a weekly basis, and you unconsciously know how to deal with them. You know how they work and what to expect. But here's the tricky part: genres blur together. A proposal often comes in the form of an essay. Reviews sometimes include a layer of profile. Like musical styles—for example, blues-rock, jazz fusion, country-rock—writing genres blend together. Still, it's valuable to understand the above distinctions.[1]

Finally, another complicating factor about genres is that they change. Even though people's expectations about a given genre (rock music, for instance) may remain somewhat stable, they also shift over time. Consider the immense difference between contemporary heavy metal and early Beatles or Elvis Presley. Pioneers in rock music consistently pushed against the expectations and, therefore, nudged the genre in different directions. It has happened in every conceivable art form: painting, photography, classical music, sculpture, and so on. But the changes usually don't happen overnight. Change takes time because people don't generally toss out their expectations quickly. They hold on to them. In this sense, genres contain a degree of tension—a friction between what people expect and what adventurous contributors offer.

The chapters in Part I of *Think About It* include a range of excerpts from published works such as magazine articles, newspaper articles, blogs, historical texts, and books. Full-length works and longer excerpts appear in Part II. And while the specific publication type may not

---

[1] We should also examine publication types. Genre is linked with how something gets published (or made public so that others can access it). An article, for example, may be part profile and part report. A blog may be part review, part memoir.

be necessarily important to your understanding, it may help to orient you. For instance, if you know that a passage came from a newspaper—and not an academic journal—you may have a better sense of what you're reading. For that reason, make sure to note the genre and publication, which are described before the works in this section.

A LOOK AT THE ACADEMIC JOURNAL ARTICLE

Chances are you will likely confront a good number of academic articles in your college career. Even your first few semesters in college will have you engaging articles from scholarly journals such as *Psychology Quarterly, College English, Nursing Quarterly*, and so on. If you're researching a project for an English course, you will likely run into—or be required to reference—at least one scholarly journal.

Like pop songs, academic articles have their own conventions. In other words, academic articles are a genre. And the more comfortable you get with the genre, the more you'll understand what's being said. While there is no universal formula or arrangement strategy, there are some repeated patterns. For instance, the following pattern, which is also the structure of many scholarly books, shows up repeatedly in academic journals across the curriculum. Academic writers from linguistics to physics, from mathematics to psychology, use this well-established formula: First, they "review the literature," or discuss what has previously been said about the topic at hand. Next, they explain a tension, problem, or debate in the literature. Then, they propose a strategy for resolving the tension, solving the problem, or settling the debate. Then, they offer support for that strategy, and finally, they call for further discussion:

- Review of the literature
- Explanation of a tension, problem, or debate

- Proposal for a new strategy
- Support for that strategy
- Call for further discussion

Of course, the overall pattern fluctuates depending on the nature of the field and the nature of the problem, tension, or debate. Often, articles begin with the debate—with a portrayal of the thing that must be addressed or solved. Still others begin with the proposal, in which case the writer assumes that the audience understands, to some degree, the need for some change. Sometimes, writers walk slowly through the second step and quickly through the first—or vice versa. In other words, *academic writers usually devote most of their energy (and time) to the information or ideas with which their colleagues will be least familiar.*

DON'T FEAR THE JARGON

When it comes to academic material, you may notice a lot of words ending in -ism: *postmodernism, structuralism, progressivism, atheism, magnetism, Dadaism, impressionism, romanticism, humanism, liberalism, modernism, classicism,* and so on. Don't be put off by such words. They are simply labels that help writers and readers to make sense of trends. The ending -ism signals a way of thinking—not a single idea, but an outlook. For example, *humanism* is an outlook that centers on human rather than divine or supernatural affairs.

These -isms often come from specific moments in time. They are, or were, movements. Romanticism, for example, evolved from a group of European writers and artists in the eighteenth century. Dadaism came from a group of artists in the early twentieth century. Impressionism came from a group of painters in the late nineteenth century. As the outlooks become popular or widely accepted ways of thinking, they get turned into descriptors: *Humanism* turns into *humanist*. *Modernism* turns into *modernist*. And the words get used to make sense out of specific positions, texts, even people:

- The argument against corporal punishment was basically humanist.

- In this work, it's easy to see a modernist approach to poetry.

- The Dadaist reflex resurfaced again in the late 1970s as punk rock.

- Michael has become such a materialist now that he's out of college.

- You don't have to be an idealist to imagine a better way of structuring schools.

It's not important to remember a list of *-isms* and *-ists* just to sound smart. Frankly, people who throw around a bunch of these terms can quickly wear down everyone's patience. But it is important that you don't leave the page (or the room) when you encounter an unfamiliar *-ist* or *-ism*. Chances are the term refers to some intellectual or cultural trend, one that might be worth looking up.

Academic articles and books are also full of words like *Johnsonian, Butlerian, Newtonian, Jeffersonian, Calvinist, Whitmanesque*—which are simply people's last names turned into adjectives. A Jeffersonian perspective, for example, takes its cues from the political vision of Thomas Jefferson. Rather than list out all the assumptions and positions that Thomas Jefferson held and then attribute them to a particular policy, we can take a shortcut and say something like "The present push against corporate power is Jeffersonian at its root." We don't have to say, "Here are all the things Thomas Jefferson believed about the role of federal governments interacting with people." We can just say *Jeffersonian*.

TALK ABOUT IT   Go online and check out Michelangelo's statue *David*, and then find Marcel Duchamp's sculpture *Fountain*. (If you're wondering, Duchamp's sculpture is, indeed, a men's restroom urinal.) These two works come from two different outlooks—from two different perspectives on art. If you prefer Michelangelo, you might be a classicist. If you prefer Duchamp, you might be a modernist. Of course, you can be both or neither. That's allowed. (And in academic life, you can even change your mind and you won't get accused of flip-flopping.) ■

SEEK COMPLEXITY
• • • • • • • • • • • • • • • • • •

Kissing Technology on the Mouth
by Steven D. Krause

STUDY THE MOVES

In the following essay, Steven D. Krause examines writing and technology. In the process, he makes several of the moves described in Chapter 1 ("Seek Complexity"), Chapter 2 ("Seek Tension"), and Chapter 3 ("Apply Sources"):

| PARAGRAPH 1 | Draws from a vital source (Ong) |
| PARAGRAPH 2 | Denies the usual association between *natural* and *long-standing practices* |

continued

Steven D. Krause, a professor at Eastern Michigan University, maintains an award-winning blog and has published in periodicals such as the Chronicle of Higher Education and Kairos.

Reprinted by permission of Steven D. Krause.

PARAGRAPH 3	Denies the usual association between *technology* and *new*
PARAGRAPH 4	Denies the usual association between *new* and *better*
PARAGRAPHS 6–7	Unpacks *literacy*, a broad term, and explains three of its traits
PARAGRAPH 8	Describes a tension—specifically, Lindstrom's concerns about technology
PARAGRAPH 9	Makes connections between Lindstrom's and Socrates's fears of technology

To say writing is artificial is not to condemn it but to praise it. Like other artificial creating and indeed more than any other, writing is utterly invaluable and indeed essential for the realization of fuller, interior, human potentials. Technologies are not mere exterior aids but also interior transformations of consciousness, and never more when they affect the word. (23)

~Walter Ong

This epigraph comes from Walter Ong's essay "Writing is a Technology that Restructures Thought." Ong, who was a student of the media theorist Marshall McLuhan before going on to become theorist and professor himself, is concerned in this essay with the implications of writing as a technology and about the differences between oral cultures (that is, cultures with no written language) and literate cultures. These can be difficult concepts for us to wrap our heads around because we have always lived literate lives where writing is ingrained and normal. To wonder what it would be like to experience the world without literacy is a bit like trying to imagine what it would be like to be a different person or even a different species.

First we have to get beyond the idea that something which has been common for a long time like reading and writing is "natural" and therefore not technological. This is not easy to do. For example, we tend to forget that things like electricity and running water are technological since they are so common and ordinary; however, if an ice storm hits and freezes pipes and takes down power lines and you're left in the dark without electricity and water on a cold winter's night, you soon recognize how these ordinary conveniences that we assume are a part of our everyday lives are in fact technologies quite separate from the natural world.

Technologies are the tools and practices we make that have always been critical in defining who we are as humans and how we live our lives. The word *technology* is often synonymous with "new," but ancient tools like wheels, axes, and levers are technology too. Humans create technology, and as such, those technologies are different from the animals, plants, and the rest of the natural world. Technologies exist outside of our bodies and beings—neither our lungs nor our imagination are technological—yet they paradoxically define in many ways who we are as a species and how we have changed. We live our lives significantly differently now from humans a million years ago, hundreds of years ago, or even a generation ago largely because of technology. We are a different species, and those differences have been formed by technologies that we ourselves have created.

"Differently" doesn't always mean "better," and here we could consider a host of technologies that have been setbacks for humanity, or at least technologies that have been both positive and negative: the use of fossil fuels immediately comes to mind. Even literacy has had its critics, notably Socrates in Plato's famous dialog *Phaedrus*. Speaking to the young and impressionable Phaedrus about the value of reading and writing, Socrates argues that literacy merely gives the *appearance* of wisdom and truth when in reality it embodies neither. "I cannot help feeling, Phaedrus," Socrates says, "that writing is unfortunately like painting; for the creations of the painter have the attitude of life, and yet if you ask them a question, they preserve a solemn silence." Worse yet, once the words of speeches are written down, there's the danger that those words will be "tumbled about anywhere among those who may or may not understand them. . . ."

5   Incidentally, it is worth noting that, according to legend, Socrates was illiterate.

But Walter Ong argues that literacy is one example—perhaps a unique example—of a technology invaluable and even essential for humans to rise to their full potential. (Note that Ong is not praising the technology of *print* as in the printing press or even writing and reading utensils, but *writing* and *literacy*.) Still, it's difficult to grasp the idea that literacy itself is akin to the wheel. After all, literacy lacks identifiable inventors and materiality: there is no Thomas Edison figure in history we credit with the origins of writing. It's easy to recognize the technological object of a book, but you can't see and hold the technology required for someone to make sense of that book because literacy is a process that is reflected but not contained in print.

It seems to me that literacy does have three traits that can help us see it as a technology. First, not all cultures are literate—though in times when global communication is the norm, it is true that fewer and fewer oral cultures exist. Nonetheless, while *all* cultures have a spoken language, not all have a written one, which is evidence that speaking is natural while reading and writing are not. Second, literacy has to be taught—in fact, we devote a great deal of time in elementary school and beyond teaching children how to read and write. In contrast, children learn how to speak by imitating the people around them; again, evidence that speaking is natural and literacy is not. Third, while the naturalness of speech requires only our bodies, the technology of literacy manifests itself with tools: paper, pens, and computers, but also the concept that the marks we make with those tools correspond to language. What are the implications of this idea, that literacy itself is technological? Ong discusses these matters in great detail. For example, besides transforming consciousness itself, literacy, he argues, makes learning and schooling possible. He also argues that literacy allows us to separate words from an author. Despite Socrates's objection to the problems of words being tumbled out everywhere like this, it does have some obvious advantages. After all, you are right now reading these words that I wrote some time ago, and I am not standing in front of you.

But beyond Ong's observations, it seems to me that an awareness of literacy as a most humanizing technology should make us hesitate to accept the critiques of contemporary writing technologies. For example, in a *New York Times* editorial titled "You Love Your iPhone. Literally," Martin Lindstrom raises concern about the feelings of "loss" that iPhone users experience when they are without their phones. "As we embrace new technology that does everything but kiss us on the mouth," Lindstrom writes, "we risk cutting ourselves off from human interaction."

Whenever I read critiques like Lindstrom's, I always remember old Socrates, 2,500 years ago, and I imagine him lecturing to a young student about the dangers of moving away from face-to-face conversation to the distancing and dehumanizing technology of reading and writing. Yet I don't think anyone would ever describe pens, papers, typewriters, newspapers, or books as "dehumanizing," nor do we think poorly of people who always have a pen at the ready. Indeed, I think there is a rather Romantic idealization of the *writer* with *pen* (maybe a *typewriter* though probably not a *computer*) and *paper* alone in a room (think Emily Dickinson) or alone in the woods (think Henry David Thoreau). We certainly would not accuse those who are kissing the technology of literacy on the mouth as less fully realized humans, would we?

Works Cited

Lindstrom, Martin. "You Love Your iPhone. Literally." *New York Times*. New York Times, 30 Sept. 2011. Web. 15 May 2012.

Ong, Walter. "Writing Is a Technology that Restructures Thought." *Literacy: A Critical Sourcebook*. Ed. Ellen Cushman et al. Boston: Bedford, 2001. 19–31. Print.

Plato. *Phaedrus*. Trans. Benjamin Jowett. *The Internet Classics Archive*. Ed. Daniel C. Stevenson. MIT, 2009. Web. 15 May 2012.

Air
by Stephanie Mills

STUDY THE MOVES

In the following essay from her book *Tough Little Beauties*, Stephanie Mills examines air. In that process, she seeks complexity in weather and wind. While Mills's writing is more poetic than a traditional academic essay, she uses a clear set of intellectual moves from Chapter 1 ("Seek Complexity") and Chapter 2 ("Seek Tension").

PARAGRAPH 1	Introduces the concept of air and explains how we might think about it
PARAGRAPH 2	Unpacks *air* by describing several qualities that might be taken for granted
PARAGRAPHS 3–5	Unpacks *air* by describing what it means, what it has meant, to human life and culture

continued

Stephanie Mills, a nature writer and ecological activist, is the author of the 2010 book *On Gandhi's Path: Bob Swann's Work for Peace and Community Economics*.

Take a deep breath. Go ahead. Inhale till you feel your diaphragm move. What do you feel? Is it the blessed breath of life? *Prana* is what the yogis call it—breath energy. The act of breathing spans the conscious and unconscious, voluntary and involuntary body functions. Hence, focus on the breath is an ageless meditative practice. Rightly understood, every breath you draw is a gift from the universe. We are air-breathing animals. To live we need oxygen. In just the right amount, Earth's atmosphere provides the oxygen molecules to help us metabolize our sustenance—and the inspiration that animates us.

The air seems almost like nothing. It is the membrane through which we perceive, and by which we are protected from, the sparkling vacuum of the cosmos. The air is the enveloping atmosphere of planet Earth, inviting our sight to seek the heavens. Sometimes (or seemingly always, depending on where you live) the air bears countless tons of water, as cloud panoramas or just as an expanse of overcast (when as far as one can see is up to the ceiling). Thanks to the jet age, many of us have had the experience of looking at clouds from both sides now. We've passed through them and flown over them and cringed as pilots threaded their ways among them. Many more of us have watched the skies, with the realms of clouds, just for pleasure. Down to Earth, on a bright day, you may look out to a clear blue vastness, all illumined by the sun, simile of an empty mind. And at night, if you are fortunate enough to live in a region where ambient light doesn't interfere, you can gaze up at the stars, knowing that there are billions of them, and possibly millions of solar systems, some that might even be hospitable to life.

Because we humans are always looking for guidance (or justification), usually in the form of a story, it is perennially human to try to read the metaphors in the night sky, to tell the myths associated with the constellations, and to seek the governance of the zodiac, or of fateful shooting stars, or comets as portents of millennial change.

Migratory birds also consult the sky for guidance, if not of the metaphysical sort. They navigate by star patterns and the position of the sun on their journeys the length of a hemisphere, or across the trackless seas. Before we ventured up in balloons or 747s, the sky was largely reserved for the stunning variety of species of birds. However common, a bird is always a bit of a wonder. Even the neighborhood birds are a delight and an amusement. One late autumn afternoon in the course of writing this essay, I watched an impromptu convention of about a dozen crows taking place in a taller-than-average tree out back in the lately bare woods. These crows were a lively crowd; they seemed a little precariously perched, bobbing in the wind as the branches swayed in the chilly breeze. I love the way crows seem to drift, float, and quiver in midair. A couple of them will slope off, casually doing a loop-de-loop together for no other purpose than fun and sociability; then others lift off and alight, taking a quick look-see around the treetops. The why of it is a happy mystery.

5   As the province of flying things, the air was, until only very recently, a realm beyond our powers. Now *we* claim to have conquered the sky—flight paths have become to us what sea-lanes were to our great-grandparents. Not only have airplanes become a commonplace means of transportation in the late twentieth century, in space capsules we have escaped Earth's ambit and traveled far enough away to have a look back at the home planet and take snapshots of Earth as Gaian mandala.

Earth's enveloping atmosphere is the caldron of planet-girdling currents of wind, humidity, and temperature, the arena of tornadoes, blizzards, and drought. The weather is a mix of weather and air driven by fire (in the form of solar radiation). Impeded and rerouted by Earth's landforms, given its dynamic by temperature differentials and the Earth's rotation, weather governs our lives. Over evolutionary time, each living thing has developed a specific relationship to the weather and climate. Most organisms are not so cosmopolitan as we are. Plants, being unable to flee, are particularly limited in their temperature ranges. Animals, being more mobile, are less limited by climate, except those creatures that are closely coevolved with a single plant species or association. And *Homo sapiens,* who can build shelter and make clothing, has extended her range throughout the planet. Because of the root-edness of plants, dramatic or sudden changes in the weather can be devastating, ecologically, to wild plant communities. Global warming, brought about by a man-made increase in the atmosphere's "greenhouse" gases, is exactly such a change. Cosmopolitan and footloose though we may be, because our civilization depends on agriculture and a relative handful of cultivated plants, also entirely subject to climate, variations in weather hold the potential to change history.

Weather is made of many forces. Among these forces, humans have come to know the winds as intimately as anything unpredictable and invisible can be known. We have been influenced by the winds, have blessed and cursed them: hot winds that make people do crazy things, winds that create conditions for wildfires or set the undertone of certain seasons, have names—chinook, simoom, samiel; foehn; khamsin, harmattan, sirocco, solano, Santa Ana—native to the places where they blow.

Some winds change the face of the Earth, working over the eons, subtly hurling grains of sand against rock faces, sculpting out magical shapes—pinnacles, needles, and arches. Winds move huge sand dunes, tons of mass, grain by grain, in sinuous ranks. The magnitude of the wind as an Earth-shaping force is plain in phenomena like windblown soils in one hemisphere that were first ground to powder by glaciers in another.

In addition to flecks of inorganic matter, winds carry other small particles—pollen and spores—moving germs of life around, colonizing new places, and abetting the great cause of genetic variation. In the back eighty, I can watch this transport as autumn gusts gather up seedheads of switchgrass and tumble them in the air. The wind delicately lifts them high overhead, then piles them in blond thatchy drifts against wire fences and borders of close-set firs. It carries wisps of milkweed floss, causes leaves to tremble, rips them free, whirls them up in little cyclones, and, after a short dance, abandons them to the Earth to settle and begin more soil.

10   Bob Dylan, the great bard of the sixties generation, sang that you don't need a weatherman to know which way the wind blows. True enough. If wind there be, you can just step right out and feel it on your face. Your breeze is a local phenomenon, local as the canyon between the high-rises or the little hill you're perched upon, local as your cheeks and their nerve endings, and the fine hairs clothing your skin. The wind that spawns the breeze may come from half a world away, however. We live in an era where technology lets us see, from twenty-two thousand miles up, which way the wind blows across the hemisphere and around the planet.

Although satellite imagery has provided us with the big picture of weather systems, it hasn't entirely supplanted land-based observers who check rain gauges and anemometers and phone the results in to a network. Other people whose lives depend, one way or another, on the dynamics of the weather—farmers and sailors—are also keen readers of the signs written in the shapes of the clouds, the hue of the dawn, the shifting of the winds. And many of us, with no training at all, can anticipate some barometric pressure changes simply by feeling them in our bones.

The Gaia Hypothesis asserts that Earth's atmosphere is continuously interacting with geology (the lithosphere), Earth's cycling weathers (the hydrosphere), and everything that lives (the biosphere). Evidently the atmosphere has always been an integral factor of the evolution of life. It seems not to have been passive, but an active chemical medium participating in evolution. The atmosphere has been changed dramatically by the appearance of certain life-forms (the cyanobacteria, for instance), which, incidentally, created conditions more favorable to other, subsequent life-forms—like us.

Thus the hope is that the living air itself will offer some forgiveness: Gaia's autopoiesis. (Autopoiesis means self-making—"The concept is that it is intrinsic in cells and organisms to maintain their organization via interactions with their environment," explains Gaia Hypothesis coauthor Lynn Margulis.) The image is that the atmosphere is a circulatory system for life's biochemical interplay. If the atmosphere is part of a larger whole that has some of the qualities of an organism, one of those qualities we now must pray for is resilience.

SEEK TENSION
• • • • • • • • • • • • • •

Was *Paul's Boutique* Illegal?
by Matthew Yglesias

STUDY THE MOVES

In the following article, originally posted on *Slate*, Matthew Yglesias considers the current state of music sampling

continued

An avid blogger, Matthew Yglesias is the business and economics correspondent for *Slate* and the author of two books on political and economic issues.

and explains how the creative process has changed as a result of intellectual property disputes. Throughout, Yglesias makes several moves described in Chapter 2 ("Seek Tension") and Chapter 3 ("Apply Sources"):

PARAGRAPH I	Examines a real event, which prompts thinking about a past example of music sampling
PARAGRAPHS 2–4	Describes the historical context of music sampling
PARAGRAPHS 5–7	Describes a tension within the music industry and synthesizes several cases of music sampling
PARAGRAPH 8	Gives a current example of the situation
PARAGRAPH 9	Describes a broad tension and reveals an insight about the creative process

The death on Friday [May 4, 2012] of Adam Yauch, best known as the Beastie Boys' MCA, surely sent many of us back to old albums we may not have heard for a while. And anyone who threw on *Paul's Boutique,* the Boys' best album, was surely struck by the sense that they don't make records like that anymore. That's not just because tastes and styles have changed. The entire album is based on lavish sampling of other recordings. "Shake Your Rump," which leads *Slate*'s #MCATracks playlist, features samples of 14 songs by 12 separate artists. In all, the album is thought to have as many as 300 total samples. The sampling gave *Paul's Boutique* a sound that remains almost as distinctive today as it was when it was released in 1989.

Perhaps the main reason—and certainly the saddest reason—that it still sounds distinctive is that a rapidly shifting legal and economic landscape made it essentially impossible to repeat.

In the late 1980s, sampling occupied a legal gray area. The principle of "fair use" of material clearly (and fortunately) allows for the quoting of copyrighted text. Music samplers argue that the same right to quote belongs to them. In the case of text, the permissibility of quoting goes essentially unquestioned. If book reviewers needed the author's permission to quote a work under review, meaningful criticism would be impossible. The back-and-forth, you-said-I-said dialogue of the blogosphere would be against the law. Historians wouldn't be able to quote historical newspaper accounts of the events they're describing. Where exactly the line is between quoting someone's writing and straight-up copying it is often unclear, but the need to preserve a healthy space for quotation is uncontroversial.

Hip-hop sampling began as a live technique, with DJs working turntables at parties and clubs. Whether it was strictly legal or not, nobody was going to try to sue anyone about it. As the genre's popularity grew, people naturally started recording performances and releasing them as albums. Early sampling tended to come fast and furious. In the '80s, short clips of existing recordings were the order of the day, often—as in the case of the Beastie Boys—lots of them, layered and shuffled in a clearly creative way. As hip-hop pushed further into the mainstream, however, the stakes got bigger and so did the samples.

5   1990 saw the release of both M. C. Hammer's "U Can't Touch This" and Vanilla Ice's "Ice, Ice, Baby." Not only did both songs sample, they each relied heavily on one particular sample—the baselines from Rick James' "Superfreak" and Queen and David Bowie's "Under Pressure"—for their main hook. Both hits resulted in legal controversy. Ultimately Hammer settled out of court with James, giving him co-composer credit and a share of royalties, and Bowie and Queen received songwriting credits for "Ice, Ice, Baby." In 1991 came the case of *Grand Upright Music v. Warner Bros. Records* in which Biz Markie and Warner were

enjoined against further distribution of his album *I Need a Haircut* on the grounds that "Alone Again" contained an unauthorized sample of Gilbert O'Sullivan's "Alone Again (Naturally)."

In the specific cases of "U Can't Touch This" and "Ice, Ice, Baby," paying off the original artists seems like a fair outcome. But the systematic consequences of these three precedents ensured that the methods of *Paul's Boutique* would vanish from mainstream music.

After the legal turmoil, record companies didn't want to expose themselves to copyright risk. Sampling was fine, but it would have to proceed on the basis retroactively agreed to by Hammer and Ice. Some form of explicit licensing arrangement would need to be worked out in advance with the rights holder of any recognizable sample. For songs in the specific mold of "U Can't Touch This"— rapping over a lengthy excerpt of a well-known tune— this model works perfectly well and gave the world hits like Puff Daddy's "I'll Be Missing You" (borrowing from the Police's "Every Breath You Take") and "Come With Me" (borrowing from Led Zeppelin's "Kashmir"). But it's neither logistically nor financially feasible to contact hundreds of separate artists to win permissions for a complicated, sample-based album. And record labels don't want to take the risk of exposing themselves to hundreds of potential lawsuits.

The art of heavy sampling survives, but only on the margins. Under the stage name Girl Talk, Gregg Michael Gillis has released a number of popular and well-regarded pure mashup albums. But he does it with a specialty record label, Illegal Art, dedicated to keeping the genre alive. And the albums are available for download on a "pay what you want" basis, with the exception of his latest, which is free.

Even as hip-hop is more mainstream than ever, one of the key musical innovations has been pushed to the margins. That should serve as a reminder that the battles over intellectual property don't merely pit the economic interests of creators against would-be freeloading consumers. The existing stock of recorded music is, potentially, a powerful tool in the hands of musicians looking to create new works. But it's been largely cut off from them—for no good reason. Congress could enact a mandatory licensing scheme in which you pay a modest fixed fee to sample an existing recording for commercial purposes. Or it could create a legislative safe harbor, stipulating that samples under some set length automatically qualify as a fair use. But it won't, because in the music and movie industries, the only kind of copyright laws Congress is willing to pass are ones that give more power to copyright holders, not less.

The Substance of Style
by Virginia Postrel

STUDY THE MOVES

In the following excerpt from her book *The Substance of Style: How the Rise of Aesthetic Value Is Remaking Commerce, Culture, & Consciousness*, Virginia Postrel takes a fresh look at a major political event: Afghani liberation from Taliban rule. In the process, she makes several moves described in Chapter 1 ("Seek Complexity"), Chapter 2 ("Seek Tension"), Chapter 3 ("Apply Sources"), and Chapter 8 ("Escape the Status Quo"):

PARAGRAPHS 1–2	Examines a real event—and its unexpected effects
PARAGRAPH 3	Describes a subtle tension related to cultural values and expectations—and applies a supportive source

continued

An award-winning columnist and speaker, Virginia Postrel is currently writing her third book on the subject of glamour.

PARAGRAPHS 4–5	Calls out quiet assumptions about aesthetics—and applies a supportive source
PARAGRAPH 6	Asks focused questions to better explain the tension
PARAGRAPHS 7–9	Describes a broad tension and reveals insights about human nature

As soon as the Taliban fell, Afghan men lined up at barbershops to have their beards shaved off. Women painted their nails with once-forbidden polish. Formerly clandestine beauty salons opened in prominent locations. Men traded postcards of beautiful Indian movie stars, and thronged to buy imported TVs, VCRs, and videotapes. Even burka merchants diversified their wares, adding colors like brown, peach, and green to the blue and off-white dictated by the Taliban's whip-wielding virtue police. Freed to travel to city markets, village women demanded better fabric, finer embroidery, and more variety in their traditional garments.

When a Michigan hairdresser went to Kabul with a group of doctors, nurses, dentists, and social workers, she intended to serve as an all-purpose assistant to the relief mission's professionals. Instead, she found her own services every bit as popular as the serious business of health and welfare. "When word got out there was a hairdresser in the country, it just got crazy," she said. "I was doing haircuts every fifteen minutes."

Liberation is supposed to be about grave matters: elections, education, a free press. But Afghans acted as though superficial things were just as important. As a political commentator noted, "The right to shave may be found in no international treaty or covenant, but it has, in Afghanistan, become one of the first freedoms to which claim is being laid."

That reaction challenged many widely held assumptions about the nature of aesthetic value. While they cherish artworks like the giant Bamiyan Buddhas leveled by the Taliban, social critics generally take a different view of the frivolous, consumerist impulses expressed in more mundane aesthetic pleasures. "How depressing was it to see Afghan citizens celebrating the end of tyranny by buying consumer electronics?" wrote Anna Quindlen in a 2001 Christmas column berating Americans for "uncontrollable consumerism."

5   Respectable opinion holds that our persistent interest in variety, adornment, and new sensory pleasures is created by advertising, which generates "the desire for products consumers [don't] need at all," as Quindlen put it, declaring that "I do not need an alpaca swing coat, a tourmaline brooch, a mixer with a dough hook, a CD player that works in the shower, another pair of boot-cut black pants, lavender bath salts, vanilla candles or a KateSpadeGucci-PradaCoach bag."

What's true for New Yorkers should be true for Afghans as well. Why buy a green burka when you're a poor peasant and already have two blue ones? Why paint your nails red if you're a destitute widow begging on the streets? These indulgences seem wasteful and irrational, just the sort of false needs encouraged by commercial manipulation. Yet liberated Kabul had no ubiquitous advertising or elaborate marketing campaigns. Maybe our desires for impractical decoration and meaningless fashion don't come from Madison Avenue after all. Maybe our relation to aesthetic value is too fundamental to be explained by commercial mind control.

Human beings know the world, and each other, through our senses. From our earliest moments, the look and feel of our surroundings tell us who and where we are. But as we grow, we imbibe a different lesson: that appearances are not just potentially deceiving but frivolous and unimportant—that aesthetic value is not real except in those rare instances when it transcends the quotidian to become high art. We learn to contrast surface to substance, to believe that our real selves and the real world exist beyond the superficiality of sensation.

We have good cause, of course, to doubt the simple evidence of our senses. The sun does not go around the earth. Lines of the same length can look longer or shorter depending on how you place arrows on their ends. Beautiful people are not necessarily good, nor are good people necessarily beautiful. We're wise to maintain reasonable doubts.

But rejecting our sensory natures has problems of its own. When we declare that mere surface cannot possibly have legitimate value, we deny human experience and ignore human behavior. We set ourselves up to be fooled again and again, and we make ourselves a little crazy. We veer madly between overvaluing and undervaluing the importance of aesthetics. Instead of upholding rationality against mere sensuality, we tangle ourselves in contradictions.

APPLY SOURCES

Why You Should Care About the Groundswell by Charlene Li and Josh Bernoff

STUDY THE MOVES

In the following excerpt from their book *Groundswell: Winning in a World Transformed by Social Technologies*, Charlene Li and Josh Bernoff use sources to develop their case about the *groundswell*, the rapidly growing influence of social media. As the essay progresses, Li and Bernoff examine the implications of the groundswell and develop insights about how we live and interact with one another. Throughout, they use

continued

An expert on social media, Charlene Li is the author of the 2010 book *Open Leadership: How Social Technology Can Transform the Way You Lead*. Josh Bernoff is an expert on technology and TV and the author of the 2010 book *Empowered: Unleash Your Employees, Energize Your Customers, Transform Your Business*.

Source: *Groundswell: Winning in a World Transformed by Social Technologies*, Boston: Harvard Business Review, 2011. Copyright 2011 Forrester Research, Inc. All rights reserved.

moves described in Chapter 1 ("Seek Complexity"), Chapter 2 ("Seek Tension"), and Chapter 3 ("Apply Sources"):

PARAGRAPHS 1–2	Applies a supportive source (Sturgeon) to explain the concept of groundswell
PARAGRAPH 3	Applies another supportive source (Kawasaki) to explain the connection between science fiction and reality
PARAGRAPH 4	Makes more connections between science fiction and reality
PARAGRAPHS 6–7	Detects subtle tensions and describes implications for workers and businesses
PARAGRAPH 8	Applies another supportive source (Anderson) to show the changing nature of commerce
PARAGRAPHS 9–11	Detects more subtle tensions and describes more implications
PARAGRAPH 12	Connects to broad social and economic tensions

In 1941, the great science-fiction writer Theodore Sturgeon wrote an amazing short story called "Microcosmic God." In it a scientist named James Kidder secretly creates a new form of life—a rapidly evolving race of three-inch-tall intelligent creatures called Neoterics. Because Neoterics have faster metabolisms and brains than humans, they experience a generation in about eight days, and James watches them develop a civilization equivalent to humankind in less than a year. As he subjects them to stresses and puts obstacles in their path, the Neoterics invent ways around these obstacles, which he turns into commercially successful inventions in the real world. He even puts groups of Neoterics in competition with each other to motivate their inventive instincts.

The Neoterics outpace any human research lab since they try, fail, and adapt so much more quickly than ordinary slow-paced humans. As in all mad-scientist stories, the creation gets way beyond the control of the creator.

This is an apt metaphor for the current state of the Internet. Web 2.0 technologies and the masses of people who connect to them allow for rapid prototyping, failure, and adaptation. For example, technology marketing whiz Guy Kawasaki put a new venture called Truemors—a site for sharing rumors—together in seven weeks, for a total investment of $12,107.09. Online entrepreneurs are highly competitive, and speed can create a dominant edge because whoever gets to an idea first gets first crack at the visitors (and the traffic). The result is an evolution of new ways for people to interact, moving forward at a blistering rate.

In attempting to deal with this rapid innovation, traditional businesses are as overmatched as ordinary humans compared to Neoterics. Offline, people don't change behaviors quickly, so companies can develop loyal customers. Online, people can switch behaviors as soon as they see something better. It's the force of these millions of people, combined with the rapid evolution of new technologies by trial and error, that makes the groundswell so protean in form and so tough for traditional businesses to deal with.

5   What does this mean to you? It means the groundswell is coming to your world very soon (if it's not already there).

If you work for a media company, look out. Advertisers are shifting more and more of their money online. The groundswell is creating its own news sites (like Google News or Digg). The very idea of news is changing, as bloggers jostle with journalists for scoops. People take entertainment properties like TV shows and movies, rip them off the airwaves and DVDs, hack them, and repost new versions on YouTube or Dailymotion.

If you have a brand, you're under threat. Your customers have always had an idea about what your brand signifies, an idea that may vary from the image you are projecting. Now they're talking to each other about that idea. They are redefining for themselves the brand you spent millions of dollars, or hundreds of millions of dollars, creating.

If you are a retailer, your lock on distribution is over. People are not just buying online; they are buying from each other. They are comparing your prices with prices all over the Internet and telling each other where to get the best deal on sites like redflagdeals.com. As Chris Anderson, author of *The Long Tail*,[1] has pointed out, shelf space creates far less power when there's nearly infinite selection online.

If you are a financial services company, you no longer dominate flows of capital. Trading happens online, and consumers get financial advice from message boards on Yahoo! Finance and the Motley Fool. Companies like Prosper allow consumers to get loans from each other, instead of from banks. Paypal makes credit cards unnecessary for many transactions.

10   Business-to-business companies are, if anything, *more* vulnerable to these trends. Their customers have every reason to band together and rate the companies' services, to join groups like ITtoolbox to share insights with each other, or to help each other out on LinkedIn Answers.

Even inside companies, your employees are connecting on social networks, building ideas with online collaboration tools, and discussing the pros and cons of your policies and priorities.

The groundswell has changed the balance of power. Anybody can put up a site that connects people with people. If it's designed well, people will use it. They'll tell their friends to use it. They'll conduct commerce, or read the news, or start a popular movement, or make loans to each other, or whatever the site is designed to facilitate. And the

---

1. Chris Anderson's blog is at <www.thelongtail.com> or <http://forr.com/gsw1-26>.

store, or media outlet, or government, or bank that used to fill that role will find itself far less relevant. If you own that institution, the groundswell will eat up your profit margins, cut down your market share, and marginalize your sources of strength.

Works Cited

Anderson, Chris. *The Long Tail: Why the Future of Business Is Selling Less of More*. New York: Hyperion, 2006. Print.

Kawasaki, Guy. "By the Numbers: How I Built a Web 2.0, User-Generated Content, Citizen Journalism, Long-Tail, Social Media Site for $12,107.09." *How to Change the World*. N.p., 3 June 2007. Web. 2011. <http://forr.com/gsw1-25>.

Sturgeon, Theodore. "Microcosmic God." 1941. *The Science Fiction Hall of Fame*. Ed. Robert Silverberg. Vol. 1. New York: Orb, 2005. 88–112. Print.

The View from the Kitchen
by Shawn Burks

STUDY THE MOVES

In the following essay, Shawn Burks explains the situation of a local chef and focuses specifically on the hard decisions chefs make when it comes to juggling between culinary trends and practical issues of supply. In the process, he makes several moves described in Chapter 2 ("Seek Tension") and Chapter 3 ("Apply Sources"):

PARAGRAPHS 1–2	Describes the context of eating, cooking, and maintaining a restaurant
PARAGRAPH 3	Describes a broad tension related to culinary trends—and uses a supportive source (Escoffier)

continued

Shawn Burks, a culinary instructor at Northwestern Michigan College, graduated from the Culinary Institute of America.

PARAGRAPH 4	Explains how the broad tension plays out in a real situation—and uses a supportive source (Waters)
PARAGRAPH 5	Applies two supportive sources (Waters and Borlaug) to better explain the tension
PARAGRAPH 6	Provides a final insight about the balancing act that chefs must learn

Eating for pure enjoyment is nearly universal. And when it's done for pleasure, eating (and cooking) is hyper-focused on the details of aroma, visual presentation, texture, temperature, seasoning, and flavor profiles. Each of these details includes a huge range of controllable and uncontrollable possibilities. This is the fun part of "chefing," planning and balancing all of the variables to make others happy through food. But how do foodservice professionals get focus? How do chefs determine a menu? The answers lie in identity—in establishing and maintaining the particular culture of a restaurant.

Professional fine-dining chefs understand that their work is tied to a *genre*—a particular culinary category that transcends but informs each individual establishment. Fine-dining restaurants adhere to certain norms of pricing and exclusivity. But each restaurant is, or should be, distinguished with a theme and internal culture. It is the chef's job to maintain that culture. And, in turn, the culture will help to guide the daily decisions—even the tough ones.

Above all else, menu decisions loom constantly. And perhaps more than anything else, the menu determines the identity of a restaurant. Technically speaking, a menu is a list of offerings with attached prices, serving the function of creating perceived value. Now that even the stuffiest of establishments have done away with the tradition of including prices only on men's menus, every diner is the focus of perceived value. Menu decisions depend on the constraints of seasonality: cost, timeline realities, and product quality. Just because a chef can have fresh New Zealand raspberries the size of a fat thumb Fed Ex'ed to the top of a mountain in Montana during January doesn't mean she should. But beyond the cost of raw materials and labor, value perception is based on far more subjective and ephemeral pleasures that present true challenges to a chef trying to maintain profitability. Of course, this is nothing new. The radical visionary Auguste Escoffier, whose influence is felt strongly today, addressed this idea in the foreword to his 1902 book, *Le Guide Culinaire*: "At a time when all is undergoing modification and change, it would be foolish to claim to establish the future of an art which is connected in so many ways to fashion and is just as changeable" (x). Escoffier, known as the chef of kings and the king of chefs, knew his royal customers well and understood the need for food evolution. Since Escoffier's time, trends and fads have continued to influence professional chefs, despite some of the counter-intuitive culinary results that sometimes come along with them (fondue, anyone?). As chefs, we are bound to fashionable food and must sway with the currents of contemporary culture, often outside of practicality and even reason.

Where I live, the current trend lending itself to these pitfalls is the push for local meats. The region has always been agrarian and has an extensive and devout local food community, whose connection to the local food movement has followed national trends. A restaurateur-philosopher and a leading voice in the local food movement, Alice Waters has changed the way Americans buy and consume food over the last forty years through her business Chez Panisse as well as her community education programs. In her book *In the Green Kitchen: Techniques to Learn by Heart*, Waters defines the role of cooking in daily life: "Cooking creates a sense of well-being for yourself and the people you love and brings beauty and meaning to everyday life" (2). She goes on to describe the holistic approach to food culture that underpins her philosophy: "And all it requires is common sense—the common sense to eat seasonally, to know where your food comes from, to support and buy from local farmers and producers who are good stewards of our natural resources, and to apply the same principles of conservation to your own home kitchen" (*In the Green Kitchen* 2). Waters's approach has been marketed through cable TV's Food Network, leading the trend toward *locavorism*, or the push for a diet of locally sourced food. And consumers, as a result, have developed a taste for local foods. But while it is an admirable endeavor, the local food movement has shortcomings that could, ultimately, undermine a restaurant's identity and survival.

5 Now that the locavore radar is on for tomatoes, turnips, and kale, a growing number of customers don't understand why they can't also get a local porterhouse steak. It looks great on a menu. The public is passionate about it. The local media focus on it. But what fine-dining chefs are finding, especially those of us running a facility larger than a couple dozen seats, is that we cannot feed customers local foods, and especially local meats, with any consistency of product, nor at a price acceptable to most consumers. The supply is just not there, and what is available is inconsistent. And yet more and more consumers have come to see products that aren't locally sourced as inadequate and inferior. Here, Waters delves further into her philosophy:

> If we choose to feed ourselves responsibility [sic], if we feed ourselves with fresh, living, local food, we have to interact with purveyors who are trying to live on the earth in a harmonious and responsible way. After several years of buying food from such people in a farmers market, one has all kinds of understanding: about agricultural economy and risk, and the heroic effort required to husband the land and its life-sustaining resources; about who the farmers are and what they grow best; and about the freshness and seasonality of food and

> what things smell and taste like. And these kinds
> of understandings contribute to the health and
> stability of local agriculture and to a real sense of
> belonging to a local community. (Letter)

According to Waters, it is irresponsible to eat food from outside regions, whether Wisconsin, California's central valley, or Peru. So the difficult questions begin: Do we rely exclusively on farmers with small land holdings, who by default must also be their own delivery drivers, marketers, and retailers? Are they more important to the community than larger operations with multiple paid employees? Do we support the culture of agricultural migrant workers or, with each menu decision, subvert it? And taken to reductio ad absurdum, is fresh living food unacceptable if not from down the street? Does distance between production and consumption always lower the quality of smell and taste? Would the town I live in, marketed heavily for decades as The Cherry Capital of the World (for good reason), and owing much of its economic base to the industry, willingly and happily step aside and encourage locavores everywhere to grow their own cherries? Suddenly, the massive national post-WWII effort to mitigate many of the risks and issues that Waters identifies, and to increase food safety and production for a steady and high-quality supply at reasonable costs, seems a fool's errand. Certainly, the humanitarian feat of Nobel Peace Prize winner Norman Borlaug in eradicating hunger for more than a billion people depended on precise measures for increasing the world's food supply. On a smaller scale, fine-dining chefs running their own restaurants are faced with similar tough decisions about how to design their menus with both supply and demand in mind.

And these daily, tough decisions, of course, shape a restaurant's identity. They determine how consumers perceive a fine-dining establishment, and whether or not it will survive. In my neck of the woods, we have more options agriculturally than most regions, but we have our backs against the wall when it comes to the center of the plate. The chefs here have the option of fish during the warmer months, albeit with some limitations in terms of availability and consistency. Local vegetables, honey, and dairy products are all highlighted on menus here as well. But local red meat? It's a tough call. And once the call is made, it may have to be unmade. The whole process becomes a balancing act—not simply between supply and demand, not simply between perceived value and profit, but also between the identity of a restaurant and the identity of its surroundings.

Works Cited

Escoffier, Auguste. Foreword. *Escoffier: The Complete Guide to the Art of Modern Cookery*. By Escoffier. Trans. H. L. Cracknell and R. J. Kaufmann. New York: Wiley, 1979. ix–x. Print.

Waters, Alice. *In the Green Kitchen: Techniques to Learn by Heart*. New York: ClarksonPotter-Random, 2010. Print.

---. Letter to Clinton and Gore. 9 Dec. 1995. *EarthLight. org*. EarthLight, 1996. Web. 15 Apr. 2012.

APPLY A CONCEPT
• • • • • • • • • • • • • • • • • •

Superconductivity: A Super Idea
by Bradford A. Smith

STUDY THE MOVES

In the following essay, Bradford A. Smith demystifies a complex concept (superconductivity) and discusses some

continued

Bradford A. Smith is an expert on magnet design and the recipient of a US patent on magnet structure for particle acceleration. He has published numerous articles about superconductivity and magnetics, which, like the following essay, cite sources using a scientific style.

real-world applications. Although he tackles a difficult subject, he uses clear language and examples to walk readers through the concept and its applications. Throughout, he uses moves described in Chapter 3 ("Apply Sources") and Chapter 4 ("Apply a Concept"):

PARAGRAPHS 1–3	Draws from a vital source (Feynman) and establishes context for superconductivity
PARAGRAPH 4	Explains the concept with a comparison and applies a supportive source (Larbalestier)
PARAGRAPH 5	Describes common applications of the concept
PARAGRAPH 6	Applies the concept to a specific situation (the author's own research)
PARAGRAPH 7	Explains new insights that come from applying the concept
PARAGRAPH 8	Describes the ongoing questions and pursuits related to the concept

Now in the further development of science, we want more than just a formula. First we have an observation, then we have numbers that we measure, then we have a law which summarizes all the numbers. But the real glory of science is that we can find a way of thinking such that the law is evident.

~Richard P. Feynman[1]

In this quote, and in his work as a Nobel Prize–winning theoretical physicist, Richard P. Feynman shares an important insight: The scientist's intellectual posture enables a process of discovery. In many ways, the scientific community is defined by the uncertainty of its work. We test, probe, experiment, observe, ponder, and discuss—but our conclusions are often tentative, unresolved, and lead to further questions whose answers depend on more thought and research. In the sciences, fundamental ideas about how the natural world works form the backbone of inquiry. They provide a starting point from which scientific research is possible. We accept that the earth is a planet among many, that polar opposites attract, and that gravity keeps us grounded. But beyond these basic truths lies a realm of possibilities, ways of thinking about natural phenomena and their implications for how we live and interact with our surroundings.

Continued exploration of accepted ideas, often from new perspectives, can reveal inconsistencies, which imply that current theories are not fully adequate. Experiments, both real and in thought (the latter being one of Einstein's favorite activities), can sometimes lead to breakthroughs that change established ways of thinking. In an ever-evolving process, current theories are again challenged and reset by the next generation of scientists.

The term *superconductivity* is often associated with the stuff of science fiction. As a case in point, the 2009 film *Avatar* names a magical superconducting substance "unobtainium," illustrating the lengths to which people will go to acquire it. But in the world of physics and engineering, superconductivity is a real phenomenon that has seen significant and widespread applications since its discovery in 1911 by Kamerlingh Onnes. Although superconductivity was discovered more than a hundred years ago, many of the phenomenon's details are still being researched today, and perhaps this leaves room for its inclusion in sci-fi and fantasy contexts.

Superconductivity might be called an "experimental fact," the existence of which has been proven but the exact workings of which are still being explored and developed. Conducting materials have little electrical resistance, while superconducting materials have zero electrical resistance.

Superconductors help to reduce wasted energy. To understand why this is important, consider the problem of moving heavy furniture: hauling a couch from one room to another becomes a far easier task when furniture rollers arrive on the scene. The rollers serve as a conduit, guiding the cumbersome furniture into place. Similarly, electrons require certain conditions in order to move smoothly and freely. Superconductivity—creating a zero-resistance path for electrons to flow—depends on specific factors, including a very low temperature and a limited magnetic field environment. By nature, electrons repel one another, but in extremely cold conditions (in the range of –300 degrees Fahrenheit in some materials), electrons actually "pair" up and move together unhindered.[2] With their potential for reducing wasted energy, superconductors have been generating interest and excitement within and beyond the scientific community since their discovery.

5   The most common application of superconductivity is in MRI (Magnetic Resonance Image) scanners, which use superconducting magnet coils to create a magnetic field in the body, enabling physicians to see patients' soft tissues in striking detail. Magnetic levitation (maglev) is another use: superconducting magnets function as "tracks" for trains and other vehicles, generating a magnetic field that can efficiently guide vehicles as they are propelled and offering passengers a fast, smooth ride. Still other applications focus on alternative energy use, such as superconducting power lines and high-efficiency wind turbines.

Modern-day physicists, like Feynman in his time, continue to dream up experiments to test current theories. Often, physicists conceptualize the requirements of the superconducting magnets that are used in some of these experiments. As an electrical engineer at MIT's Plasma Science and Fusion Center, I translate these magnetic field requirements into a real magnet design that fulfills the experimental needs.

Recently, I worked with my MIT colleagues to design a superconducting magnet for a specific application: proton radiation therapy. With this precise method of cancer treatment, a cyclotron, or particle accelerator, uses a superconducting magnet to guide an accelerated proton beam that irradiates diseased body tissue. Proton therapy pinpoints cancer and delivers radiation only where it is needed. Historically, and despite its obvious benefits, proton therapy has been more costly than other kinds of cancer treatment and has required large, expensive equipment. The superconducting cyclotron, designed by our group at MIT, has reduced the size and cost of the machine needed to accelerate protons for cancer therapy. These developments are making proton therapy a more viable alternative to earlier cancer treatment methods. In ongoing research, the goal is to better understand superconductivity so its benefits can be harnessed more easily and cheaply in more and more contexts.

Superconductivity demonstrates Feynman's sentiment: the ways we approach a problem reveal insights and possible solutions to that problem. We keep experimenting with this "experimental fact," knowing that in the unresolved questions, complexities, and inconsistencies lie the potential answers. Investigators in Onnes's day initially questioned the possibility of superconductivity—an intellectual posture that led to its discovery. The discovery and continued development of superconductivity have made possible more and more applications, but at the same time have uncovered new limitations and unknowns. In the end, we return seeking a more complete answer to the initial question: what is this thing called "superconductivity"?

References

[1]   R. P. Feynman, R. B. Leighton, and M. Sands, *The Feynman Lectures on Physics*, vol. 1. Reading, MA: Addison-Wesley, 1965, p. 26-3.

[2] D. Larbalestier. (2012). Superconductivity. *Mag Lab Dictionary*. Natl. High Magnetic Field Lab., FL. [Online]. Available: http://www.magnet.fsu.edu/education/tutorials/magnetminute/superconductivity-transcript.html

From Trickster to Heroic Savior: Jake Sully's Journey in *Avatar*
by Tiffany J. Smith

STUDY THE MOVES

In the following essay, Tiffany J. Smith transports concepts from comparative mythology and psychology to film studies. She offers a detailed analysis of a popular film, *Avatar* (2009), and explains the insights that emerge from applying concepts across disciplines. In the process, she uses moves described in Chapter 3 ("Apply Sources") and Chapter 4 ("Apply a Concept"):

PARAGRAPH 1	Introduces concepts from comparative mythology and psychology
PARAGRAPH 2	Applies the "hero myth" concept to the film *Avatar*
PARAGRAPH 3	Draws from a vital source (Campbell) to describe Jake as a hero
PARAGRAPH 4	Applies a supportive source (Clinton) to describe Jake as a trickster

continued

Tiffany J. Smith is a guest contributor to *Magazine Americana*, an online journal published by Americana: The Institute for the Study of American Popular Culture. The following essay has been excerpted from the full version that appears on Americana's website. Because Smith's essay originally appeared in a magazine, she doesn't include a bibliography for the sources cited in her essay.

Source: www.americanpopularculture.com/film.htm. Reprinted with permission.

Can mythological theories be applied to a modern day tale? The mythographer, Joseph Campbell, through his lifetime of studying myths from around the world, came to a universal conclusion: when we crack the nutshell of any myth from any part of the world, "it will always be the one, shape-shifting yet marvelously constant story that we find." In other words, all myths are basically the same story; only the characters and settings have changed. Whether intentional or not, all storytelling follows an ancient pattern which can be understood through the "Hero Myth" or "Monomyth" concepts. These concepts are based on another great mind—that of Carl Jung. By using a combination of certain mythological elements which these two great mythographers have detailed, we can apply them to the theatrical film *Avatar*. So, why is it important to understand the mythological aspects of the film *Avatar*? It is not simply to give people a better understanding and connection to the film, but to give them a better understanding and connection to themselves. Both Campbell and Jung believed the archetypes represented in all stories were in fact mirroring the human psyche—as Jung phrased it— "taking a sort of projection of the collective unconscious." By understanding the archetypes of myths and applying them to the film *Avatar*, we can begin to understand ourselves and those around us.

The film *Avatar* does an excellent job of showing how an age-old mythological hero's journey can continue the tradition of being handed down through oral traditions from one generation to the next. The symbols, archetypes, and the characters must be broken down and analyzed through a set of universal mythological lenses in order to understand this journey and what it represents. The film *Avatar* seems to best represent the concepts Joseph Campbell and Carl Jung define as the "Hero Myth." It is a modern and dynamic adaptation of an age-old story. When the plot and characters are stripped of their flashy and charismatic exteriors, we are left with a true-to-form example of a hero's journey. Joseph Campbell maps out this journey using specific stages which director and writer James Cameron followed in the plot of the film with exceptional accuracy, even down to the archetypes represented, such as the protagonist (in this case, a trickster turned hero), mother goddess, mentor, and protector. All of them serve to follow the hero cycle.

In the film *Avatar*, we watch a character by the name of Jake Sully, a paraplegic US Marine, sent to be a substitute navigator for his dead twin brother's avatar. He takes a life-changing journey as he goes from trickster to heroic savior. This transformation takes place with the help of some other very important characters such as Neytiri, who serves as his guide as well as a protector to him, her people, and the planet. Another important element is "Awa," which can be seen as the *Great Goddess* or *Great Mother* to the entire planet and its people. Awa is not a person, but referred to in the film as "[The Na'vi's] deity . . . their goddess made up of all living things." The shaman to the Na'vi believes it is the will of "Awa" to allow Jake into their tribe and teach him their ways. To do this, Neytiri is told by the clan's shaman to take Jake under her wing in order to see if his "insanity can be cured." This insanity is the typical human mindset that neglects the connection to the planet and to fellow humans.

Jake Sully starts out as a man whose only objective is to trick the Na'vi into allowing him into their world. His mission is to gain intel on their home in order to find a way to force them out and harvest the valuable metal deep in their planet. With the help of Neytiri (the protector), "Awa," (the Great Mother Goddess), and Mo'at (the shaman or "Wise Old Woman"), he is able to open his eyes to the world around him and gain a profound connection to the people, the planet, and Awa. Campbell comments on this very idea in *The Power of Myth* stating, "We have today to learn to get back into accord with the wisdom of nature and realize again our brotherhood with the animals and with the water and the sea." By doing this, Jake is transforming into the hero and savior the Na'vi truly need to fight the war with the greedy "sky people" or humans.

As stated above, Jake Sully begins his journey as a trickster. Professor of folklore, Dr. Esther Clinton, writes in her article "The Trickster, Various Motifs" that "the term trickster, when used by social scientists, refers to more than simply a deceptive character. Tricksters are destroyers and creators, heroes and villains." Using this description, we can see Jake Sully is already showing "trickster" qualities as well as destructive ones. While he is not destroying the Na'vi nation, Jake is helping to give the military first hand intel about the Na'vi. He does so in order to find weaknesses the military can use against them. The fact that Jake is being portrayed as a negative "trickster" at the start of the tale helps to set the stage for his later "rebirth," or ultimate change, described by Campbell as part of the hero's journey.

5   This sudden drop into the strange and new world called Pandora might be misunderstood as the "call to adventure" which sets in motion the "hero cycle" described by Joseph Campbell. This call to adventure can start in many different ways, but it must reveal "an unsuspected world, and the individual is drawn into a relationship with forces

that are not rightly understood." Campbell also states this "unsuspected world" usually contains "both treasure and danger . . . unimaginable torments, superhuman deeds, and impossible delight." In the case of Pandora, each of these elements are represented in the nearly invisible monsters, superhuman strength, resiliency of all the creatures, and the delights of having connections to the creatures and planet which human beings can only dream about. However, after arriving on Pandora, Jake is still within the confines of the military fortress of his own people. It is only after setting foot into the wilderness outside the military confines with the use of his "avatar" that the true "call to adventure" takes place. He finds out first hand what terrible monsters await him in this world. Jake loses contact with the scientists he is meant to protect and is chased down by a horrible creature to a place deep within the forests. It is upon his first meeting with one of the Na'vi who recognizes a sign which presents itself that the Na'vi become aware this "alien" has a strong heart and has a destiny which must be protected. Campbell's description of the actual point of "the call" states the protagonist must set "forth from his common day hut or castle, is lured, carried away, or else voluntarily proceeds, to the threshold of adventure. There he encounters a shadow presence that guards the passage." In Jake's case, he would fall into the "carried away" category after being chased into the jungle by one of Pandora's beasts. Now, the "call to adventure" has truly begun.

It is during this stage that Jake meets the person who will help him the most on his journey. Neytiri, who is introduced shortly after his first experience in the Avatar body, is a Na'vi, and member of the clan. Her main objective is to protect her people, and she does so with fury. Upon first spotting Jake, she tries to kill him, but is given a sign by Awa that she must not harm him; the sign is simple, yet extremely meaningful to her. A seed from the "sacred tree" falls on her arrow just before she releases it. Her archetype of the protector is made much more evident after she is given the task of teaching Jake the ways of the Na'vi. She teaches him how to read tracks in the forest, thank the animals killed for the food they provide, see animals as his brothers and sisters instead of simple creatures, and most of all to understand the connection to all living things through Awa. The teachings about animals at this point in the narrative are something Joseph Campbell discusses in "The Power of Myth: The First Storytellers," in which he examines the idea of referring to animals as "thou" instead of "it." Campbell states that by doing so we give a kind of consciousness to animals, thus creating a connection to them.

The next stage, as set by Campbell, is the "refusal of the call." During this stage, the hero ignores, or outright refuses, to accept his destiny. Campbell states, "the refusal is essentially a refusal to give up what one takes to be one's own interest." During this stage in Jake Sully's journey, he transitions from working for the military in order to control the Na'vi, to beginning to understand the importance of the land and seeing the Na'vi as more than just creatures, but as equals. Only after this understanding takes place does Jake begin the fight to protect the Na'vi, and ultimately fulfill his destiny as heroic savior. . . .

With the understanding in mind that myths contain symbolic expressions, the philosophical question comes to mind: why take the time to understand this journey and the archetypes presented? This film's plot, as well as its characters, resonate with us because we all have a deep connection to each archetype within our psyches. As Joseph Oziewicz explains, Jung believes that myths, like that of *Avatar*, are "stories of archetypal encounters which affect us so much because they derive from the collective unconscious—'a common psychic substrate of a suprapersonal nature which is present in every one of us.'" Bruce Allen states, "Cameron could have asked us to read *Tao Te Ching*, or *Bury My Heart at Wounded Knee*, or *1491*, or Thoreau's *Walden*, or Dian Fossey. But Cameron is a filmmaker, after all. And he knows the volatile combination of power, ignorance/indifference, and greed." James Cameron explains the true purpose of his film, "*Avatar* asks us to see that everything is connected, all human beings to each other, and us to the Earth."

While we may never wage a war and defeat a monster, saving a planet of humanoid aliens, we do wage our own internal wars every day. Like Jake, we each have spiritual helpers, mentors, protectors, heroes, saviors, and parental figures in our lives as well as in our hearts and minds. As time has changed, so have our myths. However, the morals and connections present in ancient myths have remained the same. Campbell states, "to grasp the full value of the mythological figures that have come down to us, we must understand that they are not only symptoms of the unconscious (as indeed are all human thoughts and acts) but also controlled and intended statements of certain spiritual principles, which have remained as constant throughout the course of human history as the form and nervous structure of the human physique itself."

10   Myths also serve to help us put into context our changing world. They allow us to transfer our understandings of the experiences we deal with to the next generations. Jung believes the origins of myths "can only be explained by assuming them to be deposits of the constantly repeated experiences of humanity." Because the film puts real world concerns in more fantastical light, it engages us, while implanting in our minds morals and lessons. In other words, through the use of mythological concepts, tales such as *Avatar* provide humanity with a universal way not only to understand ourselves, but also to understand those around us, both past and present.

The Implied Child Reader
by Annette Wannamaker

STUDY THE MOVES

In the following essay, Annette Wannamaker applies the concept of the "implied child reader" to specific texts. In the process, she relies primarily on the moves described in Chapter 4 ("Apply a Concept") and Chapter 5 ("Dismantle Arguments"). She also makes moves described in Chapter 1 ("Seek Complexity") and Chapter 3 ("Apply Sources"):

PARAGRAPH 1	Asks focused questions about children's literature
PARAGRAPH 2	Analyzes the audience for children's literature and introduces the concept of the "implied child reader"
PARAGRAPH 3	Applies a supportive source (Nodelman) to explain the concept
PARAGRAPH 4	Applies the concept to a historical text (*The New England Primer*)
PARAGRAPH 5	Applies the concept to a contemporary text (*Charlotte's Web*)
PARAGRAPH 6	Asks more focused questions and analyzes the reasoning behind cultural definitions of childhood

Children's literature is deceptively simple. How hard could it be, after all, to read and understand a picture book about talking bunnies or a novel about a pig and a spider who become best friends? How complex could

Annette Wannamaker, a professor at Eastern Michigan University, is an expert on children's literature and the author of the 2011 book *Global Perspectives on Tarzan: From King of the Jungle to International Icon*.

a work of literature written for an eight-year-old be? The answer depends largely upon our understanding of childhood—both what we assume children are and what they should be.

Adult authors who write for children (children's literature written by actual children is very rare) are consciously or unconsciously writing for two sets of readers. On one level, they are writing to children reading the book or having the book read to them, but, on another level, they are also writing to adult readers, who are buying the book, teaching the book, publishing and selling the book, reading the book aloud to a child, or reading the book over a child's shoulder. The second group of readers is clearly the more powerful and most certainly has greater influence. Indeed, there are so many adults involved in the production of children's literature that there hardly seems to be room for an actual child. Because adults are the ones creating, selling, and buying children's books, the child reader is a product of the adult imagination, not an accurate reflection of the actual condition of being a child. In other words, adults often have idealized visions of childhood that are sometimes far removed from the real lives of children, and it is this idealized child, what scholars in the field call the "implied child reader," that is being depicted and addressed in a work of children's fiction.

The implied child reader tells us more about what a culture believes childhood should be than about the actual, complex lives of children. In his book *The Hidden Adult: Defining Children's Literature,* Perry Nodelman writes, "Adults offer children images of childhood that they expect children to mimic in order to be the right kind of children" (187). Many works of children's literature, then, are didactic: they set out to teach children morals, how to behave, or what to believe. When we look closely at works of literature written for children, we can spot the "right kind" of child both in the characters depicted on the page and in the tone of voice directed at the book's readers.

For example, *The New England Primer*, a school textbook first published in the late 1680s, imagined a child reader born of original sin who needed to learn to submit to the authority of God. This very popular book, read by children living in the American colonies and well into the late nineteenth century, demonstrates the ways that something as "objective" as learning the alphabet can be infused with very subjective ideas about what children are (sinful) and what they should become (God-fearing). Students reading *The New England Primer* learned to memorize the alphabet by learning a poem to accompany the letters: for the letter *a*, they learned that "In Adam's Fall, We sinned all"; for the letter *f*, they learned that "The idle Fool, Is whipt at School"; and for the letter *p*, they were reminded that "Peter denies His Lord, and cries" (12–14). The implied child reader here is one who tends toward sin, and must be taught to fear the wrath of God.

5   In many other works of children's literature, these constructions of childhood are more subtle and harder to spot, but they are still there. For example, in E. B. White's popular 1952 novel, *Charlotte's Web*, we can spot the author's assumptions about the right ways boys and girls should behave according to gender roles that were commonly accepted in the 1950s. Fern, the eight-year-old protagonist of the novel, is nurturing and gentle, while her brother, Avery, owns guns and knives, is destructive, and often has a frog or some other critter stuffed into his pocket. The fact that these gender roles are never questioned and are depicted as normal and natural demonstrates the subtle way that these expectations are passed onto child readers, who also are expected to assume that girls are naturally passive and boys are naturally violent. For example, in one scene in the novel, Mrs. Arable consults the family doctor because she is concerned about the amount of time Fern is spending in the barn with the animals. After reassuring her that Fern's behavior is normal, the doctor asks Mrs. Arable how her son is doing. "Oh, Avery," she replies,

chuckling. "Avery is always fine. Of course, he gets into poison ivy and gets stung by wasps and bees and brings frogs and snakes home and breaks everything he lays his hands on. He's fine." To this, the doctor responds, "Good!" (White 111–12). The adult reader of the novel laughs at the way "boys will be boys," and the child reader learns how to behave like a properly gendered boy or girl who will fulfill these adult expectations.

Recognizing the cultural ideas that shape the content and the implied child reader of older texts is a lot easier than recognizing the ideas that shape contemporary texts, mostly because we are less aware of our own assumptions. It's easy to recognize ideologies that are not our own, but much more difficult to spot our own prejudices or misconceptions. Do we, for instance, believe that being a child is simple and that childhood is innocent, or do we acknowledge that children often have lives as complex, difficult, and varied as the lives adults lead? Based on our assumptions, do we then automatically assume that children's books should be simple, light books that convey unambiguous moral messages? By thinking very carefully about depictions of children in contemporary children's books, about the ways in which child readers are being addressed in these books, and about our own assumptions about the idealized implied child reader that we bring to our readings of these books, we can begin to understand our culture's construction of the "right kind of child." Children's books are, after all, one way we pass our values, beliefs, and cultural practices—both good and bad—onto the next generation.

Works Cited

The New England Primer. Albany: Whiting, 1805. Print.

Nodelman, Perry. *The Hidden Adult: Defining Children's Literature*. Baltimore: Johns Hopkins UP, 2008. Print.

White, E. B. *Charlotte's Web*. Illus. Garth Williams. 1952. New York: Harper, 1980. Print.

DISMANTLE ARGUMENTS
• •

Gossip, Empathy, and Uncomfortable Questions: Ashley Judd Changes the Conversation About Women
by William J. Carpenter

STUDY THE MOVES

In the following essay, William J. Carpenter dismantles an argument by Ashley Judd (search online to read Judd's article "Get Out of My Face"). Throughout, he makes several of the moves described in Chapter 1 ("Seek Complexity"), Chapter 3 ("Apply Sources"), and Chapter 5 ("Dismantle Arguments"):

PARAGRAPH 1	Asks focused questions about entertainment news
PARAGRAPH 2	Makes a connection between entertainment news and diet soda
PARAGRAPH 3	Draws from a vital source (Judd)
PARAGRAPH 4	Examines Judd's purpose for writing
PARAGRAPH 5	Examines Judd's audience
PARAGRAPH 6	Examines the context that Judd establishes
PARAGRAPH 7	Examines Judd as a writer and the language she uses to create a persona
PARAGRAPH 8	Explains how Judd builds a connection with readers

William J. Carpenter, a professor at High Point University, has published several scholarly articles and contributed to various college teaching materials.

Reprinted by permission of William J. Carpenter.

Gossip magazines and Hollywood news shows help us pass the time in airports and waiting rooms. They distract us from our daily routines and let all practice being armchair psychologists. It's all just good—though not necessarily clean—fun. Or is it? What do the trends in entertainment news say about us and our interests? More importantly, how do our interactions with this news, the things we do with it, affect how we think and behave? Take for instance the kinds of stories that invite readers to speculate about how female celebrities came to look fat or ugly or somehow less than perfect. These stories invite us into a conversation, but to what end? Are we harmlessly commenting on the exercise or eating habits of people we'll never meet? Or are we instead reinforcing debilitating and oppressive ideas about women?

Regular consumers of entertainment news probably think of it as diet soda. No sugar, no calories, no consequences. But everything we ingest does something to us, and the more we ingest, the greater the effect. Health experts warn that diet soda alters insulin levels and can lead to cravings for sweets and even obesity. Psychologists and cultural critics argue something similar about celebrity gossip. Stories and comments that harshly critique female celebrities' appearances, that make unsubstantiated claims about their physical and medical status, or that pit women against one another dehumanize all women—not just the celebrities. They promote a male-centric worldview—what scholars call *patriarchy*—and they devalue women's own voices, concerns, and accomplishments. As feminist critics make clear, such conversations about female celebrities reinforce the idea that women should be valued primarily, if not solely, for their physical traits.

Ashley Judd wants to change these conversations about women by explaining how damaging they are to everyone—men and women. She penned an open letter for *The Daily Beast*, a news aggregating website, in the wake of an

Us magazine article that compared recent photos of Judd with older photos. The magazine invited its audience to speculate about the cause of Judd's "puffy face," and the article soon went viral. It was picked up by other news outlets, most of which invited further speculation. Readers and viewers joined the discussion in droves, suggesting everything from plastic surgery to simply letting herself go. As Judd points out in her letter, the comments were far from charitable and included a great many from female readers.

Judd's purpose in writing is not to argue about the causes of her puffy face (she claims to have been ill and on steroids for treatment) but instead to analyze the very nature of the conversation. She asks directly, "Why was a puffy face cause for such a conversation in the first place? How, and why, did people participate?" In asking these questions, Judd redirects the readers' focus onto their own motives, forcing them into a reflective position. The questions demand specific answers from the readers about what they hoped to achieve by participating in the discussion about her face. Readers can no longer simply diss Judd's looks; they have to consider why they would want to in the first place.

5   Consider the possible answers to these questions. Perhaps readers were genuinely concerned for Judd's health. Fair enough. But those readers will still need to explain why they thought the comment section of a gossip magazine was the best place to respond. Maybe readers like the sense of community they feel when discussing celebrity news online. Okay, but these readers will need to explain what it means to bond over jibes about another person's looks. The point here is that the questions lay bare the self-serving, narcissistic, mean-spirited natures of celebrity gossip and social media. The questions raise the level of discourse from careless snark to intellectual meditation, and if they make readers angry or uncomfortable, well, that's fine. In that anger and discomfort lie the seeds for greater self-awareness and social change.

By turning the focus onto the readers' motives, Judd is expanding the scope of the entire issue. It's not just about her; it's about human relationships. "Patriarchy is a system in which both men and women participate," she writes, cementing the whole episode in the broader arena of gender politics. She continues to implicate women in the continuation of their own oppression, contending that the "subtle, insidious" nature of patriarchy makes women "unable at times to identify ourselves as our own denigrating abusers." The analysis encourages readers to re-see the issue as one in which important things are at stake. Daughters grow up with body image problems. Sons learn contempt for women. Men yield to limiting notions of masculinity. Women internalize stifling self-doubts. However, such analysis risks alienating those readers for whom gender and feminist theories seem too radical, as well as those who might read such a direct response from a celebrity as a scolding.

These risks epitomize Judd's difficult rhetorical position. Her own celebrity status makes her significantly different from her audience. She is simultaneously the object of study and an outsider to the conversation. Her response upsets an age-old balance between celebrities and fans, who know instinctively that gossip isn't meant to feed intellectual debate or nourish discussion. So positioning herself only as an offended, well-read actress simply wouldn't work. The ethos would be all wrong. Instead, she argues for readers to see that their actions have consequences for themselves and for people for whom they care. One notable strategy for building empathy is her use of inclusive language and personal observations. Note the pronouns in the first paragraph: "we," "us," and "our." These plural pronouns all have "women" as their antecedents, and they make no distinction for classifications such as race, sexuality, or class. Later, Judd admits to her own "obsession with women's faces and bodies," and she ends by explaining how patriarchy affects "our sense of our worth, value, and potential as human beings."

The plural pronouns throughout the letter invite readers to identify with Judd and to recognize a shared struggle. The admissions and personal examples show the human, accessible side of Judd. They show her as one of millions of women, one engaged in the same battle for equality and dignity as so many others. Judd alone cannot change the conversation. Not just because she is one voice, but also because she inhabits such a difficult rhetorical position. She needs allies, but those allies must be persuaded to see the battle as their own. It would be counterproductive to beleaguer or attack her readers—such actions are the hallmark of patriarchy. Instead, she chooses a more feminist line of persuasion: to educate and to elicit empathy.

Work Cited

Judd, Ashley. "Get Out of My Face." *The Daily Beast.* Newsweek, 9 Apr. 2012. Web. 15 July 2012.

The Sydney Opera House
by Astrid Reed

STUDY THE MOVES

In the following essay, Astrid Reed detects and describes the quiet argument made by the Sydney Opera House. Throughout, Reed examines the architectural elements that culminate in an overarching message about culture and art. In the process, she makes several of the moves described in Chapter 5 ("Dismantle Arguments"):

PARAGRAPHS 1–2   Examines the building's purpose and significance

continued

Astrid Reed, an expert on contemporary curatorial practice, recently co-developed two book projects on the photographers Martin Parr and Dorothea Lange.

PARAGRAPH 3	Examines the architect's original intention for the building
PARAGRAPHS 4–6	Describes the building's physical setting and political context
PARAGRAPH 7	Analyzes the building's exterior elements
PARAGRAPH 8	Analyzes the building's interior elements
PARAGRAPH 9	Calls out the quiet argument the building is making

To be truly great, a piece of architecture must fulfill its purpose while resonating with its surrounding environment. In the case of the Sydney Opera House, both the interior and exterior elements of the building serve a particular function and harmonize with the life that goes on within and around it. The Opera House is not only the most recognizable building in Sydney, but has also come to symbolize the entire country of Australia to the rest of the world. The design of the building was originally chosen for its extraordinary and modern elements, and the building's impact has only increased over the years as its function has evolved to make it the place that it is today. This building has put Australia on the map, not only in terms of its striking appearance, but also in terms of the creativity it cultivates within its walls.

I was born in Sydney two years before the Opera House was officially opened and dedicated in 1973 and I have no memory of the city before it was built. At age eight, I sang proudly on the concert hall stage in my school choir with hundreds of other nervous primary school children. I have since attended ballet performances, symphonies, and even rock concerts there. I've enjoyed dinner with friends at the restaurants inside and sat outside on the steps of the building eating ice cream and watching the sun set into the water. To me, the Opera House is as much a part of Sydney as any natural landmark. I can't imagine it not being there, yet I have never failed to notice it.

It was designed by a Danish architect named Jørn Utzon whose drawings beat out the entries of over two hundred other architects from around the world. His design was influenced and inspired by his own experiences growing up in a family of naval officers and ship builders in the Danish seaside city of Aalborg. What was to become a long construction process commenced in 1957. Engineering problems, budgetary issues, and political strife dragged the process on for sixteen years. The project was so riddled with setbacks that in 1966 Utzon resigned, packed up his family, and returned to Denmark. Despite its tumultuous beginnings, the Opera House was placed on the World Heritage List in 2007 alongside the Taj Mahal, the Great Pyramids, and the Eiffel Tower. Utzon knew only from afar that his building was wildly successful. He lived until 2008, but sadly never returned to Sydney to experience his accomplishment firsthand.

The physical setting of the Opera House is splendid and demanding of an equally splendid building. For the young architects submitting their designs back in the 1950s, the prospect of imagining a structure commensurate with the site must have been intimidating. The piece of land where the Opera House stands is called Bennelong Point, named for a famous Aboriginal elder. The area was sacred and important to the Aboriginal people for tens of thousands of years before English settlers arrived in the 1700s.

5   Sydney resounds with references to the country's colonial history, including British architectural styles that date back hundreds of years, lush rose gardens, and dark, cozy pubs. Over time, though, the Australians began to realize that the architecture wasn't the most practical, the rose gardens were wilting in the heat, and the pubs were, in fact, more stuffy than cozy. The Opera House symbolizes a time

when Australia began to accept and embrace its climate and its distinct identity, when the country started to become much less English and, well, more Australian.

The Sydney weather is characteristically warm and the sun shines in blue skies almost every day of the year. Harbor beaches and bays wiggle and weave their way throughout the city, making the water easily accessible to residents and tourists alike. There are more than twenty bridges that connect the many shores of Sydney. One bridge, the Sydney Harbour Bridge, links the North Shore with the city and ultimately with the southern, eastern, and western suburbs. I grew up on the North Shore of Sydney. The drive or train ride into the city or beyond meant crossing this bridge. Endless miles of colonial-style Victorian and Edwardian suburban homes suddenly gave way to the most extraordinary view. Sparkly, blue water dotted with ferries and sailboats and there—the grand and glorious sculptural splendor of the Opera House.

The exterior sections of the complex soar like yacht sails filled with wind (see fig. 1). For some, the building evokes seashells or the white tips of waves on a choppy sea. The million ceramic tiles encasing the exterior glow with heat each day at sunset as the sky turns pink and orange. Each year, on New Year's Eve, fireworks reflect a spectacular lightshow onto the spans of the white exterior shells.

The purpose of the building is, of course, to offer a striking venue for the performing arts. The Opera House provides a home not only for Opera Australia, but also for the Australian Ballet, the Sydney Symphony and Philharmonic Orchestras, and several theater companies. Each week, the building hosts an average of forty performances that are enjoyed by thousands of visitors. Each interior element of the building serves to heighten and enhance the audience's experience. A cascade of low, sweeping stairs creates a dramatic approach into the main doors, but the building can also be accessed from many different levels and balconies on all sides. Inside, the warmth of the pink granite and wooden beams contrasts and intersects with cool glass and

Fig. 1. The Sydney Opera House.

slabs of grey concrete. Striking dashes of blue sky, water, boats, ferries, and the Sydney Harbour Bridge are framed like precious snapshots by tall lengths of glass. There are more than a thousand rooms within the complex including concert halls and theaters of various sizes and purposes. Mirroring the geometrical pattern of tiles outside, all these rooms fit together inside like the chambers of a beehive. Acoustical engineering elements like huge glass disks and birch wood panels descend from the ceilings of the main concert hall like abstract sculpture.

Over the last half century, Sydney has developed into a cultural mecca. Museums, galleries, music, theater, and dance in Sydney rival the offerings of any large European or American city. The Opera House has served a real purpose for cultural enthusiasts from around the world by offering a spectacular venue for people to enjoy the arts. But the building's influence as a great architectural wonder has reached far beyond its walls, inspiring and encouraging a range of arts in Australia and throughout the world. Its very existence seems to have fostered a high bar of creative achievement. Such a place could never suffer the mediocre.

JUSTIFY YOUR POSITION
• •

Are Millennials the Screwed Generation?
by Joel Kotkin

STUDY THE MOVES

In the following essay, Joel Kotkin justifies his position that today's youth is "screwed." Throughout, he lines up the evidence to support his claim, focusing on social trends from a range of sources. In the process, he makes several of the moves described in Chapter 2 ("Seek Tension"), Chapter 3 ("Apply Sources"), and Chapter 6 ("Justify Your Position"):

PARAGRAPH 1	Asserts a claim about today's youth and applies a supportive source
PARAGRAPHS 2–4	Lines up evidence (focusing on the economy) to support the claim—and applies supportive sources
PARAGRAPHS 5–7	Lines up evidence (focusing on unemployment) to support the claim—and applies supportive sources
PARAGRAPHS 8–12	Lines up evidence (focusing on debt) to support the claim—and applies supportive sources

continued

A columnist for Forbes.com and a contributing editor to the *City Journal*, Joel Kotkin is the author of the 2010 book *The Next Hundred Million: America in 2050*. Because the following essay originally appeared in a magazine, Kotkin doesn't include a bibliography for the sources cited in his essay.

Today's youth, both here and abroad, have been screwed by their parents' fiscal profligacy and economic mismanagement. Neil Howe, a leading generational theorist, cites the "greed, shortsightedness, and blind partisanship" of the boomers, of whom he is one, for having "brought the global economy to its knees."

How has this generation been screwed? Let's count the ways, starting with the economy. No generation has suffered more from the Great Recession than the young. Median net worth of people under 35, according to the U.S. Census, fell 37 percent between 2005 and 2010; those over 65 took only a 13 percent hit.

The wealth gap today between younger and older Americans now stands as the widest on record. The median net worth of households headed by someone 65 or older is $170,494, 42 percent higher than in 1984, while the median net worth for younger-age households is $3,662, down 68 percent from a quarter century ago, according to an analysis by the Pew Research Center.

The older generation, notes Pew, were "the beneficiaries of good timing" in everything from a strong economy to a long rise in housing prices. In contrast, quick prospects for improvement are dismal for the younger generation.

5 One key reason: their indebted parents are not leaving their jobs, forcing younger people to put careers on hold. Since 2008 the percentage of the workforce under 25 has dropped 13.2 percent, according to the Bureau of Labor Statistics, while that of people over 55 has risen by 7.6 percent.

"Employers are often replacing entry-level positions meant for graduates with people who have more experience because the pool of applicants is so much larger. Basically when unemployment goes up, it disenfranchises the younger generation because they are the least qualified," observes Kyle Storms, a recent graduate from Chapman University in California.

Overall the young suffer stubbornly high unemployment rates—and an even higher incidence of underemployment. The unemployment rate for people between 18 and 29 is 12 percent in the U.S., nearly 50 percent above the national average. That's a far cry from the fearsome 50 percent rate seen in Spain or Greece, or the 35 percent in Italy and 22 percent in France and the U.K., but well above the 8 percent rate in Germany.

The screwed generation also enters adulthood loaded down by a mountain of boomer- and senior-incurred debt—debt that spirals ever more out of control. The public debt constitutes a toxic legacy handed over to offspring who will have to pay it off in at least three ways: through higher taxes, less infrastructure and social spending, and, fatefully, the prospect of painfully slow growth for the foreseeable future.

In the United States, the boomers' bill has risen to about $50,000 a person. In Japan, the red ink for the next generation comes in at more than $95,000 a person. One nasty solution to pay for this growing debt is to tax workers and consumers. Both Germany and Japan, which appears about to double its VAT rate, have been exploring new taxes to pay for the pensions of the boomers.

10   The huge public-employee pensions now driving many states and cities—most recently Stockton, Calif.—toward the netherworld of bankruptcy represent an extreme case of intergenerational transfer from young to old. It's a thoroughly rigged boomer game, providing guaranteed generous benefits to older public workers while handing the financial upper echelon a "Wall Street boondoggle" (to quote analyst Walter Russell Mead).

Then there is the debt that the millennials have incurred themselves. The average student, according to Forbes, already carries $12,700 in credit-card and other kinds of debt. Student loans have grown consistently over the last few decades to an average of $27,000 each. Nationwide in the U.S., tuition debt is close to $1 trillion.

This debt often results from the advice of teachers, largely boomers, that only more education—for which costs have risen at twice the rate of inflation since 2000—could solve the long-term issues of the young. "Our generation decided to go to school and continue into even higher forms of education like master's and Ph.D. programs, thinking this will give us an edge," notes Lizzie Guerra, a recent graduate from San Francisco State. "However, we found ourselves incredibly educated but drowning in piles of student loans with a job market that still isn't hiring."

More maddening still, the payback for this expensive education appears to be a chimera. Over 43 percent of recent graduates now working, according to a recent report by the Heldrich Center for Workforce Development, are at jobs that don't require a college education. Some 16 percent of bartenders and almost the same percentage of parking attendants, notes Ohio State economics professor Richard Vedder, earned a bachelor's degree or higher.

"I work at the Gap and Pacific Pak Ice, two jobs that I don't see myself working long term nor jobs that are specific to my major," notes recent University of Washington graduate Marshel L. Renz. "I've been applying to five jobs a week and have gotten nothing but rejections."

15   Particularly hard hit are those from less prestigious schools or with majors in the humanities, notes a recent Pew study. Among 2011 law-school graduates, half could not find a job in the legal field nine months after finishing school. But it's not just the lawyers and artists who are suffering. Overall the incomes earned by graduates have dropped over the last decade by 11 percent for men and 7.6 percent for women. No big surprise, then, that last year's class suffered the highest level of stress on record, according to an annual survey of college freshmen taken over the past quarter century.

The proliferation of graduate degrees also impacts those many Americans who don't go (or haven't yet gone) to college. High-school graduates now find themselves competing with college graduates for basic jobs in service businesses. Unemployment among 16- to 19-year-olds this summer is nearly 25 percent, while for high-school graduates between 2009 and 2011, only 16 percent have found full-time work, and 22 percent work part time.

Once known for their optimism, many millennials are turning sour about the future. According to a Rutgers study, 56 percent of recent high-school graduates feel they would not be financially more successful than their parents; only 14 percent thought they'd do better. College education doesn't seem to make a difference: 58 percent of recent graduates feel they won't do as well as the previous generation. Only 16 percent thought they'd do better.

This perception builds on the growing notion among economists that the new generation must lower its expectations. Since the financial panic of 2008, "the new normal" has become conventional wisdom. Coined by Mohamed El-Erian at Pimco, it's been used to describe our world as one "of muted Western growth, high unemployment and relatively orderly delevering."

The libertarian Tyler Cowen, in his landmark work *The Great Stagnation*, makes many of the same points, claiming that the U.S. "frontier" has closed both technologically and in terms of human capital and resources. He maintains that we've already harvested "the low-hanging fruit" and that we now rest on a "technological plateau," making any future economic progress difficult to achieve. Stagnation is not such a bad thing for people already established in college-campus jobs, think tanks, or powerful financial institutions. But it wipes out the hope for the new generation that they can achieve anything resembling the American Dream of their parents or even grandparents.

20   Inevitably, young people are delaying their leap into adulthood. Nearly a third of people between 18 and 34 have put off marriage or having a baby due to the recession, and a quarter have moved back to their parents' homes, according to a Pew study. These decisions have helped cut the birthrate by 11 percent by 2011, while the marriage rate slumped 6.8 percent. The baby-boom echo generation could propel historically fecund America toward the kind of demographic disaster already evident in parts of Europe and Japan.

The worst effects of the "new normal" can be seen among noncollege graduates. Conservative analysts such as Charles Murray point out the deterioration of family life—as measured by illegitimacy and low marriage rates—among working-class whites; among white American women with only a high-school education, 44 percent of births are out of wedlock, up from 6 percent in 1970. With incomes dropping and higher unemployment, Murray predicts the emergence of a growing "white underclass" in the coming decade.

The prospect of downward mobility is most evident in recent discussions about the future of the housing market. Since World War II the expectation of each generation was to own property, preferably a single-family house. The large majority of boomers became homeowners during the Reagan-Clinton era. Yet it is increasingly fashionable to insist this "dream" must be expunged. If millennials ever move out of their parents' house, they will live in apartments they don't own. There's a lot of talk about a "generation rent" replacing a primarily suburban ownership society with a new caste of city-dwelling renters. "I'm hoping that the millennial generation doesn't set its sights on homeownership as a benchmark of economic stability," sociologist Katherine Newman suggests, "because it's going to be out of reach for so many of them."

No doubt the prospects for homeownership will be tough in the years ahead. But it's delusional to believe millennials don't desire the same things as previous generations, note generational chroniclers Morley Winograd and Mike Hais. Survey research finds that 84 percent of 18- to 34-year-olds who are currently renting say that they intend to buy a home even if they can't currently afford to do so; 64 percent said it was "very important" to have an opportunity to own their own home.

And where do millennials see their dream house? According to research at Frank Magid Associates, 43 percent describe suburbs as their "ideal place to live," compared with just 31 percent of older generations. Even though big cities are often preferred among college graduates in their 20s, only 17 percent of millennials say they want to settle permanently in one. This was the same percentage of members of this generation who expressed a preference for living in rural or small-town America.

25   So far, the Great Recession has driven young people around the high-income world to the left. Generations growing up in recessions appear more amenable to

arguments for government-mandated income redistribution. And since so few young people pay much in the way of taxes, they are less affronted by the prospect of forking over than older voters, who do. This left-leaning tendency has been on display in recent European elections. In France, 57 percent voters 18 to 24 supported the Socialist François Hollande, one of the reasons why the conservative Nicolas Sarkozy lost. Similarly, 37 percent of those in that age category voted for Syrizia, the far-left party in Greece.

But Winograd and Hais—and Democratic strategist Ruy Teixeira—say it's not just economics working for the Democrats. Social issues such as gay marriage, women's rights, and immigration—a large proportion of millennials are children of newcomers—tend to drive younger voters toward the Democrats. Half of millennials, for example, favor gay marriage, compared with a third of boomers, and some predict the Republican embrace of draconian social conservatism will serve to harden the Democratic tilt of millennials for the foreseeable future.

Yet Republicans may take heart from some of the more conservative values embraced by the young. As a group, millennials appear to be very family-oriented—being good parents is often their highest priority—and roughly two thirds claim to believe in God. And since their long-term aspirations are not so different from those of earlier generations—they still want to own a home in a nice, secure neighborhood—Republicans could make a case that their economic model will work better with their personal goals.

Right now, politics is just another place where American millennials are getting screwed. Republicans want to deport young Latinos while cutting investments, such as roads and skills education, that would benefit younger voters. Democrats, meanwhile, seem determined to mortgage the future with high spending on pensions, predominantly for aging boomers; cascading indebtedness; and economic policies unfriendly to the rapid growth necessary to assure upward mobility for the new generation.

This suggests millennials need to force the parties to cater to them and play hard to get. Being taken for granted, as African-Americans have been, does not always produce the best results for any demographic grouping. Politicians target "soccer moms," "independents," and suburban voters precisely because they are not predictable. Millennials should not want to be in anyone's hip pocket.

30   Wanting the next generation to succeed is in everyone's long-term interest. Eventually they will constitute the majority of parents, potential homeowners, and workers. This year [2012] they will comprise 24 percent of voting-age adults, up from 18 percent in 2008; by 2020 they will amount to a third of all eligible voters. And if, by then, they are still a screwed generation, they won't be the only ones suffering. America will be screwed, too.

Think Before You Breed
by Christine Overall

STUDY THE MOVES

In the following blog post, Christine Overall considers the ethics of procreation (having children). She claims that the decision to procreate should hinge on thorough reasons. She then carefully breaks down the reasons on both sides of the decision. Throughout, Overall makes several of the moves described in

continued

An expert on feminist philosophy and bioethics, Christine Overall has published numerous articles and books, including the 2012 book *Why Have Children? The Ethical Debate*.

Chapter 5 ("Dismantle Arguments"), Chapter 6 ("Justify Your Position"), and Chapter 8 ("Escape the Status Quo"):

PARAGRAPHS 1–3	Examines the context of the procreation question
PARAGRAPH 4	Calls out quiet assumptions about the decision not to procreate
PARAGRAPHS 5–6	Asserts a claim about the decision not to procreate
PARAGRAPHS 7–8	Examines the often ignored ethics of having children
PARAGRAPHS 9–11	Questions the reasoning behind the decision to procreate
PARAGRAPH 12	States the purpose of the argument
PARAGRAPHS 13–14	Breaks down reasons for the claim
PARAGRAPH 15	Dismantles and denies the opposition
PARAGRAPHS 16–19	Supports reasons for the claim
PARAGRAPH 20	Reasserts the main claim and connects to a broad principle

As a young woman in my 20s I pondered whether or not to have children. Is there a way, I wondered, to decide thoughtfully rather than carelessly about this most momentous of human choices?

It's a tough decision because you can't know ahead of time what sort of child you will have or what it will be like to be a parent. You can't understand what is good or what is hard about the process of creating and rearing until after you have the child. And the choice to have a child is a decision to change your life forever. It's irreversible, and therefore, compared to reversible life choices about education, work, geographical location or romance, it has much greater ethical importance.

Choosing whether or not to procreate may not seem like the sort of decision that is deserving or even capable of analysis. The Canadian novelist Margaret Laurence wrote, "I don't really feel I have to analyze my own motives in wanting children. For my own reassurance? For fun? For ego-satisfaction? No matter. It's like (to me) asking why you want to write. Who cares? You have to, and that's that."

In fact, people are still expected to provide reasons *not* to have children, but no reasons are required to have them. It's assumed that if individuals do not have children it is because they are infertile, too selfish or have just not yet gotten around to it. In any case, they owe their interlocutor an explanation. On the other hand, no one says to the proud parents of a newborn, Why did you choose to have that child? What are your reasons? The choice to procreate is not regarded as needing any thought or justification.

5   Nonetheless, I think Laurence's "Who cares?" attitude is mistaken.

We are fortunate that procreation is more and more a matter of choice. Not always, of course—not everyone has access to effective contraception and accessible abortion, and some women are subjected to enforced pregnancy. But the growing availability of reproductive choice makes it clear that procreation cannot be merely an expression of personal taste.

The question whether to have children is of course prudential in part; it's concerned about what is or is not in one's own interests. But it is *also* an ethical question, for it is about whether to bring a person (in some cases more than one person) into existence—and that person cannot, by the very nature of the situation, give consent to being brought into existence. Such a question also profoundly affects the well-being of existing people (the potential parents, siblings if any, and grandparents). And it has effects beyond the family on the broader society, which is inevitably changed by the cumulative impact—on things like education, health care, employment, agriculture, community growth and design, and the availability and distribution of resources—of individual decisions about whether to procreate.

There are self-help books on the market that purport to assist would-be parents in making a practical choice about whether or not to have children. There are also informal discussions on Web sites, in newspapers and magazines and in blogs. Yet the ethical nature of this choice is seldom recognized, even—or especially—by philosophers.

Perhaps people fail to see childbearing as an ethical choice because they think of it as the expression of an instinct or biological drive, like sexual attraction or "falling in love," that is not amenable to ethical evaluation. But whatever our biological inclinations may be, many human beings do take control over their fertility, thanks to contemporary means of contraception and abortion. The rapidly declining birthrate in most parts of the world is evidence of that fact. While choosing whether or not to have children may involve feelings, motives, impulses, memories and emotions, it can and should also be a subject for careful reflection.

10   If we fail to acknowledge that the decision of whether to parent or not is a real choice that has ethical import, then we are treating childbearing as a mere expression of biological destiny. Instead of seeing having children as something that women *do*, we will continue to see it as something that simply *happens* to women, or as something that is merely "natural" and animal-like.

The decision to have children surely deserves at least as much thought as people devote to leasing a car or buying a house. Procreation decisions are about whether or not to assume complete responsibility, over a period of at least 18 years, for a new life or new lives. Because deciding whether to procreate has ethical dimensions, the reasons people give for their procreative choices deserve examination. Some reasons may be better—or worse—than others.

My aim, I hasten to add, is not to argue for policing people's procreative motives. I am simply arguing for the need to think systematically and deeply about a fundamental aspect of human life.

The burden of proof—or at least the burden of justification—should therefore rest primarily on those who choose to have children, not on those who choose to be childless. The choice to have children calls for more careful justification and thought than the choice not to have children because procreation creates a dependent, needy, and vulnerable human being whose future may be at risk. The individual who chooses childlessness takes the ethically less risky path. After all, nonexistent people can't suffer from not being created. They do not have an entitlement to come into existence, and we do not owe it to them to bring them into existence. But once children do exist, we incur serious responsibilities to them.

Because children are dependent, needy and vulnerable, prospective parents should consider how well they can love and care for the offspring they create, and the kind of relationship they can have with them. The genuinely unselfish life plan may at least sometimes be the choice not to have children, especially in the case of individuals who would otherwise procreate merely to adhere to tradition, to please others, to conform to gender conventions, or to benefit themselves out of the inappropriate expectation that children will fix their problems. Children are neither human pets nor little therapists.

15   Some people claim that the mere fact that our offspring will probably be happy gives us ample reason to procreate. The problem with this argument is, first, that there are no guarantees. The sheer unpredictability of children, the limits on our capacities as parents, and the instability of social conditions make it unwise to take for granted that our progeny will have good lives. But just as important, justifying having kids by claiming that our offspring will be happy

provides no stopping point for procreative behavior. If two children are happy, perhaps four will be, or seven, or 10.

The unwillingness to stop is dramatized by the so-called Octomom, Nadya Suleman, who first had six children via in vitro fertilization, then ended up with eight more from just one pregnancy, aided by her reprehensible doctor, Michael Kamrava. Higher-order-multiple pregnancies often create long-term health problems for the children born of them. It's also unlikely that Suleman can provide adequate care for and attention to her 14 children under the age of 12, especially in light of her recent bankruptcy, her very public attempts to raise money, and the impending loss of their home. Was Suleman's desire for a big family fair to her helpless offspring?

Consider also reality television "stars" Michelle and Jim Bob Duggar, the parents of 19 children. The Duggars claim to have religious motives for creating their large family. But it's not at all clear that God places such a high value on the Duggar genetic heritage. Unlike Suleman, the Duggars don't struggle to support their brood, but mere financial solvency is not a sufficient reason to birth more than a dozen and a half offspring, even if the kids seem reasonably content.

People like the Duggars and Suleman might respond that they have a right to reproduce. Certainly they are entitled to be free from state interference in their procreative behavior; compulsory contraception and abortion, or penalties for having babies, are abhorrent. But a right to non-interference does not, by itself, justify every decision to have a baby.

We should not regret the existence of the children in these very public families, now that they are here. My point is just that their parents' models of procreative decision making deserve skepticism. The parents appear to overlook what is ethically central: the possibility of forming a supportive, life-enhancing and close relationship with each of their offspring.

20   After struggling with our own decision about whether to procreate, in the end my spouse and I chose to have

two children, whom we adore. The many rewards and challenges of raising kids have gradually revealed the far-reaching implications of procreative decision making. In choosing to become a parent, one seeks to create a relationship, and, uniquely, one also seeks to create the person with whom one has the relationship. Choosing whether or not to have children is therefore the most significant ethical debate of most people's lives.

CHANGE THE TERMS

The Third World
by John McCormick

STUDY THE MOVES

In the following essay, John McCormick calls for a change in terms—specifically in the way that political scientists characterize economically struggling countries. You don't need to be a political science major to see (and use) the moves he's making throughout the essay, which are described in Chapter 1 ("Seek Complexity") and Chapter 7 ("Change the Terms"):

PARAGRAPHS 1–2	Examines the phrase *third world* and its historical context
PARAGRAPH 3	Explains the problem with *third world*
PARAGRAPHS 4–6	Explains how the term ignores the real complexity
PARAGRAPH 7	Describes the ongoing questions and the need for new terms

---

A professor at Indiana University, Purdue University Indianapolis, John McCormick is an expert on comparative politics and the European Union and the author of the 2010 book *Europeanism*.

Throughout the cold war (late 1940s to late 1980s), it was usual for political scientists and economists to think of the world as divided up into three groups of countries: the US-led Western alliance, the Soviet-led communist bloc, and all the rest. The division was initially driven by the military and ideological differences between the United States and the Soviet Union, and in 1952 the French demographer Alfred Sauvy coined the term *third world* to describe all the countries of Asia, Africa, and Latin America that did not align themselves with either of the cold war superpowers. Although the label was initially driven by geopolitics, it quickly came to take on economic and social qualities, and talk of the "third world" soon came to refer to the emerging states of the post-imperial era.

The term was neat and memorable, and could easily be inserted into discussions about the experiences and problems of countries outside North America, Europe, and the Soviet bloc. Even today, we still hear the occasional reference to third world conditions of poverty, underdevelopment, corruption, and political instability. The term is even sometimes used pejoratively to describe particularly backward and troubled regions of the United States and Europe. The term *fourth world* has been added on to describe more extreme cases of underdevelopment, and the nun Mother Theresa—after decades of experience working in the slums of Calcutta, India—was so horrified by what she saw during a visit to the slums of Port-au-Prince, Haiti, that she described them as the "fifth world."

People like to use labels, particularly if they can neatly summarize complex ideas or situations, and they are particularly useful for the purposes of comparative politics. When we try to study and make sense of the more than 190 independent states in the world today, it helps to have a *typology*, or a system of classification that divides states into groups with common features. This allows us to make sense of a complex world; if we can group countries according to their shared political, economic, and social features, then we can choose cases from among the groups in order to help us develop explanations and rules, and test theories. But while the term *third world* was simple and neat, it was also a dangerous oversimplification; the more than 135 countries that were once considered part of the third world had much in common, but they also had many differences.

Some were politically stable and vibrant while others were unstable and occasionally authoritarian, many of them breaking down in civil war or being governed by dictators of military governments. Some had been independent for decades and had developed a strong sense of national identity, while others became independent only after the Second World War and were struggling to build national unity. Some had dynamic industrial economies and an evolving middle class, while others were mired in poverty and dependent upon low-profit agricultural exports. Some were investing effectively in basic services such as education and health care, while others came to epitomize the worst effects of social division and dysfunction.

5   With the end of the cold war, which came some time between the fall of the Berlin Wall in September 1989 and the breakup of the Soviet Union in December 1991, it was clear that the idea of the third world had little remaining value. The continuing political and economic development of countries such as Brazil, India, Argentina, Indonesia, and Malaysia stood in stark contrast to the qualities represented by third-world poverty and instability. The Islamic world had taken on a new political significance in the wake of the 1979 Iranian Revolution, and there were the first clear indications that the balance of economic power in the world was changing. This was confirmed during the global financial crisis of 2007–10 when several emerging economies—including China, India, and Brazil—weathered the

storm while the United States and Europe underwent massive downturns.

But poverty and instability have not gone away, and in some cases the problems of the most dysfunctional states in the world have become worse. This has led to the invention of a variety of new terms, those that come closest to capturing the spirit of the third world, including *marginal states*, *failing states*, or *failed states*. There is no agreement on just how many of these there are, or where they are, or what qualities they must have, but the lists will usually include examples such as Haiti, Somalia, the Democratic Republic of Congo, Sudan, and Zimbabwe. These are countries with weak and ineffective political institutions, where organized government has sometimes collapsed altogether, with failing or failed economies, and whose people often face severe social deprivation brought by civil war, natural disasters, famine, or incompetent and corrupt government.

There is still no generally accepted typology to help guide the work of comparative political scientists, many of whom dispense with the notion of classification altogether; they prefer to compare institutions or concepts (such as democracy and development) broadly defined rather than tie them to system-types. However, the remarkable political and economic changes since the end of the cold war have not only hammered the final nails into the coffin of the term *third world*, they have also created a more pressing need for a more nuanced understanding of the political and economic differences among states. The field of comparative politics has become more complex and in some ways more disorderly, leaving political scientists undecided about how to best understand and make sense of the political world. It remains to be seen what will emerge in terms of labels that can help guide us through the maze.

Acronym Headaches
by Kathleen Schenck

STUDY THE MOVES

In the following essay, Kathleen Schenck calls for a change in terms—more specifically for a change in the acronym for her teaching field. As the essay develops, Schenck examines several common acronyms (TESOL, ESOL, ESL) and describes the flaws in each. In the process, she makes several of the moves described in Chapter 3 ("Apply Sources"), Chapter 7 ("Change the Terms"), and Chapter 8 ("Escape the Status Quo"):

PARAGRAPH 1	Introduces a range of acronyms in the field of TESOL
PARAGRAPHS 2–3	Describes the inaccuracy of *ESL*
PARAGRAPHS 4–5	Describes the quiet associations of *second*—and applies supportive sources
PARAGRAPH 6	Describes the inaccuracy of *other*
PARAGRAPHS 7–8	Describes the flawed assumptions surrounding both *second* and *other*
PARAGRAPH 9	Proposes a new term (*ELL*) and explains how it avoids problems
PARAGRAPH 10	Explains the potential damage of not changing terms

In the field of TESOL, which stands for Teaching English to Speakers of Other Languages, acronyms and abbreviations rule supreme. Both ESOL (English for Speakers of Other Languages) and ESL (English as a Second Language) refer to teaching English to students who don't

Kathleen Schenck, a poet and college instructor, holds degrees in TESOL and creative writing.

Reprinted by permission of Kathleen Schenck.

already speak it in a country where English is the primary or official language (i.e., what all the street signs are in; what the legal system uses; what the majority of people speak). But the field of TESOL also uses terms like Limited English Proficiency (LEP), English for Academic Purposes (EAP), English for Non-Native Learners (ENNL), and (too) many others to describe learning English. Imagine being a student who doesn't speak English looking through a course catalog trying to find the right class to take.

Of all these terms, ESL is used most often because more people understand its meaning. Harvard and Stanford both use it, while George Washington and Portland State eschew it. One need only peruse the course catalog at any given institution of higher learning to gain a better understanding of that institution's attention and dedication to the ever-growing field of TESOL. Plainly put, if the school still uses the term ESL, the school lags behind current thought and practice.

The field is hard-pressed to agree on its title, TESOL, much less the term to use for the classes and students taught therein. "Applied Linguistics" sometimes serves as a substitute for TESOL, and one can pursue a master's degree in either. (Indiana University solves the problem by offering a "M.A. in TESOL and Applied Linguistics.") If it is widely understood by professionals and laypeople alike, what, then, is the problem with simply using the term ESL? For openers, the term is often inaccurate. The student may already have a second language . . . and a third, fourth, eighth. A Swiss national may know Italian, German, French, and even Romansch before attempting English. A citizen of Brazil may speak Portuguese and German first, thus making English her third language. English may also be acquired simultaneously—that is, alongside one or more languages. The term ESL implies, incorrectly, that languages are always acquired separately and one at a time.

Another issue with the term ESL involves the message it sends to non-native English speakers. "Second" implies that a non-native speaker's English will always play second fiddle to a native speaker's English. A student studying the English language may feel that no matter how hard she tries, she will never achieve a native speaker fluency or dialect; she will never "sound like an American." She fears her accent will set her apart and prevent her from being understood as well as accepted. However, there is no one "appropriate" or standard dialect of English. The term *Standard American English* exists only as an "idealization" (Fromkin, Rodman, and Hyams 455). Linguists and teachers tried and failed to define a standard dialect during a conference in the 1990s (Fromkin, Rodman, and Hyams 455). In fact, as many dialects exist as speakers, which means literally millions of dialects of the English language are spoken every day (Fromkin, Rodman, and Hyams 445).

5   So what is "secondary" about an English language learner's dialect, or accent? Many Midwesterners wrongly assume they hold the monopoly in their usage of *the* proper American English, as do residents in the Great Plains and beyond. The first rule of linguistics is no one dialect trumps another; that is to say beauty is in the eye (or ear) of the beholder. Of the millions of English dialects spoken, it is up to the listener to decide what sounds "appropriate." To an American, a British accent may sound intelligent while an Italian one sounds sexy. But the United States is chock-full of accents (not to mention connotations associated with those accents) from native speakers of American English, too. Presidents Jimmy Carter and Bill Clinton fought against stereotypes of Southerners being "slow" or unintelligent while they drawled through debates and interviews. Comedian Seth Meyers held Donald Trump's accent up to scrutiny by joking, "I like that Trump is filthy rich but nobody told his accent" (C-SPAN).

Accents aside, there's also an issue with using *other* in the acronyms TESOL and ESOL. *Other* conjures up images of something that is different than the norm and therefore out of place. (Think *Sesame Street*'s "One of the these things is not like the other. . . .") A foreign exchange student from South Korea is seen as *other* in a hallway of white faces at a rural Michigan public high school. Another issue is again the inaccuracy of the term ESOL. At my high school, students chose Spanish, French, German, or Latin classes to fulfill the foreign language requirement. The token "dead" language of Latin aside, we teenagers at a Midwestern public high school qualified as "speakers of other languages" who were also, of course, taking English classes. The term ESOL fails to differentiate between those learning English as a language and those studying Shakespeare in order to gain AP status for a lighter first-year college course load.

Since the majority of Americans speak English only, the Ameri-centric assumption would follow the same logic for other countries and their inhabitants. I had a Midwestern-centric understanding of word choices before travelling to other areas of the country. I thought everyone knew what a Vernors was. Imagine my surprise when I discovered not only was Vernors unavailable outside Michigan, but that "pop" was met with scrunched eyebrows and confused looks, ending with some version of, oh, you mean a Coke/soda/soda pop. When it comes to language, we often think in terms of our own experience. Because many of us are monolingual, we wrongly assume that an immigrant to the United States must speak only one language; therefore, English would be his or her second language. But of course this simply isn't so.

Furthermore, due to recent "English only" stampedes on the political landscape, the term ESL suggests English is learned immediately—directly after the native language. This immediacy more than hints at biases toward immigrants and those speaking languages other than English in the United

States. Again the term ESL fails us in its assertion that languages are always learned one at a time, and that English must be second in line after the speaker's native language.

A new term is needed. In fact, one already exists: ELL. ELL stands for English Language Learner. This term subtracts the numbers from the equation altogether and focuses on the positive as well as the present: currently, this person is learning English. The level of proficiency is not brought into question, nor is the native language or dialect of English being learned. The logic behind the term ELL acknowledges that English is a subject to be studied, like geology or math. I did not, for example, sign up for High School Geometry for Those Who Have Never Done Well in Math, or HSGT-WHNDWM. ELL acknowledges that the English language contains a multitude of dialects—many of which are found in the United States. A non-native English speaker showcases just another dialect. This dialect is not secondary to any other dialect, nor is it indicative of the speaker being less intelligent, more of an outsider, or unfinished in some way. Furthermore, learning English is not synonymous with a promise to use only English. If the speaker knows two languages or seven, she may enjoy a more culturally and linguistically diverse life in many of America's metropolitan areas than most monolingual speakers of American English currently enjoy. With a wider acceptance into varied cultural groups comes a wider understanding of the same groups, increasing one's intercultural competence, employability, and, one could argue, compassion.

10   TESOL professionals who continue to use ESL because their employers use it or because it's simply "easier" further the acceptance of an outdated and inaccurate term riddled with political and social miscues. They do their students and the general public a disservice by not telling the truth, the full story. They fail to acknowledge and elaborate on the context in which we live in this twenty-first-century global society. We have airplanes now. The Internet. Donald Trump!

Works Cited

C-SPAN. "Seth Meyers Remarks at the 2011 White House Correspondents' Dinner." *C-SPAN Video Library*. C-SPAN, 30 Apr. 2011. Web. 21 Feb. 2012.

Fromkin, Victoria, Robert Rodman, and Nina Hyams. *An Introduction to Language*. 7th ed. Boston: Thomson, 2003. Print.

ESCAPE THE STATUS QUO
••••••••••••••••••••••••

When Race Is in the Room
by Michael Anderson

STUDY THE MOVES

In the following essay, Michael Anderson calls out widely held beliefs about race. In the process, he examines several events that prompt new thinking about the racial status quo. Throughout, Anderson makes several of the moves described in Chapter 2 ("Seek Tension"), Chapter 3 ("Apply Sources"), Chapter 7 ("Change the Terms"), Chapter 8 ("Escape the Status Quo"), and Chapter 9 ("Assess Your Thinking"):

PARAGRAPHS 1–10	Examines a real event, which prompts thinking about race
PARAGRAPH 11	Detects subtle tension in a personal encounter
PARAGRAPHS 12–15	Connects to a broader tension about race
PARAGRAPH 16	Calls out quiet assumptions that reinforce racial prejudice

continued

Michael Anderson, a communications instructor at Northwestern Michigan College, holds degrees in journalism and media studies.

PARAGRAPH 17	Applies a supportive source to explain racial literacy
PARAGRAPH 18	Describes the quiet associations of the term *they*
PARAGRAPH 19	Examines another real event, which prompts further thinking about race
PARAGRAPH 20	Calls out quiet cultural assumptions about race
PARAGRAPHS 21–22	Examines another real event to explain the impact of these assumptions
PARAGRAPH 23	Describes new thinking about the racial status quo

Even though I wasn't raised to be hateful, only colorblind, it's fortunate that my first real encounter with race was touched by both comedy and chance.

I'd decided to move downstate to attend a university in southwest Michigan and planned to live in the dorms. The housing request form had asked, "Would you be interested in living with someone from another culture?" I checked "Yes," thinking that it would be good for me. "That's what college is all about," I quipped. And during the ensuing summer of digging, planting trees, and chasing the sun, I thought about living with someone from Malaysia, or Germany, or even Gilgit-Baltistan. But when the room assignment arrived months later, bearing the name of my roommate, I saw, with some disappointment, that I had been paired instead with a "Charles Welch," who could not possibly have been from Thailand, India, or Ukraine.

Or Monrovia.

Having said final goodbyes to my family, and now standing in a tiny, empty room, I spotted the lone personal effect placed by Charles: a large, framed painting depicting the Black Jesus. Even then, as I closely examined its various panels, I assumed that momentarily, a white guy, perhaps one deeply into reggae, would walk in and introduce himself.

5   When he did arrive, my surprise was acute. Charles was black, and from Detroit. We both stood there, staring at each other. Music boomed and echoed inside the vast halls. Even with the man in front of me, I couldn't quite believe it. Charles was black. I felt dull at not even having considered the possibility.

Our confusion, it turned out, had been mutual:

"You thought I was going to be black?"

"Yeah," he said. "Sounds like a black guy's name. 'Michael Anderson?'"

Just by the way he said it, I understood. There had probably been plenty of Andersons, Johnsons, and Williamses at his school in Detroit.

10   Then he got quiet and said this: "I've never lived with a white person." There was a long silence. And I saw Charles forget that I was in the room: he disappeared inside himself to see if he could really do this.

But this impression of him privately deciding is something perceptible to me only now, many years later. In that room, my focus was on what to say or how to act—I wasn't even aware that he was deciding something. For me, race had always been easy, because it had almost always been at a distance, something I could ignore, discount, or get away from. Now it felt hard, complicated, and immediate. He knew quite a bit more about meeting Michael Anderson than I knew about meeting Charles Welch.

Conversations about race today are often about what you should and shouldn't say. It's big news when some public figure says something stupid or insensitive about race. Shaming the offender, depending on the extent and nature of the slur, is a standard social media ritual. Such stories make race seem like a simple matter of choosing one's words and so contribute to a sense of race as being "settled" in America. Betrayed especially by awkward stumbles or dimwitted slurs from politicians, actors, or comedians, race is far from settled. In fact, it feels like a collective blind spot is still growing, and it has the shape and size of a blind spot that is acquired simply from growing up white in a mostly white region.

The thing was, *they* just weren't ever around, or so it seemed. Mexican laborers worked the farms every summer, and there was a Native American reservation ten miles from where I grew up. But we hardly saw them. Seeing a black person was an event you would share with your friends. In twelve years of school, the only black classmate I can remember was Gloria, from second grade, who drew circles in crayon on her desk even when the teacher told her to stop. If I hadn't traveled so extensively, it is likely that she would have been the only black person I would have interacted with during my childhood.

In early elementary school, we learned about the "melting pot." We looked at a large, illustrated poster showing a number of different "types" of people, their "nationality" signaled by dress, hair color, the presence of a mustache or even a musical instrument, each with a big smile and all swimming in an immense, Stars-and-Stripes-themed stew pot. The metaphor has since been dropped from the State of Michigan's curriculum. While useful for explaining that difference can enrich the whole, the "melting" part of the metaphor is now seen as toxic, as it presupposed that racial difference is something ideally boiled down to a generic, indistinguishable soup.

15   Like many students at the time, we talked about the "N-word." Our class studied the word's entry in an old school dictionary, and as we weighed the pseudo-scientific language against its known cultural obsolescence, we felt secure that time had done its job. We felt sad for the ignorance of the

past and happy that things had changed. And these were some of our easiest lessons, because they jibed with other, larger stories about national progress that presented the ideal America as race-blind, which again subtly confirmed our lack of experience. Although our awareness was likely raised, race became just another subject among many in school that didn't seem to apply to our lives. The innumerable small lessons of socialization—the sublime and the squabbling, the in- and out-group training, the humiliations of hallway culture, the panic of junior-high firsts—all occurred in race-neutral settings. The false sense of race neutrality made it easier to regard race as a non-factor—even to think that's the way it should be in an ideal world.

One way we did encounter race, at a distance, was through sports. Like most of my friends, I worshipped sports stars, especially those who played basketball, most of whom were black. Our chatter about players and the big games included discussions about why black people dominated sports. We took a rational, common-sense position on the matter: for reasons of history, geography, and culture, black people were "natural" athletes, built of leaner muscle and longer bones, graced with agility and speed. In addition to *their* having hunted and gathered so recently, the selectivity and trials of hundreds of years of slavery, it was reasoned, had made *them* stronger, bigger. When it came to "jumps" or "hops," *they* had more of them, and not because they were black, but for reasons that were so safe, so easy to accept, so not about race. At the same time, when these ideas were uttered by some hapless, soon-to-be-fired commentator for NBA Gameday, we shook our heads and said, "There are some things you just don't say."

Minding one's words is good advice but isn't an adequate substitute for genuine racial literacy. Nor can our ignorance be "forgiven" for lacking malicious intent: since we didn't know we were being racist, how could we be faulted? According to

Shannon Sullivan, author of *Revealing Whiteness: The Uncon-scious Habits of Racial Privilege*, this conventional under-standing of ignorance is misleading, and "ha[s] the effect of excusing people for their racism" (18). Nor can racial illiteracy be solved simply by providing accurate information, argues Sullivan, who goes on to say, "Even though logical arguments about race might lead a person to consciously decide to endorse non-racist ideas, such a decision does not necessarily have much, if any, impact on his or her unconscious habits" (22). In other words, if we truly want to understand racial thinking, our good intentions may be put to their best use mining our hidden personal histories with race.

What we didn't see was our own way of processing, our own collective blindness, our own intellectual habits: we were dealing with race by accepting another way to ignore it. It didn't occur to us to challenge the broad, gaping generalization represented by the collective pronoun *they* because it seemed so very obvious: black people. The label was unexamined, incontrovertible, totalizing. Maybe we needed to hear a deep and perhaps menacing voice inquire, "Who do you mean by *they*?" Or perhaps we needed a black friend who was good at radio-controlled cars, racing bikes, and chess, which were other things we enjoyed.

And there was this: my first race against a black kid, who attended a private school nearby. While stretching near the starting line before the two-mile race, I remember feel-ing intimidated and outmatched by his "natural" ability. At the time, running was very important to me, and his was a physique I coveted—a long, thin, feral silhouette, which I wasn't ever going to have, owing to my stocky build. I fin-ished in the middle of the pack, as usual, but I had beaten *him*. I remember feeling good about having outrun him partly because he was black . . . and then in the next instant feeling hot guilt. I sought him out to bump hands and say "good race" when he finished. It felt awkward, like I was being polite on principle.

20   The revealing truth is that when we did encounter people of other races growing up in Northern Michigan, real communication didn't often happen. It seemed like there was always something in the way, something that preceded them, marked them in our minds. And since our actual encounters with race were so fleeting, we didn't get enough practice seeing beyond the expectations given to us—expectations about the progress of culture and the end of racism. We were so saturated in advertising, news media, and history class that we measured each real encounter against the bigger story of progress, and even against our wills. With hindsight, this dissonance seems to result from being raised to think that the ideal meeting of races occurs when race is somehow not a factor at all.

As a child, I did have one native friend: Matt Lewis. We became friends because our fathers were both Vietnam veterans and members of the Army Reserve station in Traverse City. Matt and I met there at the annual picnic, during summer, far away from school and our usual hangouts. We climbed on top of the trucks, threw water balloons, ate too many hotdogs, and watched our dads get into formation and yell in unison. I can still see Matt's face in front of me, with its chiseled features and crooked teeth, laughing. He was big like his father and as healthy as a raccoon. Matt was the biggest kid in class, and I, being small, admired him for his power and his bravery.

Somehow, during sixth grade, his last name became a joke. Just to goad Matt, one kid started saying it "Looo-Whee!" This went on for a few months. One day, the situation climaxed during a game of twenty-one. After taking a hard foul, and with the jokester saying "Looo-Whee," Matt stood to take his free throws, and the joke had finally gone on too long. Matt told him to stop it. Urged on by the others, and, to my shame, I joined them. Matt took it for a while, then turned to me and said—and I will never forget this— "Hey man, you don't need to be that way." But I laughed and continued to chant the same, stupid nonsense. "Looo-whee! Looo-whee!" Matt put the ball down and walked away.

Twenty-five years later, I still cringe when I think about it. We may not have targeted him because he was native, but if I'm honest with myself, I can't say that race hadn't been there, though in a way that we eleven-year-olds couldn't fathom. Maybe the quiet racial assumptions beneath our taunting had been clear to him. I don't know. Though we talked again, we didn't talk about what happened because it seemed easier not to. From time to time, I try to look him up, but his name, so common like my own, resists tracking down.

Work Cited

Sullivan, Shannon. *Revealing Whiteness: The Unconscious Habits of Racial Privilege.* Bloomington: Indiana UP, 2006. Print.

The "Scientific" Argument for Cheer by Barbara Ehrenreich

STUDY THE MOVES

In the following essay, Barbara Ehrenreich interrogates the often-assumed connection between positive thinking and cancer survival. Throughout, Ehrenreich applies a range of sources to dismantle and deny the opposition and to build toward a new way of thinking. In the process, she makes several of the moves described in Chapter 3 ("Apply Sources"), Chapter 5 ("Dismantle Arguments"), Chapter 6 ("Justify Your Position"), Chapter 8 ("Escape the Status Quo"), and Chapter 9 ("Assess Your Thinking"):

continued

A widely published political activist and feminist, Barbara Ehrenreich is the author of the 2011 book *Complaints and Disorders: The Sexual Politics of Sickness.*

Source: *Bright-Sided: How the Relentless Promotion of Positive Thinking has Undermined America* © 2009 by Barbara Ehrenreich. Used by Permission. All rights reserved.

There was, I learned, an urgent medical reason to embrace cancer with a smile: a "positive attitude" is supposedly essential to recovery. During the months when I was undergoing chemotherapy, I encountered this assertion over and over—on Web sites, in books, from oncology nurses and fellow sufferers. Eight years later, it remains almost axiomatic, within the breast cancer culture, that survival hinges on "attitude." One study found 60 percent of women who had been treated for the disease attributing their continued survival to a "positive attitude."[1] In articles and on their Web sites, individuals routinely take pride in this supposedly lifesaving mental state. "The key is all about having a positive attitude, which I've tried to have since the

1. <http://www.cfah.org/hbns/newsrelease/women3-07-01.cfm>.

beginning," a woman named Sherry Young says in an article entitled "Positive Attitude Helped Woman Beat Cancer."[2]

"Experts" of various sorts offer a plausible-sounding explanation for the salubrious properties of cheerfulness. A recent e-zine article entitled "Breast Cancer Prevention Tips"—and the notion of breast cancer "prevention" should itself set off alarms, since there is no known means of prevention—for example, advises that:

> A simple positive and optimistic attitude has been shown to reduce the risk of cancer. This will sound amazing to many people; however, it will suffice to explain that several medical studies have demonstrated the link between a positive attitude and an improved immune system. Laughter and humor has [sic] been shown to enhance the body's immunity and prevents against cancer and other diseases. You must have heard the slogan "happy people don't fall sick." (Russell)

No wonder my "angry" post was greeted with so much dismay on the Komen site: my respondents no doubt believed that a positive attitude boosts the immune system, empowering it to battle cancer more effectively.

You've probably read that assertion so often, in one form or another, that it glides by without a moment's thought about what the immune system is, how it might be affected by emotions, and what, if anything, it could do to fight cancer. The business of the immune system is to defend the body against foreign intruders, such as microbes, and it does so with a huge onslaught of cells and whole cascades of different molecular weapons. The complexity, and diversity, of the mobilization is overwhelming: Whole tribes and subtribes of cells assemble at the site of infection, each

---

2. <http://www.nugget.ca/webapp/sitepages/content.asp?contentid=537743&catname=Local+News>.

with its own form of weaponry, resembling one of the ramshackle armies in the movie *The Chronicles of Narnia*. Some of these warrior cells toss a bucket of toxins at the invader and then move on; others are there to nourish their comrades with chemical spritzers. The body's lead warriors, the macrophages, close in on their prey, envelop it in their own "flesh," and digest it. As it happens, macrophages were the topic of my Ph.D. thesis; they are large, mobile, amoebalike creatures capable of living for months or years. When the battle is over, they pass on information about the intruder to other cells, which will produce antibodies to speed up the body's defenses in the next encounter. They will also eat not only the vanquished intruders but their own dead comrades-in-arms.

For all its dizzying complexity—which has kept other graduate students toiling away "at the bench" for decades—the immune system is hardly foolproof. Some invaders, like the tuberculosis bacillus, outwit it by penetrating the body's tissue cells and setting up shop inside them, where the bacilli cannot be detected by immune cells. Most diabolically, the HIV virus selectively attacks certain immune cells, rendering the body almost defenseless. And sometimes the immune system perversely turns against the body's own tissues, causing such "autoimmune" diseases as lupus and rheumatoid arthritis and possibly some forms of heart disease. It may not be perfect, this seemingly anarchic system of cellular defense, but it is what has evolved so far out of a multimillion-year arms race with our microbial enemies.

5   The link between the immune system, cancer, and the emotions was cobbled together somewhat imaginatively in the 1970s. It had been known for some time that extreme stress could debilitate certain aspects of the immune system. Torture a lab animal long enough, as the famous stress investigator Hans Selye did in the 1930s, and it becomes less healthy and resistant to disease. It was apparently a short leap, for many, to the conclusion that positive feelings

might be the opposite of stress—capable of boosting the immune system and providing the key to health, whether the threat is a microbe or a tumor.

One of the early best-selling assertions of this notion was *Getting Well Again,* by O. Carl Simonton, an oncologist; Stephanie Matthews-Simonton, identified in the book as a "motivational counselor"; and psychologist James L. Creighton. So confident were they of the immune system's ability to defeat cancer that they believed "a cancer does not require just the presence of abnormal cells, it also requires a *suppression of the body's normal defenses*" (43). What could suppress them? Stress. While the Simontons urged cancer patients to obediently comply with the prescribed treatments, they suggested that a kind of attitude adjustment was equally important. Stress had to be overcome, positive beliefs and mental imagery acquired.

The Simontons' book was followed in 1986 by surgeon Bernie Siegel's even more exuberant *Love, Medicine, and Miracles,* offering the view that "a vigorous immune system can overcome cancer if it is not interfered with, and emotional growth toward greater self-acceptance and fulfillment helps keep the immune system strong" (77). Hence cancer was indeed a blessing, since it could force the victim into adopting a more positive and loving view of the world.

But where were the studies showing the healing effect of a positive attitude? Could they be duplicated? One of the skeptics, Stanford psychiatrist David Spiegel, told me he set out in 1989 to refute the popular dogma that attitude could overcome cancer. "I was so sick of hearing Bernie Siegel saying that you got cancer because you needed it," he told me in an interview. But to his surprise, Spiegel's study showed that breast cancer patients in support groups—who presumably were in a better frame of mind than those facing the disease on their own—lived longer than those in the control group. Spiegel promptly interrupted the study, deciding that no one should be deprived of the benefits provided by a support group. The dogma was affirmed and remained so at the time I was diagnosed.

You can see its appeal. First, the idea of a link between subjective feelings and the disease gave the breast cancer patient something to *do*. Instead of waiting passively for the treatments to kick in, she had her own work to do—on herself. She had to monitor her moods and mobilize psychic energy for the war at the cellular level. In the Simontons' scheme, she was to devote part of each day to drawing cartoonish sketches of battles among buglike cells. If the cancer cells were not depicted as "very weak [and] confused" and the body's immune cells were not portrayed as "strong and aggressive," the patient could be courting death, and had more work to do (Simonton, Matthews-Simonton, and Creighton 144–45). At the same time, the dogma created expanded opportunities in the cancer research and treatment industry: not only surgeons and oncologists were needed but behavioral scientists, therapists, motivational counselors, and people willing to write exhortatory self-help books.

10   The dogma, however, did not survive further research. In the nineties, studies began to roll in refuting Spiegel's 1989 work on the curative value of support groups. The amazing survival rates of women in Spiegel's first study turned out to be a fluke. Then, in the May 2007 issue of *Psychological Bulletin,* James Coyne and two coauthors published the results of a systematic review of all the literature on the supposed effects of psychotherapy on cancer. The idea was that psychotherapy, like a support group, should help the patient improve her mood and decrease her level of stress. But Coyne and his coauthors found the existing literature full of "endemic problems" (367). In fact, there seemed to be no positive effect of therapy at all. A few months later, a team led by David Spiegel himself reported in the journal *Cancer* that support groups conferred no survival advantage after all, effectively contradicting his earlier finding. Psychotherapy and support groups might improve

one's mood, but they did nothing to overcome cancer. "If cancer patients want psychotherapy or to be in a support group, they should be given the opportunity to do so," Coyne said in a summary of his research. "There can be lots of emotional and social benefits. But they should not seek such experiences solely on the expectation that they are extending their lives" (qtd. in Molnar).

When I asked Coyne in early 2009 whether there is a continuing scientific bias in favor of a link between emotions and cancer survival, he said:

> To borrow a term used to describe the buildup to the Iraq war, I would say there's a kind of "incestuous amplification." It's very exciting—the idea that the mind can affect the body—and it's a way for the behavioral scientists to ride the train. There's a lot at stake here in grants for cancer-related research, and the behavioral scientists are clinging to it. What else do they have to contribute [to the fight against cancer]? Research on how to get people to use sunscreen? That's not sexy.

He feels that the bias is especially strong in the United States, where skeptics tend to be marginalized. "It's much easier for me to get speaking gigs in Europe," he told me. . . .

It could be argued that positive thinking can't hurt, that it might even be a blessing to the sorely afflicted. Who would begrudge the optimism of a dying person who clings to the hope of a last-minute remission? Or of a bald and nauseated chemotherapy patient who imagines that the cancer experience will end up giving her a more fulfilling life? Unable to actually help cure the disease, psychologists looked for ways to increase such positive feelings about cancer, which they termed "benefit finding" (Tennen and Affleck 584). Scales of benefit finding have been devised and dozens of articles published on the therapeutic interventions that help produce it. If you can't count on recovering, you should at least come to see your cancer as a positive experience, and this notion has been extended to other forms of cancer too. For example, prostate cancer researcher Stephen Strum has written: "You may not believe this, but prostate cancer is an opportunity. . . . [It] is a path, a model, a paradigm, of how you can interact to help yourself, and another. By doing so, you evolve to a much higher level of humanity" (qtd. in Cerulo 118).

But rather than providing emotional sustenance, the sugar-coating of cancer can exact a dreadful cost. First, it requires the denial of understandable feelings of anger and fear, all of which must be buried under a cosmetic layer of cheer. This is a great convenience for health workers and even friends of the afflicted, who might prefer fake cheer to complaining, but it is not so easy on the afflicted. Two researchers on benefit finding report that the breast cancer patients they have worked with "have mentioned repeatedly that they view even well-intentioned efforts to encourage benefit-finding as insensitive and inept. They are almost always interpreted as an unwelcome attempt to minimize the unique burdens and challenges that need to be over-come" (Tennen and Affleck 594–95). One 2004 study even found, in complete contradiction to the tenets of positive thinking, that women who perceive more benefits from their cancer "tend to face a poorer quality of life—including worse mental functioning—compared with women who do not perceive benefits from their diagnoses" (Dittmann).

Besides, it takes effort to maintain the upbeat demeanor expected by others—effort that can no longer be justified as a contribution to long-term survival. Consider the woman who wrote to Deepak Chopra that her breast cancer had spread to the bones and lungs:

> Even though I follow the treatments, have come a long way in unburdening myself of toxic feelings, have forgiven everyone, changed my lifestyle to include meditation, prayer, proper diet, exercise, and supplements, the cancer keeps coming back.

> Am I missing a lesson here that it keeps reoc-
> curring? I am positive I am going to beat it, yet
> it does get harder with each diagnosis to keep a
> positive attitude.

She was working as hard as she could—meditating, pray-
ing, forgiving, but apparently not hard enough. Chopra's
response: "As far as I can tell, you are doing all the right
things to recover. You just have to continue doing them
until the cancer is gone for good. I know it is discouraging
to make great progress only to have it come back again, but
sometimes cancer is simply very pernicious and requires the
utmost diligence and persistence to eventually overcome it."

15   But others in the cancer care business have begun to
speak out against what one has called "the tyranny of
positive thinking." When a 2004 study found no survival
benefits for optimism among lung cancer patients, its lead
author, Penelope Schofield, wrote: "We should question
whether it is valuable to encourage optimism if it results
in the patient concealing his or her distress in the mis-
guided belief that this will afford survival benefits. . . . If
a patient feels generally pessimistic . . . it is important to
acknowledge these feelings as valid and acceptable" ("Positive Attitude").

Whether repressed feelings are themselves harmful, as
many psychologists claim, I'm not so sure, but without
question there is a problem when positive thinking "fails"
and the cancer spreads or eludes treatment. Then the patient
can only blame herself: she is not being positive enough;
possibly it was her negative attitude that brought on the disease in the first place. At this point, the exhortation to think
positively is "an additional burden to an already devastated
patient," as oncology nurse Cynthia Rittenberg has written
(37). Jimmie Holland, a psychiatrist at Memorial Sloan-
Kettering Cancer Center in New York, writes that cancer
patients experience a kind of victim blaming:

It began to be clear to me about ten years ago that society was placing another undue and inappropriate burden on patients that seemed to come out of the popular beliefs about the mind-body connection. I would find patients coming in with stories of being told by well-meaning friends, "I've read all about this—if you got cancer, you must have wanted it. . . ." Even more distressing was the person who said, "I know I have to be positive all the time and that is the only way to cope with cancer—but it's so hard to do. I know that if I get sad, or scared or upset, I am making my tumor grow faster and I will have shortened my life."

Clearly, the failure to think positively can weigh on a cancer patient like a second disease.

I, at least, was saved from this additional burden by my persistent anger—which would have been even stronger if I had suspected, as I do now, that my cancer was iatrogenic, that is, caused by the medical profession. When I was diagnosed I had been taking hormone replacement therapy for almost eight years, prescribed by doctors who avowed it would prevent heart disease, dementia, and bone loss. Further studies revealed in 2002 that HRT increases the risk of breast cancer, and, as the number of women taking it dropped sharply in the wake of this news, so did the incidence of breast cancer. So bad science may have produced the cancer in the first place, just as the bad science of positive thinking plagued me throughout my illness.

Breast cancer, I can now report, did not make me prettier or stronger, more feminine or spiritual. What it gave me, if you want to call this a "gift," was a very personal, agonizing encounter with an ideological force in American culture that I had not been aware of before—one that encourages us to deny reality, submit cheerfully to misfortune, and blame only ourselves for our fate.

Works Cited

Cerulo, Karen A. *Never Saw It Coming: Cultural Challenges to Envisioning the Worst.* Chicago: U of Chicago P, 2006. Print.

Chopra, Deepak. "Positive Attitude Helps Overcome Cancer Recurrence." *Health Experts.* Yahoo! Health, 17 Apr. 2007. Web. 2009. <http://health.yahoo.com/experts/deepak/92/positive-attitude-helps-overcome-cancer-recurrence>.

Coyne, James C., Michael Stefanek, and Steven C. Palmer. "Psychotherapy and Survival in Cancer: The Conflict between Hope and Evidence." *Psychological Bulletin* 133.3 (2007): 367–94. Print.

Dittmann, M. "Benefit-Finding Doesn't Always Mean Improved Lives for Breast Cancer Patients." *APAOnline.* Amer. Psychological Assn., Feb. 2004. Web. 2009. <http://www.apa.org/monitor/feb04/benefit.aspx>.

Holland, Jimmie. "The Tyranny of Positive Thinking." *Leukemia & Lymphoma Society.* LLS, n.d. Web. 2009. <http://www.leukemia-lymphoma.org/all_page?item_id=7038&viewmode=print>.

Molnar, Amy. "Cancer Survival Is Not Influenced by a Patient's Emotional Status." *Bio-Medicine.org.* Bio-Medicine, 21 Oct. 2007. Web. 2009. <http://www.bio-medicine.org/medicine-news-1/Cancer-survival-is-not-influenced-by-a-patients-emotional-status-4214-2/>.

"A Positive Attitude Does Not Help Cancer Outcome." *Medical News Today.* MediLexicon Intl., 9 Feb. 2004. Web. 2009. <http://www.medicalnewstoday.com/medicalnews.php?newsid=5780>.

Rittenberg, Cynthia N. "Positive Thinking: An Unfair Burden for Cancer Patients?" *Supportive Care in Cancer* 3.1 (1995): 37–39. Print.

Russell, Michael. "Breast Cancer Prevention Tips." *EzineArticles.com.* EzineArticles, 16 May 2006. Web. 2009. <http://ezinearticles.com/?Breast-Cancer-Prevention-Tips&id=199110>.

Siegel, Bernie S. *Love, Medicine, and Miracles: Lessons Learned About Self-Healing from a Surgeon's Experience with Exceptional Patients*. New York: Harper, 1986. Print.

Simonton, O. Carl, Stephanie Matthews-Simonton, and James L. Creighton. *Getting Well Again*. New York: Bantam, 1992. Print.

Tennen, Howard, and Glenn Affleck. "Benefit-Finding and Benefit-Reminding." *Handbook of Positive Psychology*. Ed. C. R. Snyder and Shane J. Lopez. New York: Oxford UP, 2002. 584–97. Print.

ASSESS YOUR THINKING

Math vs. English
by Ann-Marie Paulin

STUDY THE MOVES

In the following essay, Ann-Marie Paulin considers the common labels "math person" and "English person." As the essay develops, Paulin interrogates the assumptions that lump people into either category and builds toward a newer, richer way of thinking. In the process, she makes several of the moves described in Chapter 2 ("Seek Tension"), Chapter 6 ("Justify Your Position"), and Chapter 9 ("Assess Your Thinking"):

PARAGRAPH 1	Uses a past event to introduce the tension between math and English
PARAGRAPH 2	Examines past assumptions about math and English
PARAGRAPH 3	Lines up evidence for the tension between math and English

continued

An instructor at Owens Community College, Ann-Marie Paulin holds degrees in English and biology.

Reprinted by permission of Ann-Marie Paulin.

When I was in college, my best friend and I sat in the cafeteria between classes while she told me about her nightmare of the night before. She was alone on a desolate plain, running through dry grass trying to escape monsters. She could feel their hot breath on her neck and hear them gnashing their long teeth as they got closer and closer. Then, she tripped and fell into a pit. As the monsters surrounded the pit and closed in on her, dripping monster slobber on her and preparing to tear her to bits, she woke up screaming, "The numbers are going to get me!" Did I mention my best friend had a real phobia about math?

To tell the truth, I was no fan of math either. Like many people, I assumed you were a math person or an English person, and I was definitely an English person. I was fascinated by brilliantly written stories, challenging and well-supported arguments. Whether I did well on a test depended on how well I thought, researched, and expressed myself. There were so many ways to get it right. On the other hand, math seemed so rigid. It was right or it was wrong, and I usually ended up in the Wrong camp, feeling stupid and bewildered. Why was it the examples on the board are so clear while the problems for homework seem to follow completely different rules?

Years have gone by, and I have been teaching college English for over twenty years, and I have often noticed that students and faculty still hold on to the old math/English duality. I notice this most often in literature classes when we discuss poetry. The students who enjoy playing with language and who are comfortable with several different meanings being possible all at once tend to catch on to working with poetry fairly quickly. Students who are math or science majors often seem alarmed and bewildered by the idea that a line of poetry can mean multiple things at once. How can three interpretations be different and all correct!?

But are things really as clear-cut as this seems? Is it really a duality? We often get the message in our culture that things are black or white, liberal or conservative, beautiful or ugly, smart or dumb. Not all cultures see things this way. Think of the yin and yang. While the symbol recognizes certain dualities, it also recognizes they are not absolute: there is a bit of the light in the dark and a bit of the dark in the light. But recognizing the subtleties requires a willingness to pay attention, to question, to stop and think. It requires time. These activities are not as popular as they once were in our moving-at-the-speed-of-technology society.

5   To go back to my college friend, she can do math that matters to her. She balances her checkbook, calculates appropriate tips, measures fabrics for sewing, and can measure a room to determine how many gallons of paint to buy. Same for me. (Well, my checkbook is a mess, but you get my point.) And I know there are plenty of math people who write wonderful letters and web page updates, who can tell a story that keeps everyone crying with laughter. So is the issue one of ability or desire?

I figure it is a bit of both. It would be foolish to say that everyone starts out with equal potential to do everything; it is just a matter of applying oneself. For example, I'm old and built like a fireplug. I can practice till doomsday, yet I'll never be good at jump shots. And anyone who has watched *American Idol* knows not all humans are blessed with a lovely voice, no matter how hard they try. But I am absolutely in love with language. And learning new ways to use it and play with it is fun for me.

But we are not doomed to be rotten at something just because it does not come easily to us. Most skills will improve if we work on them. I was waiting in line at Starbucks the other day, when I noticed the young woman ahead of me was holding an algebra book. And, since I had been thinking about the whole math/English thing, I asked her if she liked algebra. She said that she did enjoy it, but she had to work on it a lot to get it.

So maybe there is a clue in what this young math fan said. She is pretty good at math because she works hard at it. Well, that sounds obvious, but let's be honest. Many of us do not want to do things that are hard. We often automatically assume hard equals unpleasant. When we are having difficulty learning material, especially in a classroom where others appear to be gliding through it, we question ourselves. We feel stupid, unfairly, when a bit more work would get us gliding too, like a swan: all calm glory where it shows, paddling like the dickens below the surface. Most activities look easy when others who have worked long and consistently do them. But no one likes to feel stupid or lost, so maybe we give up too soon rather than deal with those feelings long enough to gain the expertise to get past them.

As a student, I embodied this way of thinking. I could actually do math, but it felt like work, and there didn't seem to be any satisfaction in the completion. Somehow, that got translated into "I can't do math" or "I'm not a math person." I could be if I worked at it, but I don't like working at it. Likewise, many of my students who claim they can't figure out poetry have never really tried, or they tried once, didn't like it, and never tried again. When they work with a partner on explicating a poem, they often find when they learn certain strategies for approaching the form, they can make sense of it. Will they leave my class and stock their libraries (or Kindles) with poetry? Probably not, but they leave with the confidence to know that, should they ever want to read a poem someday, they can. The point is, learning to think and function in ways one is not automatically comfortable with makes people grow and expand their horizons. And that growth and confidence can help a person learn all sorts of new skills, practical or impractical.

10   Given the fact that the more knowledge and skills we have, the more flexibility we develop in life, why are we so quick to decide we "can't" do something when really we mean we don't want to? Well, as mentioned earlier, we are raised on dualities, and sadly, rather than asking us to question them, most schools reinforce them. For example, seeing the math/English thing as gender based: For years many schools felt there was nothing wrong with teaching students that boys were best at math because men are the logical sex, while women, the emotional ones who desire connection, are more verbal, and therefore better at English. My friends, Barb and Anna, went to a high school that tried to force them into home economics classes, saying girls did not need physics. It was only when their father stormed the school and demanded his girls be allowed to study physics that they got into the class. How many children had no parents to push for their right to learn as much as they could? Fortunately, things seem to be changing in this area. Remember the big controversy a few years ago over the talking Barbie doll that said, "Math is hard"? That doll had to be taken off the market due to parental outrage. So maybe one cause of our duality is fading.

I believe it was the business community that started the expression "thinking outside the box." As annoying as that cliché has become, it became a cliché because there is truth to it. When we challenge ourselves to think in ways that don't come "naturally" to us, we grow. We force our mind to work muscles it has not used much before. We can imagine in new ways, which is the only way the human race can move forward. Now, if you'll excuse me, I'm going to make another run at my checkbook.

A Hard Look at Parking Lots
by Teresa Scollon

STUDY THE MOVES

In the following essay, Teresa Scollon examines the identity of American car culture. Throughout, she considers the complexities and tensions that underlie group behavior—and the ways we can and can't escape such behavior. In the process, she makes several of the moves described in Chapter 1 ("Seek Complexity"), Chapter 2 ("Seek Tension"), Chapter 7 ("Change the Terms"), and Chapter 9 ("Assess Your Thinking"):

PARAGRAPH 1	Examines the tension between daily hopes and realities
PARAGRAPH 2	Examines assumptions about belonging to parking culture
PARAGRAPH 3	Uses a metaphor to illustrate parking culture
PARAGRAPH 4	Explains how people have adapted to and function within parking culture
PARAGRAPH 5	Examines the tension between interior and exterior college culture
PARAGRAPH 6	Makes an analogy between commuters and geese
PARAGRAPH 7	Explains the ecological damage of car culture
PARAGRAPH 8	Examines daily life before the onset of car culture

Teresa Scollon, a poet and college instructor, holds degrees in creative writing, business administration, and international relations.

When I roll out of bed in the morning, I'd like to align my day with what's really important: the people I love, or poetry, or prayer—another day's gesture toward becoming a better person. But the reality is more mundane: when I get up the first thing on my mind is getting the dogs outside before they make a mess in the house. The second thing is parking.

If I correctly time my arrival at the college, there'll be a parking space next to the building in which I teach an early class, a space which will set me up for the rest of the day. If I leave my house a little too late, I send urgent good juju ahead of me, asking the universe for an empty spot. Otherwise, I'll have to park in a faraway lot, which means I'll be rolling breathlessly into the classroom in the nick of time, which means I'll have to rush out again after class in order to get to the next thing on schedule. And I'll have to lug heavy bags of student papers clear across campus. Having a nearby parking spot just makes everything easier.

In fact, I prefer early classes because it's easier to get a parking spot before 7:30 a.m. If I had to arrive on campus later in the day, I'd join the ranks of those hovering, idling vultures, vultures in big tin cans, sizing up each person walking by, waiting for a spot to open up, to seize it. I've seen people in cars behave with astonishing rudeness, giving the finger, yelling, zooming dangerously into a spot before someone else can take it.

You might say that parking brings out the worst in us: aggression, recklessness, competitiveness. It taps into our fears of scarcity and our doubts about abundance. You might say parking brings out our creative juices as well. Seems like everybody has a personal strategy for getting the ideal spot—internal tiered maps of possibilities, favorite little-known spots. Timing is critical. Observation is key. Prayer and cursing are invoked in equal measure. Even risk—of parking tickets—is factored in.

5   Whatever the specifics of our individual plans or our commitment to manners, we all seem to share a common focus: park the damned car. Meanwhile, inside its buildings and its digital forums, the college has tried valiantly to instill a supportive culture revolving around the phrase "Can I help you?" It works up to a point. But the parking lots strewn around campus trump the collaborative vibe. It doesn't matter how high-minded you are; if you can't park, you can't get in here to teach or learn. That necessity fosters a climate that is anything but collegial.

At least the college parking lots are set among nice scenery and greenery. When I get out of my car, I see trees and birds—things I like to pay attention to. Today I saw geese flying overhead on their way north for the summer, long-distance commuters off on their biologically imperative journeys. Tonight they will no doubt be looking for a wetland in which to rest and refuel—their own version of a parking lot.

Is it really the same for geese? Yes and no. They fly together, but they compete, too, for limited resources. Like us. But geese work with the natural system at hand, and leave behind things—need I define this?—that contribute to the ecosystem in digestible ways. A wetland is more than just a parking lot—it's a water filtration system, a food supply, and a nursery for varied forms of new life. In contrast, our parking facilities—lots, garages, even houses, if you think about it—cover over other forms of life in broad, stinking swaths. From an ecological perspective, parking lots are a disaster. They form an impermeable surface—which doesn't allow rain to soak into the ground or replenish the water table. Instead, water collects in a stream, which in turn collects pollutants—motor oil, coolant, other garbage—and dumps it all in a flood, called runoff, into the lowest spot around and, eventually, into water bodies. Parking lots and other impermeable surfaces—like the expanded roof surface and perfect lawns of McMansions—have direct negative impacts: increased erosion and water pollution, and declining lake health. The big box stores and parking lots that ring most towns not only are huge impermeable surfaces, but are often built on former wetlands: a double whammy. And there's the emissions and petroleum use from all the driving we do. In sum: an ecological disaster.

Cars didn't used to be so much our everything. Our common public spaces were our pride and source of social connection. Shops and businesses were collected in towns, which were connected, even in the country, by trolleys and trains. When I was a kid, my tiny little hometown had everything it needed: bakery, dairy, butcher, clothing stores, pharmacy, lumberyard. We could walk downtown, do our shopping, and chitchat with our neighbors—the merchants—at the same time. The health of those little stores wasn't dependent on the spreadsheets of some Texas corporate accountant, and small business owners were part of the community. Parents told their kids to go outside to play in the village park, or to go downtown to the movie theatre. We rode our bikes everywhere. The town was ours.

But the car culture that emerged with the interstate highway system built in the 1950s has changed everything. The highways gave rise to fast food chains, shopping malls, and big box retailers. The result: more driving, the emptying of town centers, less walkable shopping areas, and urban sprawl. While it was fun to travel with my family on car trips—singing in the car, a little brother's or sister's head on my lap, watching power lines swoop and rise, going to drive-ins bundled up in our pajamas—for the most part, that feeling of family togetherness isn't really the focus of car culture. It's more focused on moving units of one around as quickly as possible. We don't walk very much. We're getting fatter. We buy too much stuff. Our town centers are boarded up. Parents, afraid to let their kids walk to school, spend half their time driving kids around. Driving seems to lead inexorably to more driving. The air is bad, the traffic congested, and we don't seem to have enough time to get together with people we love. Driving all of the time is a social disaster. When's the last time an employee at a big box store acted like your neighbor? Those parking lots out at the malls aren't even *safe*: they're trolled by security because of the risk of assault or kidnappings. And huge as they are, most of the time those lots are at least half empty.

10   There's a term for those oversized underused parking lots: underperforming asphalt. Planners and thinkers are suggesting ways to rethink our sloppy use of space, energy, and habitat. An artist in Toronto succeeded in getting permission to remove her driveway and replace it with a garden, and in the process, drew attention to the absurd city regulations preventing her from doing so. For me, that's good news. Other minds are at work. But what about *my* mind? It's hard to look at how I'm tied to all of this. I don't like to think that parking, or driving, is really that important to me. Apparently, I'm both subject and attuned, at a deep level, to stresses and conflicts imposed on me from without. And my response is no more noble than anyone else's. Like it or not, I can get competitive. I may refrain from honking or obscene gestures or fisticuffs, but the truth is, tomorrow morning, if I can ease into a parking spot before you do, I'll feel fine.

Maybe it's too hard to be different. Maybe this is just what it means to be part of a culture, when the forces that get us acting in congruent directions are too hard to fight every day all the way. If I don't want to be part of the collective parking obsession, then I have to think of ways to live outside the lines. I could drag the bike out of the garage, pump up the tires, and start biking to the college. But then, again, I'll have to arrive early to get a spot in the bike rack.

Recently, while I was thinking about all of this, I traveled to Chicago. At rush hour, Chicago is a river of people flowing out of office buildings, down the sidewalks to train stations, and out of the trains to the suburbs. To live and work here means timing one's individual arrivals and departures with the mass movements of people, becoming part of a living hive. In general, Americans think they don't want to be controlled this way, preferring to stick with the myth of individual autonomy. But whether it's watching a train schedule or worrying about parking spaces or traffic jams, most of us are part of a bigger scene. The habits of the mass influence how we move; one is part of the whole, one of the many. And frankly, there can be a certain joy, a certain comfort in being one of the mass. On my trip, I traveled by train and enjoyed it. I relaxed and looked out the window and thought that sometimes it feels all right to let the culture carry me once in a while.

So what do I need here? Like it or not, I'm part of a culture, a huge and multi-faceted one, which sometimes serves and sometimes appalls me. Sometimes it's my own participation that appalls me. It takes energy to fight it or change it and my energy is limited. But maybe I can be smarter about which parts I submit to, and my reasons. Riding my bike to work is an accommodating gesture towards the planet and the other creatures I value. If that means I'm still subject to college traffic patterns, all right. I can live with that. And if

I'm part of a culture, that means my small efforts to change are part of it, too. Contributing to the development of a more connected culture—that's something worth getting up for in the morning.

PART III

Apply the Moves

THE FOLLOWING PAGES offer outlines for structuring your writing. There are many possible approaches that depend on your assignment, purpose, and topic. Remember that these outlines provide general steps that can be drawn out, minimized, or even skipped depending on your specific project. The idea here is that the moves we've explained in the main chapters (1–9) can be used in combinations that accommodate a range of projects. The outlines are not meant to be restrictive or confining but to provide a path—a way forward. Of course, once you're writing, you might turn back, redirect, and reshape. But having an initial pattern in front of you will help to focus your energy—to aim your thinking so that you don't struggle to imagine the next step. As you'll see, we've grouped the outlines under typical assignment types:

- Explanatory and Descriptive Projects
- Analytical Projects
- Argumentative Projects
- Reflective Projects

As you begin your own projects, consider the purpose—the motivating drive behind your writing. While an assignment may establish a broad purpose, for instance an *informative* or *persuasive* essay, you might get better traction if you define your purpose as narrowly and specifically as possible. For example, you might set out to reveal flawed thinking about a particular issue; to report the details of a certain experience or observation; to evaluate a text, film, or product; to describe new thinking on a subject; or to convince others to take a particular course of action. There are many purposes, but all forms of academic writing seek to develop insights. The goal is always to understand something in a new or better light—not merely to perform an assigned set of moves but to generate an idea worthy of sharing.

EXPLANATORY AND DESCRIPTIVE PROJECTS

The purpose of these projects is to think through an issue—to bring a topic, person, or field of study into better focus. The goal is not to argue against or for a position but to look closely, to develop a keen awareness, and to generate meaning about something, someone, or some place. Such assignments include ethnographies, histories, profiles, and observation essays. The following outlines illustrate common approaches. They rely on moves described in Chapter 1 ("Seek Complexity"), Chapter 2 ("Seek Tension"), Chapter 3 ("Apply Sources"), and Chapter 4 ("Apply a Concept").

✔ If your assignment asks you to examine a term or concept, you can use a source as a doorway into your essay. Explain how the source uses the term or concept you are focusing on. Give some examples of the concept: how it works in daily use or within a specific discussion. Seek complexity by denying the usual associations (page 26) that come along with the term or concept. Explain how those usual associations misdirect or hinder people's thinking. Then, unpack the term (page 17). Show the qualities that people might overlook. Show the traits or parts that are often ignored. Finally, explain how this process has changed your thinking.

Explain a term or concept.

- Integrate a source that uses the term or concept.
- Give an example of the term or concept being applied.

Deny a usual association.

- Explain how the association is misleading.
- Explain how the association is limited.

Unpack the term or concept.

- Describe qualities that might be taken for granted.
- Describe effects that aren't immediately apparent.

Explain how you see things differently.

- Explain how you now understand the term or concept.
- Describe questions or uncertainties you still have.

🔖 <u>READ:</u> Steven D. Krause (page 193) and Charlene Li and Josh Bernoff (page 210)

✔ Or you can start without a source. First, describe the ways people normally use a term or concept. Compare it to something familiar to help your readers understand how it functions. Then, seek complexity by unpacking: take the term or concept apart (page 17). Try to discover three, four, or more major components. And use separate paragraphs to thoroughly explain what others might overlook. Ask yourself if there are any dualities at work (page 39). If so, take a paragraph to explain the middle ground, the gray area between the two extremes. Finally, come back around to the term or concept and explain how your thinking has changed.

Explain a term or concept.

- Explain how the term or concept gets used.
- Compare the term or concept to something familiar.

Unpack the term or concept.

- Describe qualities that might be taken for granted.
- Describe effects that aren't immediately apparent.

Bust up a duality.

- Describe the duality: on the one side, there's _____, and on the other, there's _____.
- Explain how the duality is misleading or limited.
- Describe the gray area: between the two extremes, there's another possibility: _____.

Explain how you see things differently.

- Explain how you now understand the term or concept.
- Describe questions or uncertainties you still have.

READ: Stephanie Mills (page 198)

✔ Explanatory assignments may ask you to examine the state or condition of something—to understand the subject well enough to offer clarity and insight. Start with a real situation or event. Give readers enough information to understand what has happened. Then, seek tension in the situation or event. Consider both the subtle tensions and the broad tensions at play (page 36). Integrate sources to help describe the tension in detail. Help readers to understand the tension by making connections to other situations, events, or issues they may be familiar with. Finally, come back to the original situation or event and explain how you now see it differently or more fully.

Describe a real situation or event related to the subject.

- Give details about the situation or event.
- Explain a subtle tension at play.

Draw from a vital source.

- Describe how it characterizes the situation or event.
- Describe how it characterizes the tension.

Describe the tension.

- Use specific language to describe the tension.
- Integrate a source that describes the tension.
- Connect to a broad tension.

Explain how you now see the situation or event.

- Explain why it matters to those involved.
- Explain what new questions or problems emerge.

◆ **READ:** Matthew Yglesias (page 203) and Virginia Postrel (page 207)

✔ In examining the state or condition of something, you can start with a broad tension related to your subject. Think about the various layers of the tension—the historical, philosophical, or political friction at play (page 36). Bring in a supportive source that characterizes the tension. Then, describe a specific situation from your experience or from your research that relates to the broad tension. Also make connections between the situation you are focusing on and another situation or event that readers might identify with. Finally, come back to the broad tension that you started with and explain how you now see it differently or more fully.

Describe a broad tension related to the subject.
- Use specific language to describe the tension.
- Integrate a source that describes the tension.

Show the tension in a real situation.
- Give details about the situation.
- Integrate a source that characterizes the situation.

Find patterns in other situations or events.
- Describe a similar situation or event.
- Describe a dissimilar situation or event.
- Explain an idea you can draw from the comparison.

Explain how you understand the tension differently.
- Explain why it matters to those involved.
- Explain what new questions or problems emerge.

READ: Shawn Burks (page 214)

ANALYTICAL PROJECTS
••••••••••••••••••••••••

These projects aim to break something down, to take apart or dismantle a specific subject such as a photograph, an advertisement, a written argument, a piece of literature, even a concept or theory. The goal is not to judge or celebrate the subject but to examine it so closely that you come to a better understanding. Such assignments include rhetorical analyses and literary analyses. They primarily rely on moves described in Chapter 1 ("Seek Complexity"), Chapter 2 ("Seek Tension"), Chapter 3 ("Apply Sources"), Chapter 4 ("Apply a Concept"), and Chapter 5 ("Dismantle Arguments").

✓ Some analytical assignments ask you to dissect particularly complex concepts. Start by explaining the concept in detail, giving readers background information to understand the various layers. Compare the concept to something that is common or familiar to readers. Explain how the concept normally gets used. What does it help people to do or understand? Here, you can apply sources to show how writers use the concept. Then, apply the concept to a particular situation, text, or case (page 72). What does this application reveal? Finally, explain how you now understand the concept differently.

Explain a concept related to the subject.
- Use specific language to describe the concept.
- Compare it to something familiar.

Explain how the concept gets used.
- Give an example of the concept being applied.
- Integrate a source that uses the concept.

Apply the concept to a real situation.
- Explain what problems the application solves.
- Explain what insights emerge.
- Explain what new questions or problems emerge.

Explain how you see things differently.
- Explain how you understand the concept more fully.
- Describe questions or uncertainties you still have.

READ: Bradford A. Smith (page 219) and Annette Wannamaker (page 231)

✔ Some projects ask you to analyze a concept outside your discipline. Begin by examining the concept, describing it in detail. For especially complex concepts, make connections to other, familiar ideas. Explain where the concept comes from, how it shows up in daily life, writing, and speaking. Integrate a source that uses the concept. Then, transport the concept into another discipline (page 78). Apply the concept to a particular situation, text, or case in the new discipline. What does this application reveal? Finally, explain how the concept creates a better way of thinking, a more accurate vision, or a more thorough understanding.

Explain a concept related to the subject.

- Use specific language to describe the concept.
- Compare it to something familiar.

Explain how the concept gets used.

- Give an example of the concept being applied.
- Integrate a source that uses the concept.

Transport the concept into another discipline.

- Explain what problems the concept solves.
- Explain what insights emerge.
- Explain what new questions or problems emerge.

Explain how you see things differently.

- Explain how you understand the concept more fully.
- Describe questions or uncertainties you still have.

READ: Tiffany J. Smith (page 224)

✓ Often, analytical assignments ask you to break down the ideas in a written text. Start by summarizing the ideas in the text (page 54). What specific issue does the text deal with? What particular insight or idea does the writer offer? What is the purpose of the text (page 98)? Then, examine the context of the work: under what circumstances was the text written? Finally, analyze the reasoning of the work (page 93). Consider the claim the writer is making and the ways he or she justifies that claim. What specific words and arrangement strategies does the writer use to achieve a certain effect? Finally, explain how you now have a richer understanding of the work.

Summarize the ideas in a text.

- Explain an issue that the text explores.
- Examine an insight that the writer offers.
- Describe the writer's purpose.

Consider the context of the work.

- Describe the cultural atmosphere.
- Describe the political climate.

Analyze the reasoning of the work.

- Describe the claim the work is making.
- Explain how the claim relates to the context or tension surrounding the work.

Explain how you now understand the text.

- Explain its significance to the subject.
- Describe questions or uncertainties you still have.

📘 <u>READ:</u> William J. Carpenter (page 235)

✔ Or instead of focusing on a written text, you might be asked to analyze the elements of a nontextual work, such as a work of art or architecture. Start by investigating the purpose of the work. Make connections between the work you are focusing on and another work, event, or situation that readers might identify with. Then, examine the cultural context of the work. Finally, examine the quiet argument that the work is making (page 104). What artistic elements contribute to an overall point?

Examine the purpose of a work.
- Explain the original intention for the work.
- Explain how the purpose has changed over time.

Find patterns in other works.
- Explain how the work resembles something similar.
- Explain how the work resembles something dissimilar.
- Explain an idea you can draw from the comparison.

Consider the cultural context.
- Describe the physical setting.
- Describe the prevailing attitudes, values, or beliefs.
- Describe the political climate.

Analyze the quiet argument of the work.
- Describe the message of the work.
- Explain how the message relates to the work's purpose.
- Explain how the message relates to the cultural context.

📗 <u>READ:</u> Astrid Reed (page 239)

ARGUMENTATIVE PROJECTS

The purpose of these projects is to make a case for your position. The goal is usually to persuade others to see a subject in a certain way or to propose a particular course of action. These assignments ask you first to think critically about the current state of things or about common terminology, and then to argue for something new or better. Often, you will need to take on opposing positions and carefully dismantle their reasoning. Such assignments include proposals, argumentative research essays, and literary arguments. They rely mainly on moves described in Chapter 1 ("Seek Complexity"), Chapter 2 ("Seek Tension"), Chapter 3 ("Apply Sources"), Chapter 6 ("Justify Your Position"), Chapter 7 ("Change the Terms"), and Chapter 8 ("Escape the Status Quo").

✔ Argumentative assignments often ask you to assert a claim and to support that claim with evidence. Begin by explaining the situation. Describe the issue or tension that needs to be addressed. Offer your position, your particular claim. Then, line up the evidence (page 114) that supports your claim, bringing in supportive sources to back up your points. Slowly walk readers through the information, devoting entire paragraphs to complex ideas. (In other words, don't just drop tons of data on your readers. Explain the most significant information in your own words.) Then, take on opposing positions (page 122). Carefully explain and dismantle the reasoning in their arguments (page 93). Finally, come back to your original claim and explain the value of your position.

Explain the situation.

- Describe the issue or tension that needs to be addressed.
- Offer your position, your specific claim.

Line up the evidence to support the claim.

- Explain the evidence.
- Integrate a source that describes the evidence.

Dismantle and deny the opposition.

- Identify an opposing position.
- Analyze the opposition's reasoning.
- Explain how the opposition is limited or flawed.

Explain the value of your position.

- Explain how your position matters to others.
- Explain how your ideas create new or helpful questions.

◆ <u>READ:</u> Joel Kotkin (page 244)

✔ Or you can focus on the reasons that justify your position. Start by explaining the situation. Describe the issue or tension that needs to be addressed. Offer your position, your particular claim. Then, break down reasons for your claim (page 117). If your reasons are especially complex, devote an entire paragraph to each. Support your reasons and integrate sources to help back up your points. Explain how your reasons connect to a broad principle related to your subject. Then, take on opposing positions (page 122). Carefully explain and dismantle the reasoning in their arguments (page 93). Finally, come back to your original claim and explain the value of your position.

Explain the situation.

- Describe the issue or tension that needs to be addressed.
- Offer your position, your specific claim.

Break down reasons for the claim.

- Explain each reason.
- Integrate a source that supports the reason.
- Connect to a broad principle.

Dismantle and deny the opposition.

- Identify an opposing position.
- Analyze the opposition's reasoning.
- Explain how the opposition is limited or flawed.

Explain the value of your position.

- Explain how your position matters to others.
- Explain how your ideas create new or helpful questions.

◆ READ: Christine Overall (page 252)

✔ Argumentative assignments may ask you to question a problematic term or phrase. Start by defining the term or phrase as it is commonly used. How does it show up in writing and speaking? How does it function in normal practice? Draw from a source or two to show how writers use the term or phrase. You might also explain its origin and how its use has changed over time. Then, evaluate the term or phrase. What does it get wrong? Consider how the term or phrase distorts or overly simplifies something, how it conceals or ignores something. Finally, explain the need for a new term or phrase, and what it might mean for thinkers and writers.

Examine a key term or phrase.
- Define the term or phrase.
- Explain how the term or phrase gets used.
- Refer to a source that uses the term or phrase.

Describe the inaccuracy of the term or phrase.
- Explain how the above definition is misleading.
- Explain how the above definition is incomplete.

Describe what the term or phrase conceals.
- Describe qualities that might be taken for granted.
- Describe effects that aren't immediately apparent.

Explain the need for a new term or phrase.
- Explain what function the new term or phrase would serve.
- Describe whom the new term or phrase would benefit.

🔖 READ: John McCormick (page 258)

✔ Or you can propose an actual change in terms (page 139). Begin by examining the original, problematic term or phrase. Explain what it gets wrong, how and why it is inaccurate. Then, go a step further and describe the quiet associations that come along with the term or phrase (page 135). Examine how these associations misdirect or infect people's thinking. Finally, offer a new term or phrase, explaining how it prompts richer, more accurate, more sophisticated thinking.

Examine a key term or phrase.

- Define the term or phrase.
- Explain how the term or phrase gets used.
- Refer to a source that uses the term or phrase.

Describe the inaccuracy of the term or phrase.

- Explain how the above definition is misleading.
- Explain how the above definition is incomplete.

Describe the associations of the term or phrase.

- Explain how the term or phrase reinforces a bias.
- Explain how the term or phrase limits thinking.

Propose a new term or phrase.

- Define the new term or phrase.
- Explain how the new term or phrase is more accurate than the original.
- Describe the positive associations of the new term or phrase.
- Acknowledge any limitations of the new term or phrase.

READ: Kathleen Schenck (page 262)

✔ Argumentative projects may ask you to challenge the status quo, or usual state of affairs. Start by describing a real event or situation. Give readers enough information to understand what has happened. Then, seek tension in the situation or event. What friction does the situation call to the surface? Think about the various layers of the tension—the historical, philosophical, or political friction at play (page 36). Bring in a supportive source that characterizes the tension. Call out quiet assumptions about your subject (page 157). How do they misdirect or shut down thinking? Return to the original situation or event and explain how these quiet assumptions reinforce the status quo. Finally, explain why your position on the subject matters.

Describe a real situation or event related to the subject.
- Give details about the situation or event.
- Explain a subtle tension at play.

Describe a broad tension related to the subject.
- Use specific language to describe the tension.
- Integrate a source that describes the tension.

Describe quiet assumptions related to the subject.
- Explain how the quiet assumptions reinforce a bias.
- Explain how the quiet assumptions limit thinking.

Explain the value of your position.
- Explain why your position matters to those involved.
- Explain how your ideas create new or helpful questions.

🔖 **READ:** Michael Anderson (page 267)

✔ Or you can start by questioning a maxim, or common statement, related to your subject (page 160). Examine the reasoning behind the maxim and explain what it misses or gets wrong. Bring in a vital source that helps you to explain the problem with the maxim. Then, call out quiet assumptions about the subject (page 157). Consider how they misdirect or shut down thinking. Come back to the maxim that you started with and explain how it gets reinforced by these quiet assumptions. Finally, explain why your position on the subject matters.

Question a maxim related to the subject.

- Explain how the maxim is inaccurate.
- Explain how the maxim is misleading or limited.

Draw from a vital source.

- Examine an insight that the writer offers.
- Describe how the source dismantles the reasoning behind the maxim.

Describe quiet assumptions related to the subject.

- Explain how the quiet assumptions reinforce a bias.
- Explain how the quiet assumptions limit thinking.

Explain the value of your position.

- Explain why your position matters to those involved.
- Explain how your ideas create new or helpful questions.

READ: Barbara Ehrenreich (page 274)

REFLECTIVE PROJECTS
• •

These projects get writers inside their own thinking. The goal is for writers to focus on their own progress, their struggles and breakthroughs as they relate to particular writing assignments. Reflective projects include reflective memos and essays, literacy narratives, cultural identity projects, and critical memoirs. The following outlines illustrate common approaches. They rely on moves described in Chapter 1 ("Seek Complexity"), Chapter 2 ("Seek Tension"), Chapter 5 ("Dismantle Arguments"), Chapter 6 ("Justify Your Position"), and Chapter 9 ("Assess Your Thinking").

✔ Reflection is often prompted by a real situation or event that gets writers thinking differently about a particular subject. Start by describing the situation or event, giving readers enough information to understand what has happened. Then, seek tension in the situation or event. What friction do you detect between what you expected and what you experienced? Describe your past assumptions about the subject. Where did they come from? Consider how they have limited or misdirected your thinking. Ask yourself if there are any dualities at work (page 39). If so, take a paragraph to explain the middle ground, the gray area between the two extremes. Finally, come back to the original situation or event and explain how your thinking has changed.

Describe a real situation or event related to the subject.

- Give details about the situation or event.
- Explain a subtle tension at play.

Examine past assumptions about the subject.

- Explain where the assumptions come from.
- Explain how the assumptions are flawed or biased.

Bust up a duality.

- Describe the duality: on the one side, there's _____, and on the other, there's _____.
- Explain how the duality is misleading or limited.
- Describe the gray area: between the two extremes, there's another possibility: _____.

Explain how you see the subject differently.

- Explain why it matters to those involved.
- Explain what new questions or problems emerge.

◀ **READ:** Ann-Marie Paulin (page 285)

✔ Reflective projects often reveal broad tensions that writers struggle with, often on a personal level. Start by thinking about the various layers of the tension—the historical, philosophical, or political friction at play (page 36). Bring in a supportive source that characterizes the tension. Then, examine your past assumptions about the subject. Consider their origin and the way they've shaped your view of the subject. Then, seek complexity in the subject and examine the quiet associations (page 135), the qualities or effects that you've overlooked or ignored in the past. Finally, explain how this process has changed your thinking.

Describe a broad tension related to the subject.

- Use specific language to describe the tension.
- Integrate a source that describes the tension.

Examine past assumptions about the subject.

- Explain where the assumptions come from.
- Explain how the assumptions are flawed or biased.

Describe the quiet associations of the subject.

- Describe qualities that might be taken for granted.
- Describe effects that aren't immediately apparent.

Explain how you see the subject differently.

- Explain why it matters to those involved.
- Explain what new questions or problems emerge.

📘 **READ:** Teresa Scollon (page 290)

Index

Page numbers in blue indicate definitions.